Ellen Augarten

MICHAEL T. KLARE is the author of fourteen books, including *Resource Wars* and *Rising Powers, Shrinking Planet*. A contributor to *Current History, Foreign Affairs,* and the *Los Angeles Times,* he is the defense correspondent for *The Nation* and the director of the Five College Program in peace and world security studies at Hampshire College in Amherst, Massachusetts.

ALSO BY MICHAEL T. KLARE

THE RACE FOR WHAT'S LEFT

THE RACE FOR WHAT'S LEFT

THE GLOBAL SCRAMBLE FOR
THE WORLD'S LAST RESOURCES

MICHAEL T. KLARE

PICADOR

A METROPOLITAN BOOK   HENRY HOLT AND COMPANY   NEW YORK

www.picadorusa.com
www.twitter.com/picadorusa • www.facebook.com/picadorusa
picadorbookroom.tumblr.com

Picador® is a U.S. registered trademark and is used by Henry Holt and Company
under license from Pan Books Limited.

For book club information, please visit www.facebook.com/picadorbookclub
or e-mail marketing@picadorusa.com.

Maps by Glenn Ruga based on designs by Michael T. Klare
Designed by Kelly S. Too

The Library of Congress has cataloged the Henry Holt edition as follows:

Klare, Michael T., 1942–
    The race for what's left: the global scramble for the world's last resources / Michael T.
Klare.—1st ed.
        p. cm.
    Includes bibliographical references and index.
    ISBN 978-0-8050-9126-7
    1. Nonrenewable natural resources. 2. Natural resources. 3. Nonrenewable natural
resources—Management. 4. Nonrenewable natural resources—Political aspects.
I. Title.
    HC85.K63 2012
    333.7—dc23

2011035151

Picador ISBN 978-1-250-02397-1

First published in the United States by Metropolitan Books, an imprint of Henry Holt
and Company

First Picador Edition: January 2013

10 9 8 7 6 5 4 3 2 1

For Andrea and Sasha—always

CONTENTS

THE RACE FOR WHAT'S LEFT

INTRODUCTION

At 1:36 p.m. Moscow time on August 2, 2007, the robotic arm of a Russian mini-submarine planted a titanium replica of the Russian flag on the seabed of the North Pole, two and half miles below the ocean's surface. "Why did we place it?" asked Artur Chilingarov, the leader of the Russian expedition. "Well, any time a country wins something, it installs its flag." Explorers throughout history have planted their nations' banners at prominent locations such as the South Pole and the top of Mount Everest, he explained, so the Russian team—the first to reach the polar floor—was resolved to do likewise. "I'm proud the Russian flag is there," said Chilingarov. "If a hundred or a thousand years from now someone goes down to where we were, they will see the Russian flag."[1]

Chilingarov and his fellow crew members took substantial risks in piloting their vessel to the North Pole floor. Even in the middle of summer the polar ice cap is many feet thick, and the only way for the expedition's small submersible to enter the water—and to return to the surface when the dive had been completed—was to find a natural hole in the drifting ice sheet. When the team located an opening and began their descent, they could not know with any certainty that they would find a similar aperture on their return. Chilingarov admits that he feared for his life, rating his chances of survival at only 30 percent. But after planting the Russian flag and spending an hour and a half exploring the seabed, the team came back to the surface and, after some frantic searching, located the necessary opening in the ice. Nine hours after starting their dive, the expedition members returned to the (relative) safety of the icebreaker *Rossiya*.[2]

"I am not crazy to dive there again," Chilingarov said of the 2007 polar expedition. Still, he has not been able to conceal his pride in the achievement. "There have been almost 500 people in outer space; thirteen people have been on the Moon. But we were the first to travel under the North Pole."[3]

Chilingarov, who was awarded a Hero of Russia medal for his exploits, has spent most of his life exploring the Arctic and Antarctica on behalf of Soviet and Russian state agencies. From 1979 to 1992 he was part of the USSR State Committee of Hydrometeorology, becoming its deputy chairman in 1986; after the breakup of the Soviet Union, he served on various Russian scientific bodies and in 1993 was elected to the lower house of the Duma, the Russian parliament. Although the August 2007 expedition to the North Pole was privately organized and financed, Chilingarov has consistently affirmed that he was acting as a representative of the Russian state and its people. "Our main aim is to remind the whole world that Russia is a great polar and scientific research power," he said on the eve of the polar descent.[4]

But while national pride no doubt played a major role in his decision to plant a Russian flag on the polar seabed, Chilingarov has also made it clear that the expedition was driven in large part by pragmatic considerations. Long considered a frozen wasteland with little to attract human interest, the Arctic region is now believed to harbor vast deposits of oil, natural gas, and valuable minerals—resources that will become increasingly accessible as global warming melts the polar ice cap. Even during the Soviet era, Russian leaders insisted that the portion of the Arctic Ocean bordering Russia was part of its national territory; now that climate change is making this area (and its underground riches) ever more accessible, they are reasserting these claims. Indeed, maintaining control over this vast region and extracting its material riches have been declared strategic national priorities. But to do so, Russia must first establish its rightful ownership of these offshore territories in accordance with international law—and it was to *this* end that Chilingarov descended to the floor of the North Pole.

Since 1982, the determination of offshore boundaries and territorial waters has been governed by the United Nations Convention on the Law of the Sea. The treaty allows each coastal nation to establish an "exclusive economic zone" (EEZ) extending two hundred nautical miles out from its shoreline, within which it is entitled to control the exploitation of all natural resources, including those lying beneath the ocean bottom. In addition, the convention allows a coastal state to claim ownership of its outer continental shelf, even if it extends beyond two hundred nautical miles. To acquire such rights, however, a claimant must provide scientific evidence to demonstrate that its continental shelf does, in fact, reach beyond its EEZ. For Russia to acquire legal control over a large stretch of the Arctic, therefore, it must show that its northern landmass extends to the North Pole. This, in turn, requires undersea mapping and the collection of geological samples—exactly the activities that Chilingarov's expedition was designed to undertake. "We must determine the border, the most northerly of the Russian shelf," he explained on national television.[5]

As it happens, the Chilingarov mission did not return with conclusive evidence that the polar seabed—a geological feature known as the Lomonosov Ridge—is an extension of the Russian landmass. Nevertheless, Moscow insists that the Lomonosov Ridge is indeed a part of Russia and says that it will undertake additional polar surveys to establish the legitimacy of its claim. The Russians have also made it clear that they will use force, if necessary, to protect their vital interests in the region. "We have immediately started the revision of our combat training programs for military units that may be deployed in the Arctic in case of a potential conflict," General Vladimir Shamanov, the head of the Defense Ministry's combat training board, said in June 2008.[6]

REVERBERATIONS ELSEWHERE

Chilingarov's expedition and Russia's subsequent moves to assert control over a vast slice of the Arctic produced alarm and indignation among leaders of the other Arctic nations, all of which have announced plans of their own to exploit the region's great hydrocarbon potential. Besides Russia, four nations—Canada, Greenland (administered by Denmark), Norway, and the United States—border the Arctic Ocean and claim significant chunks of its total expanse. And, like Russia, all four have recently taken steps to reinvigorate their claims.

The first to act was Canada, the country with the second largest Arctic coastline and long-standing Arctic interests. Scarcely had Chilingarov's mini-submarine stuck its flag into the polar seabed when Canada's foreign minister, Peter MacKay, issued a blistering response: "You can't go around the world and just plant flags and say, 'We're claiming this territory.'" [7] Of course, Chilingarov had not exactly laid claim to the North Pole based on the flag planting, but rather had argued that the surrounding seabed was an extension of Russian territory as defined by the UN convention. But this distinction did not prevent the Canadians from responding with an Arctic mission of their own. "The Russians sent a submarine to drop a small flag at the bottom of the ocean," a senior government official told the Associated Press six days after the Russian descent. "We're sending our prime minister to reassert Canadian sovereignty." [8]

Shortly after this announcement, Prime Minister Stephen Harper left for one of Canada's northernmost settlements, the frigid hamlet of Resolute Bay, located on Cornwallis Island in the Canadian Arctic Archipelago. Speaking in a storage shed to protect him from the icy, howling winds, Harper announced a series of moves aimed at bolstering Canada's strategic presence in the Arctic region. Resolute Bay itself, he indicated, would become the home of a new Canadian Army training center for cold-weather operations. In addition, the government would establish a deepwater port for military and civilian use on Baffin Island, at the eastern end of the Northwest Passage between the Atlantic and Pacific Oceans.[9] "Today's announcements tell the world that Canada has a real, growing, long-term presence in the Arctic," Harper told reporters accompanying his visit.[10]

Russia's Arctic initiatives also prompted a vigorous response from Denmark, which exercises ultimate authority over Greenland. On August 11, 2007, while Prime Minister Harper was in Resolute Bay to reassert Canada's claims to the region, a Danish scientific expedition aboard the Swedish icebreaker *Oden* headed into far northern waters in an attempt to collect data showing that the Lomonosov Ridge was an extension of Greenland, rather than Russia. Although the Danish mission had been planned before Chilingarov began his expedition to the ocean floor, it was now portrayed as a necessary counter to Russia's territorial claims. "The preliminary investigations done so far are very promising," declared Helge Sander, Denmark's minister of science, technology, and innovation, as the *Oden* set sail. "There are things suggesting that Denmark could be given the North Pole."[11]

Norway, too, has paid increased attention to the Arctic region. In 2007, it began operation of the first liquefied natural gas facility above the Arctic Circle, at Hammerfest, 825 miles north of Oslo. This $7.7 billion facility converts gas from the offshore Snøhvit (Snow White) field in the Barents Sea into a supercooled liquid and transports it by ship to customers in the United States and southern Europe.[12] Buoyed by the success of their Snøhvit project, the Norwegians have announced plans to develop oil and natural gas fields in even more northerly waters of the Barents Sea, laying claim to large swaths of Arctic territory. To better defend its Arctic domains, moreover, Norway has relocated its joint military headquarters to Boda—550 miles north of Oslo and well above the Arctic Circle.

In the United States, the official response to Chilingarov's polar mission was muted, with little more than a sarcastic comment by a State Department representative. "I'm not sure of whether they've put a metal flag, a rubber flag, or a bed sheet on the ocean floor. Either way, it doesn't have any legal standing or effect on this claim," the department's deputy spokesman told reporters at the time.[13] Behind the scenes, however, there was considerable concern, leading to increased vigilance over Arctic affairs by the National Security Council. After devoting many months to a review of U.S. interests in the region, the council released a new strategic assessment of the Arctic in January 2009, shortly before President George W. Bush left office. Known officially as National Security Presidential Directive 66, this document now governs U.S. policy for the region. Among its key provisions is a call for intensified government effort to assert American sovereignty over a stretch of the continental shelf extending north from Alaska toward the North Pole. The directive also promises federal support for efforts to undertake the extraction of oil and natural gas from Arctic reserves.[14]

WHY THE ARCTIC? WHY NOW?

Why this sudden burst of interest in the Arctic? For decades, the region elicited little interest from surrounding nations, except insofar as it played a role in the Armageddon scenarios of the U.S.-Soviet nuclear competition. (Most Soviet and American intercontinental missiles and long-range bombers were expected to fly over the polar region on the way to their intended targets, prompting the United States to establish radar stations and jet interceptor bases in Canada, Iceland, and Greenland.) After the Cold War, most military bases in the region were closed or downgraded, and, aside from the region's native Inuit inhabitants and an occasional fishing crew, few souls have been willing to brave the Arctic's frequent storms and bitterly cold weather to establish much of a presence there. But this historic neglect is now changing: the Arctic is attracting immense interest from the world's major energy firms, and the Snøhvit project in Norway is a harbinger of many more oil and gas facilities to come.

Driving all of this interest is the release of geological studies indicating that the Arctic may contain some of the world's largest untapped reserves of oil and natural gas. Until recently very little was known about the region's hydrocarbon potential, but a few years ago the U.S. Geological Survey undertook a systematic assessment of oil and gas reserves in the land and sea areas north of the Arctic Circle. The results, published in July 2008, were nothing short of astonishing: this region, which occupies a mere 6 percent of the earth's surface, was said to account for 22 percent of the "undiscovered, technically recoverable [oil and gas] resources in the world." This includes 13 percent of the world's undiscovered oil reserves and 30 percent of its undiscovered natural gas— together, the equivalent of 412 billion barrels of oil, or 56 times the current rate of U.S. annual petroleum consumption.[15]

This report, combined with similar studies commissioned by private firms, has triggered a rush by giant energy companies to acquire development rights in promising Arctic drilling zones. Most of this activity, at present, is concentrated in the Barents Sea, above Norway and northwestern Russia; the Chukchi Sea, between northwestern Alaska and eastern Siberia; and the Beaufort Sea, above northeastern Alaska and Canada's Northwest Territories. In the Barents, near Norway's Snøhvit project, the Russians are preparing to develop an even larger gas field, called Shtokman, in an area they control. In Alaska's portion of the Chukchi Sea, exploratory drilling is being planned by ConocoPhillips and Royal Dutch Shell; at a 2008 auction, these companies spent $660 million and $2.1 billion, respectively, for the right to develop certain areas of the territory. Farther east, in the Beaufort Sea, Shell is preparing to explore for oil in American waters while BP, ExxonMobil, and Imperial Oil of Canada will search in nearby Canadian waters.[16]

Many analysts believe that this is just the beginning of what has been termed an energy "gold rush" in the Arctic region. As the demand for energy rises and global warming makes the far north more accessible to survey and drilling vessels, additional fields are likely to be developed. With this in mind, giant energy firms are spending ever-increasing sums on Arctic exploration and acquiring especially hardened ships that can safely navigate ice-clogged seas.[17] "Despite grueling conditions, interest in oil and gas reserves in the far north is heating up," Brian Baskin reported in the *Wall Street Journal*. "Virtually every major producer is looking to the Arctic sea floor as the next—some say last—great resource play."[18]

That the major energy firms are rushing to secure development rights in the Arctic is hardly surprising, given that they are always searching for new sources of supply as older fields become depleted. But the urgency of this northward drive, and the importance that these companies attach to it—as reflected in the vast sums that they are spending on complex and technologically challenging projects—is the product of something more profound. Until now, the energy industry has been able to tap into giant, easily exploited oil and gas reservoirs in relatively accessible locations, providing the world with cheap and abundant power. This vast profusion of affordable energy drove the great worldwide industrial expansion of the post–World War II era and allowed new economic dynamos to emerge in the developing world. But the era of readily accessible oil and gas has come to an end: from now on, vital energy supplies will have to be drawn from remote and forbidding locations, at a cost far exceeding anything experienced in the past. The world is entering an era of pervasive, unprecedented resource scarcity.

NOT JUST THE ARCTIC, AND NOT JUST OIL

The drive to acquire oil and gas leases in the Arctic region is by no means the only sign that we have entered a different age. The giant energy companies are also pursuing resource "plays" in northern Siberia, in the deep waters of the Atlantic, in remote corners of Africa, and in other previously avoided areas. And similarly forbidding, hard-to-access locations are increasingly becoming the primary focus for the mining industry and agricultural enterprises.

In Russia, for example, a major effort is now under way to develop oil and gas deposits off the east coast of Sakhalin, a large island in the Sea of Okhotsk in the North Pacific. Sakhalin Island is below the Arctic Circle, and so is spared the extreme temperatures of more northerly locations. Nevertheless, it is not an easy place to operate in. Temperatures in the winter often reach 40 degrees below zero, and the island lies in an area prone to typhoons. What's more, Sakhalin's offshore oil and gas platforms are often exposed to massive ice floes pushed toward the island by powerful currents in the Sea of Okhotsk. To withstand these floes, as well as the earthquakes that often rattle the area, the platforms have to be specially reinforced. And because an ice sheet surrounds much of Sakhalin in the winter, supply ships and oil tankers can reach the oil-production zone only during certain times of the year.[19] The island's vulnerability to severe weather was made especially evident in December 2011, when the *Kolskaya* oil rig capsized and sank in a fierce storm while being towed into a Sakhalin harbor, resulting in the death of most of the sixty-seven crewmen aboard.[20]

Equally daunting challenges face the developers of Brazil's new off-shore oil discoveries, including the giant Tupi field in the deep waters of the South Atlantic. Known as "pre-salt" deposits because they lie buried beneath a thick layer of salt, Tupi and neighboring offshore fields are thought to hold as much as 100 billion barrels of oil, making them the largest untapped reservoir to be exploited since wells in the North Sea were brought online in the 1970s. But extracting oil from the pre-salt area will not be easy or inexpensive. The offshore deposits lie beneath 1.5 miles of water and another 2.5 miles of compressed salt, sand, and rock. New drilling technologies will have to be developed to operate at these ocean depths and to penetrate the salt dome below. The subsalt reserves are also believed to contain high concentrations of natural gas, and the separation and handling of this gas will pose additional challenges.[21] Successful development of Tupi and other pre-salt fields will require hundreds of billions of dollars and many years of effort.

Innovative technologies are also the key to developing another kind of resource frontier now eagerly being explored by the major energy producers: dense rock formations that cannot be exploited by traditional drilling methods. Historically, most hydrocarbons have been produced from deposits in highly porous rocks such as sandstone, which readily release their oil and gas riches once a wellbore provides an opening to the surface. Less porous rocks, like shale, do not naturally allow trapped oil and gas to escape, so these formations must be artificially broken up by some means before the hydrocarbons can be extracted—an approach that had generally been considered too difficult and expensive to be practical. However, with the introduction of new techniques such as hydraulic fracturing, which uses high-pressure water blasts to crack the underground shale seams, major energy companies are increasingly looking to such "tight" rock formations as a promising new source of oil and gas. Likewise, engineers are finding new ways to extract usable fuel from the "tar sands" of Canada's Athabasca wilderness, turning the solid bitumen found there into synthetic crude oil. Some energy experts believe that new technologies such as these will help alleviate the future scarcity of conventionally produced oil and gas, but many scientists warn that the extraction of "unconventional" hydrocarbons will accelerate the rate of global warming and produce widespread environmental destruction.[22]

The harsh conditions that confront oil and gas corporations in Brazil, on Sakhalin, and in challenging geological formations are typical of the difficulties that the energy industry faces as it is increasingly forced to turn to reserves in remote, forbidding locations. And what is true of the oil and gas companies is also true of the mining industry. With many existing sources of key minerals facing exhaustion, giant mining firms such as BHP Billiton, Rio Tinto, and Freeport-McMoRan are obliged to search for new deposits in the same sort of distant, hazardous frontiers as their energy brethren. "Like oil, most of the easy-to-reach deposits of basic materials like copper, nickel, and gold have already been found and exploited," Patrick Barta noted in the *Wall Street Journal*. "That has left lower-grade deposits in remote, politically volatile countries that will cost more to develop than the mother lodes of yesteryear."[23]

Take copper, a vital component of electrical wiring, roofing, plumbing fixtures, and a host of other industrial products. The global consumption of copper has soared in recent years—largely thanks to an ongoing building boom in Asia—and every leading producer has struggled to keep up with demand. With many of the largest mines in Canada, Chile, and Indonesia having reached their peak levels of output (or having long since passed that peak), mining companies have been forced to look elsewhere for new sources of supply. For the most part, this means developing new deposits in remote and uninviting areas of Siberia, Mongolia, and the Arctic, or returning to war-torn areas in Africa where mines had been abandoned due to recurring violence.[24]

A similar picture prevails in the case of cobalt, nickel, titanium, and other vital minerals that are in heavy demand because of strong economic growth in Asia but, like copper, are largely derived from mines that have passed their prime. To supplement the output of these aging mines, major producers are pursuing the same strategies employed for copper: seeking new deposits in frontier areas such as Mongolia, or plunging back into conflict-torn countries like the Democratic Republic of the Congo. Following the lead of Artur Chilingarov, some firms and governments are also looking at the ocean bottom as a source of valuable resources. In July 2011, a Chinese submersible, the *Jiaolong*, dove 16,500 feet below the surface of the Pacific Ocean—a near-record depth—in a test of deep-sea mining techniques. "China's economy is developing, and the central government finally realizes that it's not nearly enough only to develop mining on land," said Professor Wang Pinxian, head of the State Laboratory of Marine Geology at Shanghai Tongji University. "So this is a big step that we are starting to pay attention to exploring oceanic mineral exploration."[25] Whether on land or at sea, the outlook is the same: with existing sources of critical materials facing exhaustion, more and more of our essential supplies will have to come from places that are risky for reasons of geography, geology, politics, or some combination of all three.

And in the near future, the most precious natural resource of all—food—will also become scarce in many parts of the world. While the planet is currently capable of satisfying the basic nutritional requirements of the existing world population (although transportation difficulties and inequitable pricing often prevent food from reaching those in need), this capacity will come under threat in the decades ahead, as the population grows and climate change reduces the amount of rainfall in many areas. To guard against inevitable food shortages, government-backed agricultural firms in China, South Korea, Saudi Arabia, and the United Arab Emirates are already buying vast tracts of arable land in Africa and elsewhere to produce food for consumption at home. Many private investors and hedge funds in the West are pouring money into similar ventures. Such "land grabs" are being greeted with growing anxiety and hostility in the developing world, where land is scarce and hunger never absent. As the planet warms, the pursuit of these overseas food factories will no doubt become more intense—as will resistance from those who see them as a threat to their survival.

THE RACE FOR WHAT'S LEFT

The pursuit of untapped oil and mineral reserves in remote and hazardous locations is part of a larger, more significant phenomenon: a concerted drive by governments and resource firms to gain control over whatever remains of the world's raw materials base. Government and corporate officials recognize that existing reserves are being depleted at a terrifying pace and will be largely exhausted in the not-too-distant future. The only way for countries to ensure an adequate future supply of these materials, and thereby keep their economies humming, is to acquire new, undeveloped reservoirs in those few locations that have not already been completely drained. This has produced a global drive to find and exploit the world's final resource reserves—a race for what's left.

At stake in this contest is the continuation of the Industrial Age. Ever since the onset of the Industrial Revolution, the major economies have consumed ever-increasing quantities of basic raw materials—wood, iron, copper, tin, and coal to begin with; oil, natural gas, uranium, titanium, and other specialized minerals in more recent times. Vast quantities of these materials were extracted over the years to satisfy the needs of the major industrial powers, producing an incessant search for new sources of supply. As more and more countries have become industrialized, the demand for these materials has risen exponentially, so that current consumption rates are the highest in history. But many of the reserves that were developed in the previous century to meet the world's ravenous resource requirements have been substantially depleted, so the extractive industries' capacity to satisfy the needs of the existing industrial powers—let alone provide for the newly industrializing ones—is in serious doubt. Only by acquiring new sources of supply, wherever they might be found, can the industrialized nations continue to prosper.

The continued availability of energy and mineral supplies is also essential for political and military survival. No nation can maintain a robust military defense without a wide array of modern weapon systems, and most such systems—from warships to fighter jets—are fueled by oil. The U.S. military, with multiple overseas commitments and a significant combat presence in Southwest Asia, is especially dependent on petroleum, consuming as much oil every day as the entire nation of Sweden.[26] Other nations that seek to project military power beyond their immediate territory, such as Britain, China, France, and Russia, also require substantial petroleum supplies. Any nation that seeks to sustain a significant arms-making capability, moreover, must possess ensured supplies of iron, cobalt, nickel, titanium, and various specialty metals. And, of course, any country seeking to join the "nuclear club"— whether for political or for military reasons, or a combination of both—must have a reliable supply of uranium.

Eventually, perhaps, substitutes will be found for some of these materials. Intensive research is now under way, for example, to develop liquid fuels from cornstalks, prairie grass, wood chips, and other biological matter. Significant energy may also be provided in the future by hydrogen, a plentiful element incorporated into the molecular structure of water and many other substances. But these efforts will take a long time to mature, and it is not yet certain that they will be able to replace existing fuels on a one-for-one basis. Many of the new energy systems, moreover, require the use of resources that are themselves scarce or difficult to obtain. Any increase in biofuels production, for example, risks a reduction in global food output as more of the world's supply of farmland is devoted to producing energy crops. The wider use of hydrogen fuel cells will require increased supplies of the rare metal platinum to act as a chemical catalyst; likewise, most electrical cars and hybrids use batteries made in part of lithium, another rare metal. The development of these alternatives could, therefore, add further momentum to the race for what's left.

Under these circumstances, it is hardly surprising that the major industrial powers have embarked on an extended, calculated drive to gain control over the world's remaining preserves of vital natural resources. Governments and giant corporations—or the two acting in conjunction—have adopted ambitious plans to explore uncharted areas, pursue legal claims to disputed territories, acquire exploration and drilling rights in promising resource zones, introduce new technologies for extractive operations in extreme and hazardous environments, and develop military forces that can operate in these regions.

Some of the most elaborate of these plans concern the development of the Arctic region and deep-offshore resource reserves. All five of the Arctic powers have devised detailed blueprints for the exploration and demarcation of their northern territories and the eventual exploitation of any hydrocarbon and mineral resources detected there. Other nations have adopted similar plans to exploit their offshore reserves (in the case of countries with a substantial coastal presence) or to forge alliances with other states that possess an abundance of such resources. The government of Brazil, for example, has adopted legislation establishing a new national agency, Petrosal, to oversee development of all new discoveries in the country's pre-salt basin in deep Atlantic waters and giving control over the fields to the state-owned company Petrobras.[27] Angola, Indonesia, and Nigeria are also proceeding with ambitious plans to develop their ultra-deep oil and natural gas reserves. China, too, seeks to develop its offshore fields and—knowing that it cannot hope to satisfy its ever-growing needs solely from domestic reserves—has embarked on a multibillion-dollar drive to acquire a significant stake in the offshore energy operations of other countries.[28]

The extent of these plans makes it clear that the race for what's left is not simply the product of many individual actions—all those forays into the Arctic, Siberia, and elsewhere—but rather something far more calculated and organized. National and corporate leaders are painfully aware that existing reserves of many vital resources are disappearing and that urgent action is needed to ensure that *their* country or *their* company will have sufficient supplies to survive. They are determined, therefore, to put in place whatever measures are needed in the coming decades to replace existing reservoirs with new sources of supply.

INVADING THE LAST FRONTIERS

Human societies have, of course, been competing with one another for control over remote, undeveloped resource zones for a very long time. During the eighth and seventh centuries B.C., for example, the various Greek city-states established colonies throughout the Mediterranean basin and as far as the Black Sea to disperse excess population, acquire raw materials, and promote foreign trade.[29] The Romans kept expanding their empire as Italy's population grew and it became necessary to acquire grain and other foodstuffs from increasingly distant locations.[30] Later, in the fifteenth century, the European powers commenced a 400-year-long competition for control of overseas colonies in resource-rich areas of Africa, Asia, and the Americas. So the contemporary pursuit of vital materials in the Arctic, the deep seas, and on other resource frontiers can be viewed as part of a process that began thousands of years ago. But the race for what's left is not just a continuation of past behavior; rather, it represents a new stage in humanity's relentless hunt for critical materials—a drive without true precedents.

Several factors distinguish the current push from those of the past. To begin with, there are no other, as-yet-undetected frontiers lying beyond those now under assault. Until now, participants in the depletion of a particular resource zone could always comfort themselves with the thought that undeveloped lands lie somewhere else, still awaiting human exploitation. When the earliest American settlers exhausted the soils of New England and New York State, they moved West—first to Ohio and Indiana, then to the Great Plains, and eventually to the Pacific coast; some, in time, moved even farther afield, to Latin America and Hawaii. Likewise, the giant oil and mining companies have continuously extended their spheres of operation from traditional sites in Europe, North America, and Russia to remote and forbidding regions of Africa, Asia, and Latin America. Today, however, there exist no untilled lands or untapped oil reserves awaiting fresh development. Virtually all accessible resource zones are now in production; except for the extreme areas such as the Arctic, the Congo, the ocean bottom, and unyielding rock formations, there is nowhere else to go.

For this reason, the invasion of the world's final frontiers has unique significance. What we expropriate from these areas represents all that remains of the planet's once abundant resource bounty. In all likelihood, we are looking at the last oil fields, the last uranium deposits, the last copper mines, and the last reserves of many other vital resources. These materials will not all disappear at once, of course, and some as-yet-undeveloped reserves may prove more prolific than expected. Gradually, though, we will see the complete disappearance of many key resources upon which modern industrial civilization has long relied.

And it is not just the most common resources like oil and copper that are likely to be exhausted in this final resource drive, but also the more exotic materials that are needed for specialty purposes, such as the chromium used in making stainless steel and the cobalt used in high-strength alloys. Demand is also outpacing the supply of the "rare earth elements," including dysprosium, lanthanum, neodymium, and terbium, used in making superconductors and hybrid car motors. Likewise, the growing popularity of "plug-in" hybrids and all-electric cars has increased the demand for lithium, an ultra-lightweight metal used in advanced battery designs. The remaining deposits of rare earths, lithium, and other exotic—but vital—materials will come under increasing assault as existing mines are depleted and demand rises around the world.

The current drive is also different from those of the past because of the sudden emergence of powerful new competitors in the global resource hunt. Until relatively recently, the pursuit of overseas energy and mineral resources was largely the prerogative of a few established industrial powers, led by the United States, Japan, Germany, Britain, and France. These countries dominated the global commodity markets and accounted for the bulk of foreign investment in large-scale resource ventures in Africa, Latin America, and the Middle East. But now, due to their impressive rates of economic growth, Asian dynamos such as

China, India, South Korea, and Taiwan have become major resource consumers as well. China, for example, is now the world's leading consumer of coal, iron, copper, and aluminum ore, and the second leading consumer of petroleum. Like the older industrial powers, these new economic powerhouses are contributing to the rapid depletion of existing resource deposits and the drive to penetrate and exploit the planet's last undeveloped preserves.

This suggests that once the development of these final reserves begins, their depletion could occur very rapidly—producing a sharp contraction in the global supply of many critical resources. Under these circumstances, it is reasonable to assume that the various consuming powers will seek to gain control over as much as possible of what remains of these materials, producing an intense competitive struggle. This could lead to territorial disputes in areas where boundaries or ownership rights are contested—as is already evident in the Arctic region. In the past, such disputes have often erupted in armed combat, and there is no reason to believe that this will not happen in the future; indeed, the countries involved are already preparing for such combat by beefing up their capacity to operate in the Arctic and other contested resource zones, such as the East and South China Seas. The pursuit of vital materials in remote and marginal areas will also pose extraordinary environmental challenges, and will lead to intensified clashes between outside powers and the indigenous peoples who occupy these areas.

Needless to say, all of this will be profoundly affected by the accelerated warming of the planet and associated climate effects—although not necessarily in ways that can be foreseen. It is possible that global warming will increase the availability of some resources, for instance by making the Arctic more accessible to oil and gas extraction; it is more likely, however, that it will constrict the supply of many key materials. Agriculture appears to be at particular risk: some key growing regions will suffer from a decline in annual precipitation, making the production of food increasingly precarious; others will receive more rain, but often in the form of intense downpours that result in floods and the loss of valuable cropland. In addition, rising sea levels will wash away many coastal farming areas, including important rice-growing lands in South and Southeast Asia. True, we have encountered climate effects like these before—but never on this scale, or with such far-reaching consequences.

Thus, while the current assault on remote resource frontiers bears some similarities to historical exploitation of undeveloped territories, it is in many important ways different from anything that has come before. Never have we seen the same combination of factors that confronts us today: a lack of any unexplored resource preserves beyond those now being eyed for development; the sudden emergence of rapacious new consumers; technical and environmental limitations on the exploitation of new deposits; and the devastating effects of climate change. In many cases, the commodities procured during this new round of extraction will represent the final supplies of their type. The race we are on today is the last of its kind that we are likely to undertake.

1 ► DRIVEN BY DEPLETION

In 1971, a Mexican fisherman named Rudesino Cantarell encountered an annoying problem while plying his trade off the Yucatán Peninsula: clots of oil, apparently seeping from underground seams in the Bay of Campeche, were clinging to his nets and reducing his catch. After putting up with this inconvenience for some time, Cantarell described his difficulties to officials of the government-owned oil company Petróleos Mexicanos, known as Pemex. This prompted Pemex to conduct an exploratory survey of the area where Cantarell's nets had been contaminated—and at this spot, in 1976, the company found the second most prolific oil field in the world. Whether the fisherman ever received any financial reward for his role in the discovery is not recorded, but the giant field was called "Cantarell" in his honor.[1]

For nearly three decades, the oil gushing from the Cantarell field was a veritable fountain of gold for the Mexican government. By 1981 the field was yielding an impressive 1.2 million barrels per day, and that amount continued to rise in the years that followed. Cantarell's prolific output allowed the Mexican state to significantly increase public spending and helped ensure the extended tenure of the Institutional Revolutionary Party (known as PRI for its initials in Spanish). Indeed, no

CANTARELL OIL FIELD, MEXICO

other asset has contributed more to Mexico's economic vigor in modern times than the discovery and exploitation of Cantarell.[2]

Lying under shallow water some fifty miles off the western coast of the Yucatán Peninsula, the Cantarell field is located in the Chicxulub Crater, produced by a giant asteroid that struck the Earth some 65 million years ago. (Many scientists believe that this asteroid, one of the largest ever to hit the Earth, produced a global cloud of ashes and dust that blocked sunlight and destroyed the food supply for many species, including the dinosaurs, leading to their extinction.)[3] The crater is filled with shattered rock and rubble, and this highly fractured geology has made it easy to extract the field's extensive oil reserves. In its best years, Cantarell yielded over 2.1 million barrels of oil per day—more than any other field in the world except the colossal Ghawar deposit in Saudi Arabia.[4]

But the same conditions that made it easy to pump out Cantarell's petroleum bounty also contributed to its rapid decline. As more and more petroleum was drawn from Cantarell, the field's underground cavities emptied out and the ambient pressure dropped, reducing the outflow of oil. By 1995, the yield had fallen to 1 million barrels per day, the lowest recorded in more than fifteen years. To restore higher levels of production, Pemex spent $6 billion on a daring scheme to inject massive volumes of nitrogen into the Cantarell reservoir, intending to boost the underground pressure. For a time, the plan worked as designed, and output rose again—reaching just over 2 million barrels a day in 2003 and 2004. But the use of extraordinary means to increase production only hastened the depletion of the field. By 2005, Cantarell was again in sharp decline, and in 2010 the field produced only 558,000 barrels per day—an astonishing 74 percent reduction from its 2004 peak. At this point, engineers at Pemex possess few options to reverse the slide, and so Cantarell's output is expected to keep falling.[5]

The rapid decline of the Cantarell field has profound implications for Mexico, the United States, and the world at large. In Mexico, the reduction in oil profits has meant a substantial loss of state revenue just as the government is trying to grapple with the global economic crisis and an escalating drug war. The problem is all the greater because Cantarell provided such a large share of Mexico's total oil output. With no other fields capable of replacing it, the country's total oil production has fallen from an average of 3.8 million barrels per day in 2003–06 to 2.9 million barrels in 2010.[6] Since Mexican demand for oil is rising even as the production levels continue to fall, sometime before 2015 the country will switch from being a net oil exporter to a net importer, significantly damaging the country's economy.[7] Meanwhile, the United States, which imported much of the oil produced at Cantarell, faces the loss of one of its most trusted and reliable sources of energy; as a result, more and more of America's imports will have to come from distant, unreliable suppliers in the Middle East and Africa.

The magnitude of Cantarell's decline—and the speed with which it has occurred—has understandably been a shock for Mexican officials, who must now grapple with the consequences. "I don't recall seeing anything in the industry as dramatic as Cantarell," said Mark Thurber, an energy researcher at Stanford University.[8] But the field's degeneration also troubles global oil experts, who see in it a premonition of production declines at other major reservoirs, including Ghawar and similar "supergiants" in the Middle East. "The demise of Cantarell highlights a global issue," noted David Luhnow of the *Wall Street Journal*. "Nearly a quarter of the world's daily oil output of 85 million barrels is pumped from the biggest 20 fields.... And many of those fields, discovered decades ago, could soon follow in Cantarell's footsteps."[9]

In many ways, the story of Cantarell's rise and fall provides a microcosm of the global resource dilemma. Many of the world's principal sources of oil—and of coal, natural gas, uranium, copper, and assorted other vital materials—were, like Cantarell, discovered several decades ago and are now becoming less and less productive. According to the International Energy Agency (IEA), all but a few large oil fields have already reached their peak output levels and now face long-term decline.[10] Unless new reservoirs of comparable size and productivity are discovered in the years ahead, the global supply of oil will inevitably contract. The outlook is similar for other raw materials, even if the details vary slightly case by case. Since few discoveries can be expected in the world's existing, well-explored resource zones, any increase in worldwide output will require the development of untapped reserves in new and often inhospitable locations.

The decline of existing sources of supply and the hunt for new reserves in more remote and more dangerous areas is not a new phenomenon. Virtually all of the minerals and fossil fuels at the core of modern industrial civilization are finite materials that exist in deposits of varying degrees of size, richness, and accessibility. Almost always, producers begin by drawing on the deposits that are the easiest to find and exploit—typically, those that lie close to the surface, are located near major markets, and require minimal refining and processing. When these high-quality, easily accessed deposits are exhausted, resource firms inevitably must seek fresh reserves in places that are less convenient—usually deeper underground, farther offshore, in smaller and less concentrated deposits, or in far-flung areas of the globe. For a time, the development of new technology allows resources to be profitably extracted from these harsher, more difficult locations. But the logic of depletion is unyielding. Every fresh advance in mining and drilling techniques leads to the exploitation of hard-to-reach reserves, until those deposits, too, are exhausted—and then the cycle of exploration and production begins anew in even *more* demanding circumstances.

The depletion of existing resource deposits and the search for new sources of supply was in large measure the driving force behind European colonialism in Africa, Asia, and the Americas from the fifteenth century onward. But what occurred in the past over a lengthy span of time is now happening very rapidly: many of the world's main reservoirs of vital materials are facing systemic depletion at the same time, leaving corporations and governments urgently scrambling to find replacements. As the wholesale exhaustion of the world's natural resource base coincides with unprecedented demand for these materials, the race for what's left is set in motion.

THE GREAT POSTWAR RESOURCE BOOM

The Cantarell oil field in Mexico, the Ghawar field in Saudi Arabia, and many of the other giant oil reservoirs that we rely on today for a large share of our petroleum supply—along with the biggest reserves of natural gas, copper ore, and other vital materials that we depend on—were mostly discovered in the decades after World War II, when giant energy and mining companies scoured the world in search of new reserves to supply the booming world economy. Between 1950 and 2001, the world's combined gross domestic product (GDP) increased by 600 percent in real terms, jumping from \$5.3 to \$37.2 trillion in 1990 dollars.[11] This extraordinary surge in global economic activity produced an insatiable need for resources of all types: energy for transportation, manufacturing,

TABLE 1.1: PRODUCTION OF SELECTED COMMODITIES, 1950, 1975, AND 2000

(In thousand metric tons, unless otherwise noted)

	PRODUCTION			PERCENT INCREASE, 1950–2000
	1950	1975	2000	
Bauxite	8,370	25,401	135,000	1,513
Cobalt	7	30	33	371
Copper	2,645	6,960	13,200	399
Iron ore	250,000	887,389	1,061,148	324
Nickel	146	787	1,250	756
Titanium	814	3,298	5,187	537
Crude oil (billion barrels)	3.8	19.5	27.3	618
Natural gas (trillion cubic feet)	7.2	55.8	85.1	1,082

Source: U.S. Geological Survey, *Minerals Yearbook 2000*, vol. 1; and editions for 1976 and 1952. Oil and gas data for 2000 from BP, *Statistical Review of World Energy 2009*.

and electricity generation; minerals for buildings, infrastructure, and consumer products; and food and water to sustain a growing (and increasingly urbanized) global population. As Table 1.1 shows, production of most of the basic resources rose dramatically during the postwar years. The amount of copper mined in 2000 was almost five times what it had been in 1950; the production of natural gas increased nearly twelvefold; and other natural resources showed similarly impressive gains during those decades.[12]

To achieve these mammoth increases in resource output, the world's extractive industries had to expand beyond the well-established reservoirs that they had been exploiting at the end of World War II— reservoirs located largely in North America, Europe, and the Soviet Union. Those existing mines, oil fields, and gas reserves were not remotely large enough to support the ever-increasing levels of output demanded by the burgeoning world economy, so the resource firms were obliged to seek new reserves in other parts of the world. As a result of this drive, many resource-rich areas were explored and brought into production for the first time.

In the case of oil, for instance, more than half of the world's production in 1950 was derived from wells in the United States—with much of that oil coming from onshore sources in Texas, Oklahoma, Louisiana, and California. But U.S. reserves had grown by very little since the 1930s, and most geologists believed that it would be difficult to find significant amounts of oil elsewhere in North America. Accordingly, petroleum firms set out to develop new reserves in other oil-producing regions—or "provinces," as they are termed by oilmen—seeking to locate and exploit fields previously thought beyond their reach.[13]

This effort had its greatest initial successes in Saudi Arabia and neighboring areas of the Middle East. Although British geologists who first studied the region believed that there was little petroleum in Saudi Arabia, a number of American prospectors had higher hopes for the kingdom, and in 1933 the Standard Oil Company of California (SOCAL) acquired a concession to a large chunk of Saudi Arabia's Eastern Province, on the southern rim of the Persian Gulf. The outbreak of World War II made full-scale exploration of the area impossible, but once the war ended, SOCAL teamed up with Texaco, Mobil, and Exxon to form the Arabian-American Oil Company (Aramco) and began intensive development of the concession.[14] In 1948, the joint venture made the greatest find in the entire history of oil: Ghawar, the world's largest field, which at its peak produced 5.6 million barrels per day. Three years later, Aramco found Safaniya, the world's third largest field (after Ghawar and Cantarell), with peak output of 2.1 million barrels per day.[15]

Eager to duplicate Aramco's great success, other oil producers undertook concentrated drives to find petroleum deposits in new producing areas. The French government, wary of excessive reliance on "Anglo-Saxon" oil firms like Aramco, British Petroleum, and Royal Dutch Shell, created oil companies of its own, which soon made major discoveries in the French colonies of Gabon and Algeria. Russian efforts to find more oil, meanwhile, succeeded in locating the giant Samotlor field in western Siberia, a major new producing area.[16] Other large oil fields were also found during the 1950s in Libya, British-controlled Nigeria, and the Neutral Zone between Saudi Arabia and Kuwait.[17]

Even with these new fields gushing oil, however, the continuous growth in international demand kept pushing the energy firms to seek out additional deposits. With many of the most promising landward sites already fully explored by 1960, they began exploiting oil reserves in coastal waters, usually adjacent to existing onshore fields. Major reservoirs of this kind were developed in the Gulf of Mexico and the Persian Gulf.[18] Over time, improvements in technology gradually allowed the companies to venture deeper; in 1969, the North Sea field, one of the world's largest offshore oil deposits, was discovered in an area of that ocean shared by Norway and the United Kingdom.[19]

Technological innovation was also crucial for a few other petroleum projects at the time, such as the effort to exploit the mammoth Prudhoe Bay field in Alaska's North Slope area. Transporting the oil by pipeline from ice-clogged Prudhoe Bay to an open port in southern Alaska proved unusually challenging. Because the Prudhoe Bay crude oil is warmer than the Alaskan permafrost, any conduit laid directly on the ground could turn the frozen soil into mush, risking a rupture in the line and massive oil spills; to overcome this danger, much of the 800-mile Trans-Alaska Pipeline eventually had to be built on stilts.[20] But throughout the twentieth century, such elaborate, costly efforts were very much the exception rather than the rule. For the most part, the newly discovered fields were located in fairly accessible territories, with most new oil wells being installed on shore or in relatively shallow waters.

A similar pattern is evident in the development of natural gas over the second half of the twentieth century, with production spreading from a mere handful of suppliers to a much larger constellation of major players. In 1950, the United States, a pioneer in the development of natural gas, accounted for an astonishing 85 percent of total worldwide output.[21] But as the demand for gas rose, new fields were developed in Europe, Asia, Africa, and especially the Soviet Union.

In 1952, Soviet gas output was only 258 billion cubic feet, or roughly 3 percent of the 8 trillion cubic feet produced that year in the United States.[22] Soon, though, Soviet energy commissars launched a systematic campaign to locate additional sources of natural gas—focusing in particular on western Siberia, where many of Russia's newest oil deposits had been discovered. In the 1960s, this search resulted in the discovery of a number of enormous fields, including Urengoy and Yamburg, currently the world's second and third largest gas reservoirs (exceeded only by the mammoth South Pars/North Dome field that is shared by Iran and Qatar). Major discoveries were also made in the Kazakh and Turkmen Soviet Socialist Republics (now the independent nations of Kazakhstan and Turkmenistan). As these fields were brought on line, Soviet production soared, reaching 21.1 trillion cubic feet in 1990, just before the breakup of the USSR.[23]

The search for natural gas also led prospectors to North Africa and the Middle East, producing major discoveries in Algeria, Iran, and Saudi Arabia. The discovery of giant fields in the North Sea area, meanwhile, made Europe a leading gas producer for the first time. By 1975, gas wells in the Dutch, British, and Norwegian sectors of the North Sea allowed those three countries to produce about 4.5 trillion cubic feet of gas altogether; in 2000, their combined total had reached 7.6 trillion cubic feet.[24]

And the pattern was the same when it came to industrial minerals. The great upsurge in industrial output after World War II encouraged mining firms to seek and develop fresh reserves around the world. This was true both for common industrial ores, such as copper, iron, and bauxite (used to make aluminum), as well as for rare specialty metals needed by the aerospace and electronics industries. Whereas the production of most basic ores was once concentrated at historic mines in North America, Europe, and certain colonies in Africa, before long mining companies began expanding their search to remote areas of the world. The hunt for new sources of copper, for example, led prospectors to Irian Jaya, the Indonesian half of the island of New Guinea. In 1969, the American firm Freeport-McMoRan began development of the Ertsberg mine, a mammoth copper and gold deposit found near the summit of Irian Jaya's 16,535-foot Puncak Jaya peak; later, Freeport developed a second mine, Grasberg, on an adjacent mountain.[25]

The specialty metals needed by burgeoning high-tech industries—such as titanium, a strong, lightweight metal widely used in aircraft and missile manufacture—were initially produced in only a handful of mines. But soon new sources of these minerals were being ferreted out worldwide. To satisfy the rising demand for titanium, for example, new or expanded mines for ilmenite and rutile (the ores containing titanium) were established in Australia, Egypt, India, and South Africa.[26] A similar effort was conducted to develop new sources of cobalt, nickel, and manganese.

Mining companies paid special attention to columbium and tantalum, two rare minerals used in the production of high-strength steel alloys. The U.S. Bureau of Mines observed that these materials were "among the rare metals most vital in 1952 to the United States defense program," thus justifying special government efforts to secure adequate supplies of them.[27] In subsequent years, tantalum also found increasing use in the manufacture of compact capacitors for lightweight electronic devices, including laptop computers and cellular telephones.[28] To satisfy this growing need, new deposits were developed in Australia, Brazil, British Guyana, Mozambique, and South-West Africa (later Namibia).[29]

The development of the nuclear power industry, along with the continuing manufacture of nuclear weapons, produced a frantic search for new sources of uranium—the principal fuel for both reactors and bombs. In the postwar years, the United States obtained much of its uranium from the Belgian Congo and the Union of South Africa, two problematic areas (one the site of civil strife and UN intervention, the other ruled by a white supremacist regime) whose importance to the American nuclear program played a significant role in early Cold War politics.[30] France, determined to secure uranium under its own control for both military and electricity-generating purposes, scoured its colonies in Africa, eventually finding rich deposits in Niger.

Whether petroleum or natural gas, copper ore or cobalt, tantalum or uranium, the pattern over the second half of the twentieth century was the same: growing worldwide demand prompted a global search for additional sources of supply, leading to the development of new deposits in previously unexplored areas. Between 1950 and 2000, these efforts led to a substantial increase in the production of raw materials of all kinds, allowing for the tremendous expansion in industrial activity around the world.

WHOLESALE DEPLETION

Today, the demand for natural resources continues to trend upward, driven in large part by surging economic growth in China, India, and other Asian dynamos. As before, this increasing demand places enormous pressure on producers to increase their output of raw materials. But while some of the existing reservoirs may prove capable of increased output, many are showing signs of starkly diminishing capacity.

The most worrisome signs concern the future availability of oil. Between 1950 and 2000, the discovery of giant new fields in Africa, Alaska, Iran, Kuwait, Mexico, Russia, Saudi Arabia, and the North Sea led to a nearly eightfold increase in oil output, from 10 million to 76 million barrels per day. As this period drew to a close, however, it became increasingly clear that many of these fields had passed the moment of maximum production—their "peak"—and were now in decline.

The first major oil province to exhibit signs of profound enfeeblement was the United States. Up until 1970, ever-increasing production in California, Louisiana, Oklahoma, and Texas allowed this country to lead the world in total oil output. That year, total oil production in the Lower 48 states reached 9.4 million barrels per day—an impressive amount even by today's standards. After 1970, though, crude oil production in the Lower 48 suddenly stopped growing and then began a rapid decline, dropping to 7.1 million barrels in 1985 and a mere 4.9 million barrels in 2000.[31] For a time, increased production at Prudhoe Bay in Alaska helped stem the decline in total U.S. crude output. But in 1988, Alaskan petroleum production reached its own peak, and then also began to drop off. Total Alaskan yield fell below 1.0 million barrels per day in 2000, and was running at about 650,000 barrels per day in 2009.[32]

Other oil-producing regions around the world have followed a very similar pattern: steady gains after World War II, an eventual peak in output, followed by relentless decline. The diminishing production at the Cantarell field in Mexico, for example, has been paralleled by a slide in output in Venezuela, another major exporter to the United States. Venezuela's oil production reached a peak of 3.5 million barrels per day in 1998, but it fell to 2.4 million barrels in 2009, and further declines are likely.[33] Production in Russia, meanwhile, reached a peak of 12.5 million barrels per day in 1988, dropped to less than half that level following the collapse of the USSR, and has never fully recovered since then. While the introduction of fresh capital and advanced technologies has restored some of the lost capacity—Russian oil wells produced 9.9 million barrels per day in 2008, and their output has edged up slightly since then—many of the country's giant fields are not capable of further increases.[34]

Signs of exhaustion are also widespread in the North Sea area, one of the greatest discoveries of the postwar era. Combined production in the British and Norwegian sectors of the region peaked in 1999 at 6.1 million barrels per day,[35] but it is expected to drop to less than half that level in the near future. According to the most recent projections from the U.S. Department of Energy, the total British and Norwegian output is expected to fall to 2.8 million barrels per day in 2020 and only 2.6 million barrels per day in 2030.[36]

The decline in these and other major producing areas has generated considerable alarm among energy officials, since it means that the world will require new sources of petroleum on a large enough scale to both satisfy growing demand and compensate for the loss of output from existing fields. To calculate just how much additional production will be needed to offset the decline at existing fields, the International Energy Agency recently conducted a systematic analysis of the world's major producing reservoirs. The study examined historical production records at nearly all of the world's oil fields containing proven and probable reserves in excess of 500 million barrels; together, these reservoirs accounted for more than two-thirds of global crude output in 2007. The results, published in the 2008 edition of the *World Energy Outlook*, were startling.[37]

Extrapolating from their sample to calculate the average decline rate for all fields, the IEA concluded that between 2003 and 2007 the average "natural" decline rate for reservoirs that have passed their peak production was approximately 9.0 percent per year—substantially greater than many had assumed. Because oil companies often employ artificial means to boost production rates at declining fields (the way nitrogen was injected into Cantarell), the actual, "observed" rate of decline was somewhat smaller, an estimated 6.7 percent per year. Still, even the lower "observed" rate means that in the IEA's baseline year of 2007, the net decline from existing fields was about 4.7 million barrels per day, out of a total output of 82 million barrels. This is the amount of new production that had to be obtained from new fields in 2007 simply to maintain consumption at current levels; a like amount, of course, will be needed in every forthcoming year to replace lost output.[38]

Not only is production at existing fields declining more than previously suspected, the IEA discovered, but this rate of decline is itself getting faster every year. In 2003, the natural rate of decline was 8.7 percent per year, whereas by 2007 it had risen a full percentage point, to 9.7 percent annually.[39] IEA analysts attributed this increase in the rate of decline to the progressive depletion of the world's giant oil fields and the resultant reliance on newer and generally smaller fields—which typically reach their peak and start declining much more swiftly than bigger fields.[40] All in all, their analysis points to an inescapable conclusion: the major oil finds of the postwar era—those mammoth discoveries whose prolific output sustained rising global energy needs for nearly half a century—are no longer capable of satisfying the world's requirements. The combined output of the world's ten biggest oil fields (see Table 1.2) has already fallen by 30 percent, and this decline appears irreversible.[41]

The accelerating depletion of existing oil fields, along with doubts

TABLE 1.2: THE WORLD'S TEN BIGGEST OIL FIELDS BY PRODUCTION

(As of 2007)

FIELD	COUNTRY	YEAR OF DISCOVERY	PEAK ANNUAL OUTPUT		2007 OUTPUT Kb/d
			YEAR	Kb/d	
Ghawar	Saudi Arabia	1948	1980	5,588	5,100
Cantarell	Mexico	1979	2003	2,054	1,675
Safaniya	Saudi Arabia	1951	1998	2,128	1,408
Rumaila North and South	Iraq	1953	1979	1,493	1,250
Greater Burgan	Kuwait	1938	1972	2,415	1,170
Samotlor	Russia	1960	1980	3,435	903
Ahwaz	Iran	1958	1977	1,082	770
Zakum	Abu Dhabi	1964	1998	795	674
Azeri-Chirag-Guneshli	Azerbaijan	1985	2007	658	658
Priobskoye	Russia	1982	2007	652	652

Source: International Energy Agency, *World Energy Outlook 2008*, Table 10.1.

Kb/d = thousand barrels per day

about how many new deposits the oil companies will find in frontier regions, has led to growing reliance on "unconventional" oil—Canadian tar sands, shale oil, extra-heavy crude, and other materials obtained from nonstandard petroleum deposits. According to the IEA, such materials will constitute 9 percent of the total world supply in 2035, up from a mere 3 percent in 2009.[42] If this forecast proves accurate, the unconventionals will add 7.2 million barrels per day to global production. But this is not nearly enough to compensate for the expected decline in conventional production from known reserves, so pressure to develop new fields in problematic areas—such as the Arctic, Siberia, and the deep oceans—will only continue to grow.

A CONSISTENT PATTERN

The same pattern seen in the case of oil—a substantial increase in production in the second half of the twentieth century, followed by the wholesale depletion of existing reserves in the early years of the twenty-first—also holds true for many other resources, including natural gas and numerous key minerals.

Because natural gas was developed as an energy source later than petroleum and because the technology to exploit it has lagged behind that of oil, many of the large gas fields discovered in the second half of the twentieth century still retain a large share of their initial supply. Huge quantities of "unconventional" gas can also be extracted from shale rock and other challenging deposits. Even so, a number of the world's most intensely developed natural gas fields are now showing signs of pronounced decline.

The European producers are seeing some of the most dramatic indications of gas-field depletion. In 2000, the United Kingdom produced 3.8 trillion cubic feet of gas, making it the world's fourth largest producer (after Russia, the United States, and Canada). But UK production has diminished steadily since then, falling to 2.1 trillion cubic feet in 2009. The Netherlands, another major North Sea producer, has also experienced declining output as the giant Groningen field has been exhausted. The development of the Snøhvit field, located above the Arctic Circle in the Barents Sea, has so far allowed Norway to compensate for the decline in its other fields, but even with the addition of Arctic gas, net production in western Europe is expected to remain flat over the next five to ten years and then commence a long-term decline.[43]

Parallel declines have been occurring in many key Russian fields. Although Russia's net output continues to grow through the development of previously untapped reserves, the country's two largest gas fields, Urengoy and Yamburg, are clearly becoming depleted. Engineers from Gazprom, the Russian state natural gas monopoly, are trying to sustain output at these fields by drilling deeper into the earth and employing sophisticated production technologies, but this cannot halt their continuing decline. This means that Russia, too, will be able to increase its gas output in the future only if it develops new fields in the Barents Sea, the Kara Sea, and remote, nearly inaccessible regions of Siberia.[44]

The picture is roughly similar in the case of many key minerals. The worldwide hunt for new reserves that accompanied the great economic boom of the postwar era resulted in the discovery and development of rich deposits around the globe, substantially adding to international supplies. But many of these mineral deposits have been so intensively exploited over the past half century that—just like gas fields and oil reservoirs—they are now facing wholesale depletion.

Take the case of copper, one of the world's most important industrial materials. Propelled by soaring demand from China, world copper output jumped from 8.1 million metric tons in 1985 to 15.4 million in 2007.[45] But many existing mines are showing signs of significant decline, often characterized by the exhaustion of high-grade ores and a growing reliance on less-productive, lower-quality supplies. Chile, the world's leading copper producer—accounting for as much as 36 percent of the world's total supply in recent years—has seen its total copper output level off even as world demand continues to grow.[46] With ore qualities in steady decline, the Chilean Copper Commission predicted in 2008 that the country's net output would face an inevitable downturn.[47]

The situation in Indonesia is even more dire. In 2005, Indonesia produced 1.1 million metric tons of copper ore, nearly as much as the United States, the world's second leading producer after Chile. But production has fallen substantially since then, largely as a result of diminishing yields at Freeport-McMoRan's giant Grasberg mine. According to the U.S. Geological Survey, Indonesia's net output in 2008 was just 650,000 metric tons, down more than 40 percent in only three years.[48] With the quality of ores in Grasberg continuing to decline, it is unlikely that Indonesia will be able to reverse this slide. A similar reduction in ore quality and net output has also been recorded in other key copper-producing countries, including Australia, Canada, Mexico, and South Africa.[49] Several other suppliers, including Peru and Zambia, have so far succeeded in boosting their output, but any future expansion of the world copper supply will require the development of new mines in less-explored areas.

What is true for copper is true for other vital minerals, including bauxite, cobalt, nickel, titanium, and specialty metals such as tantalum and platinum. Existing supplies of these minerals may be sufficient for current requirements, but many key sources of supply are in decline even as worldwide demand is rising. Cobalt and nickel, for instance, are increasingly being used as alloys in steel manufacture; both are also used for making long-lasting batteries for hybrid and all-electric cars. Yet even with production of both minerals achieving record highs in recent years, their supply is barely sufficient to satisfy international demand.[50] The hunt for new supplies of these metals has already sent miners to Cameroon, Kazakhstan, Madagascar, New Caledonia, and Papua New Guinea, among other places, and the scope of the search can only increase.[51]

The global demand for titanium is also likely to outpace supply. Prized by many industries for its low weight and high strength, titanium is derived from ilmenite and rutile, which are found in just a handful of locations. At present, the leading suppliers of these ores are Australia, Canada, China, India, Norway, and South Africa. But with many existing mines approaching depletion, production from current titanium sources is not considered sufficient to satisfy future requirements, inspiring efforts to develop new mines in Kenya, Madagascar, Mozambique, and a number of other countries.[52] The situation is roughly the same for lithium, tantalum, and the platinum group metals: demand is rising, output from existing mines is falling, and new reserves will inevitably have to be found in the future.[53]

Looming shortages of rare earth elements—cerium, europium, lanthanum, neodymium, and other exotic metals critical for many high-tech applications—are a particularly worrisome matter. At one time these minerals were produced in significant quantities in the United States, but extracting them from their constituent ores typically requires using large amounts of acids and other toxic chemicals, so most U.S. rare earth mines have now been closed due to environmental concerns. In recent years, China has accounted for more than 95 percent of the world's rare earth supplies, but now it, too, is curbing production out of environmental (and other) concerns. That means that these indispensable minerals will be consistently scarce until new mines can be opened in such locations as Australia, Mongolia, and Greenland.[54]

Not every single mineral is destined to face depletion in the years immediately ahead; modern industrial societies consume a wide variety of metals, and some of them are not currently in short supply. By and large, however, the world's stockpiles of the most widely used minerals are facing a significant risk of contraction. As the Hague Centre for Strategic Studies suggested in a 2010 assessment, "there is no denying that the exhaustion of many existing mines and the shrinking size, increasing remoteness, greater depth, and lower ore grade of new mineable deposits pose a significant challenge to expanding global supplies" of many essential minerals.[55]

UNRELENTING DEMAND

Wherever one looks, therefore, the picture remains the same: the key resource stockpiles that have sustained global economic expansion for the past sixty-five years are approaching wholesale exhaustion. Even if the global economy suddenly stopped growing altogether, the world would be on its way to painful shortages of critical materials. But aside from occasional bouts of recession, the world economy is likely to continue growing in the years ahead. According to a projection by the U.S. Department of Energy, worldwide GDP will grow by an estimated 3.4 percent per year between 2008 and 2035, climbing from $66 trillion to $162 trillion over the course of this period (in constant 2005 dollars).[56] Demand for basic resources is bound to expand at a comparable pace, placing extraordinary pressure on energy and mineral producers to find and develop new sources of supply.

This search will be driven most urgently by the need for added supplies of energy, especially oil and natural gas. According to the most recent projections from the DoE, between 2008 and 2035 the world's consumption of liquid fuels will rise by 31 percent (to a total of 112 million barrels per day) and the consumption of natural gas will grow by 52 percent (to 169 trillion cubic feet per year).[57] To meet this rise in demand, the energy industry must substantially increase the production of these resources. Some of the additional oil and gas will be extracted from fields in existing hydrocarbon provinces, such as the Persian Gulf and West Africa, but much of it will have to come from newly developed fields in the Arctic, Siberia, and ultra-deep waters.

The need to develop new sources of oil and natural gas will be particularly important for China and the United States, the world's leading consumers of energy. In 2035, the DoE predicts, China and the United States will jointly consume 39 million barrels of oil per day, or about 35 percent of total world consumption.[58] Neither country is capable of satisfying its energy requirements from existing domestic sources, so both China and the United States will have to develop as-yet-untapped reservoirs within their own territories and gain access to new deposits abroad. To a considerable degree, the need for supplemental energy sources will push these countries to develop reserves in remote and challenging areas, and to place greater weight on unconventional hydrocarbons such as oil sands and shale gas.

The task of finding and exploiting these new deposits will be carried out to a large extent by the major private energy companies, which have long taken the lead in seeking out new sources of supply. Giant corporations such as BP, Chevron, ExxonMobil, and Royal Dutch Shell are set to spend hundreds of billions of dollars over the next few decades to explore promising reservoirs in the Arctic, the deep oceans, and other formerly inaccessible areas. But governments, too, will become involved in the hunt for fresh reserves. Chinese leaders, wary of depending too much on Western-owned private firms for access to new sources of energy, have been pushing state-owned Chinese energy firms to undertake similar searches. This will mean a more conspicuous international role for the China National Petroleum Corporation (CNPC), the China National Offshore Oil Corporation (CNOOC), and the China National Petrochemical Corporation (Sinopec).[59]

A similar pattern is emerging in the case of industrial minerals. As with oil and gas, the demand for mineral ores is growing rapidly: in the first decade of the twenty-first century the global consumption of copper rose by 23 percent, while iron ore and aluminum each increased by 68 percent.[60] With industrialization and urbanization continuing apace in much of the developing world, there is every reason to assume that such demand will continue to grow at comparable rates in the years ahead. The consumption of many specialty minerals—including lithium, platinum, tantalum, and the rare earth elements—is likely to experience even faster rates of growth, as various high-tech devices that rely on these metals become increasingly popular.[61]

Here, too, as in so much else, China is expected to play a dominant role. In recent years, the Chinese have been the first or second leading consumers of aluminum, copper, iron ore, nickel, tin, tungsten, and other vital minerals.[62] While some of China's mineral requirements can be satisfied by its domestic mines, such rapidly growing demand has meant that an ever-growing share of the country's supplies must come from foreign sources.[63] Many of the world's leading mining firms—BHP Billiton, Rio Tinto, and Vale of Brazil, among others—are scouring the world for new ore deposits in order to satisfy China's soaring mineral requirements. Just as in the energy field, however, the Chinese government is seeking to ensure a prominent role in these endeavors for the country's state-owned firms, such as the Aluminum Corporation of China (Chinalco) and the China Metallurgical Group Corporation (MCC).

But China is hardly alone in relying on government-backed enterprises to spearhead the search for vital resources. With demand growing for many critical materials and supply often failing to keep pace, other countries have also created special programs to enhance or supplement the endeavors of private companies. The Japanese government, for example, has established the Japan Oil, Gas, and Metals National Corporation (JOGMEC), whose stated aim is to ensure "a stable supply of natural resources for Japan." Among its principal functions is to finance efforts by Japanese mining companies to produce key minerals needed by the nation's industries, including copper, uranium, and the rare earth elements. Recognizing that Japan itself possesses few of these materials and that many traditional sources of supply have been exhausted,

JOGMEC encourages Japanese firms to pursue mining opportunities in remote and unfamiliar locations abroad.[64]

Even the most basic necessities of life are not exempt from this hunt for the world's remaining resources. With world population expected to increase from approximately 7 billion people in 2011 to more than 9 billion in 2050,[65] simply meeting the world's minimum food requirements will prove an extraordinary challenge. Currently existing farmland is wholly inadequate to support population growth on this scale, so new lands will have to be cultivated. Meanwhile, existing fields will be pressed to produce bigger yields—increasing the global demand for water, fertilizer, pesticides, and other inputs. All this will add to the pressure on commodity suppliers to seek out and develop new deposits of natural resources wherever they can be found.

As in the case of energy and minerals, the hunt for prime farmland and other ingredients in the production of food is being spearheaded by large private companies with particular expertise in the field. In recent years, vast tracts of agricultural land have been bought by such firms as Black River Asset Management, Bunge North America, Emergent Asset Management, and Hancock Agricultural Investment Group—companies that regard cropland as yet another dwindling natural resource, every bit as valuable as oil fields, copper mines, and the like. But here, too, government-backed entities are playing a conspicuous role. Fearing that their nations' domestic food output will prove inadequate to feed growing populations, the leaders of some countries—particularly in the water-scarce Persian Gulf area—have established special agencies to acquire farmland abroad. For the most part, these lands are being sought in poor and war-torn African countries, whose own leaders are desperate to attract fresh investment no matter how problematic the circumstances.[66]

This, then, is where we stand: many of the major resource reserves that have sustained global economic growth over the past sixty years are facing systemic depletion. Merely replacing the lost output from these exhausted deposits will require a major effort of exploration and development, while achieving any further growth will demand a truly unprecedented and often perilous undertaking. Because most of the world has already been scoured for readily accessible resource reserves, the only hope for finding more oil, natural gas, minerals, and farmland will lie in extending the search to previously inaccessible or inhospitable areas—the Arctic, the deep oceans, and countries long torn by war and internal strife.

2 ► DEEP-OFFSHORE OIL AND GAS

At the onset of the twenty-first century, the BP corporation—once known as British Petroleum—announced that it would stop focusing primarily on oil and natural gas and instead concentrate on the development of renewable energy sources such as wind, solar, and biofuels. John Browne, then BP's chief executive officer, proclaimed that the company needed "to look beyond oil and gas to fuels which can be produced locally and which do not threaten the sustainability of the world's climate."[1] An advertising campaign rebranded BP as "Beyond Petroleum," and the company changed its logo to a green-edged sunburst.

BP's focus on renewables delighted politicians and environmentalists, and Browne was knighted by Queen Elizabeth II for his enlightened leadership on energy matters. But the "Beyond Petroleum" campaign contributed little to the company's bottom line, and was soon deemphasized. In 2008, Browne was replaced as CEO by Tony Hayward, who immediately announced plans to restore the company's traditional focus on petroleum.[2] "The energy of the future will be more than oil, but oil will still be a major part of it," Hayward declared in February 2010.[3] He closed the company's "alternative energy" office and ramped up investment in the oil and gas sector.

In seeking to restore BP's emphasis on oil, however, Hayward encountered an intractable problem: most of the world's large, easy-to-reach oil fields were already depleted, or were under the control of state-owned firms like Saudi Aramco and the National Iranian Oil Company. (Originally private entities and known, respectively, as Aramco and the Anglo-Iranian Oil Company, these two firms were brought under state control from 1970 onward.) Like other private oil companies, BP therefore had no choice but to concentrate its search for new reserves in remote, inhospitable, or hard-to-reach areas. "We have learned how to find and produce oil and gas in challenging surroundings from the Arctic to the Sahara, from the Gulf of Mexico to western Siberia," BP's chief of exploration and production said at a March 2010 industry conference. "We operate at the frontiers of geography, geology, environment, and geopolitics."[4]

Of all these initiatives, the highest priority was given to expanding BP's drilling operations in the deep waters of the U.S. Gulf of Mexico. BP was not the first company to drill in the deepwater Gulf—Shell, Chevron, and several others had arrived there long before—but it quickly became a major player in the region. "BP is the leading operator in the deepwater Gulf of Mexico," the company boasted in its 2009 *Annual Review.* "We are the biggest producer, the leading resource holder, and have the largest exploration acreage position."[5] Intent on maintaining its dominance, BP drilled at ever-increasing distances from the shore and at ever-greater depths.[6] In September 2009, the *Deepwater Horizon*, a mobile drilling rig leased by BP, dug the deepest well ever recorded: the 35,055-feet Tiber prospect, located 300 miles off the Texas coast. Initial test results indicated that Tiber contained as much as six billion barrels of oil, making this one of the largest fields ever discovered on U.S. territory.[7]

Elated by the Tiber discovery, BP officials sought to continue their exploration of the Gulf's deepwater reserves. At the beginning of 2010, they moved the *Deepwater Horizon* to another promising location: the Mississippi Canyon 252 block, located some fifty miles south of the

Louisiana coastline. After several months of drilling, this well, named Macondo—after the fictional town of that name in Gabriel García Márquez's novel *One Hundred Years of Solitude*—also reached a large reservoir of oil. Having completed their assigned task of drilling down to the petroleum layer, the crew of the *Deepwater Horizon* began to seal the Macondo well (to be reopened later by a regular production platform) as they prepared to relocate to yet another exploration site in the Gulf. However, on April 20, 2010, as they attempted to complete the seal, a volatile mix of petroleum and gas escaped from the well and raced up a connecting tube to the rig. The resulting explosion killed 11 of the 126 workers on board and produced a gigantic underwater oil gusher.[8]

The *Deepwater Horizon* disaster focused extraordinary attention on oil company operations in the deepwater Gulf. Many commentators, especially those drawn from within the oil industry itself, portrayed the disaster as an exceptional, one-of-a-kind event. In their view, negligent oversight at BP headquarters led to a chain of mistakes that together caused the explosion; had these mistakes not been made, the disaster could have been avoided.[9] Further analysis, however, presents a far different picture. It is now clear that drilling in deep offshore waters poses enormous dangers to any company that undertakes it. Nonetheless, with most other oil fields suffering from depletion, the major energy firms see no choice but to keep expanding their presence in deep-offshore areas, multiplying the risks of another major accident.

The challenges posed by drilling in deep-offshore locations are partly a product of the physical environment itself: the immense pressures encountered at these depths produce unique and often unforeseen stresses on personnel and equipment. Beyond that, offshore rigs are also particularly vulnerable to the elements, including hurricanes, typhoons, and, in the far northern latitudes, floating ice. In addition, many offshore fields lie in politically contested waters, leading to fierce disputes between neighboring powers over the exploitation of these undersea deposits. As the world comes to rely on deepwater oil and gas for more and more of its energy, such difficulties will assume ever-greater importance.

INVADING THE DEEP WATERS

It is important to emphasize the distinction between offshore drilling in general and the specific practice of *deepwater* drilling. Oil companies have been extracting oil from coastal areas for more than fifty years, essentially placing ordinary (onshore) drilling towers onto platforms installed in shallow water. But "deepwater" drilling, generally defined as drilling at depths greater than 1,000 feet, is a relatively new phenomenon, involving the use of sophisticated technologies that had to be developed specifically for this purpose. Even newer is the practice of drilling "ultra-deepwater" wells, lying at depths of over one mile. Producing oil at such depths requires highly specialized rigs that can cost hundreds of millions or even billions of dollars.

Extracting oil from ultra-deepwater wells is so challenging and expensive that it has drawn comparisons with space exploration. As the national commission assigned to investigate the *Deepwater Horizon* points out, in 1996—six months before NASA launched the celebrated *Pathfinder* probe to planet Mars—Shell had deployed an oil platform called *Mars* in the deepwater Gulf. "At a total cost of $1 billion, Shell's *Mars* was more than three times as expensive as the Mars *Pathfinder*, and its remote technologies and engineering systems were arguably more sophisticated," the commission noted.[10]

But however costly and complicated, such investments are considered essential by the major oil companies as they attempt to maintain the pace of production in the face of declining output elsewhere. According to a March 2010 report by energy expert Michael Smith of Datamonitor, the giant oil companies will spend an estimated $387 billion on offshore drilling operations between 2010 and 2014—a 33 percent increase over the amount spent in the previous five-year period. Smith also projected that between 2010 and 2014, the major energy firms will drill a record 20,000 offshore wells, with an ever-increasing share of these to be located in deep and ultra-deep waters.[11]

With such vast efforts being devoted to offshore production, and with the major onshore fields continuing to be depleted, more and more of the world's oil and natural gas will come from offshore fields. According to a recent assessment by energy analyst John Westwood, offshore oil output will contribute 35 percent of global supplies in 2020, up from about 28 percent in 1995. More important, the share of world oil provided by deep and ultra-deep wells will grow from only 1 percent in 1995 to a projected 10 percent in 2020. Westwood further predicts that after 2015, onshore and shallow-water oil wells will not yield any further increases in output, leaving deep-offshore fields as the *only* source of growth to power the world's expanding economy. A similar prospect holds for natural gas: whereas in 2000 approximately 27 percent of the world's gas supplies came from offshore fields, by the year 2020 that share will rise to 41 percent.[12] Any energy firm that intends to continue being involved in the production of hydrocarbons must, therefore, establish a significant presence in the major deepwater drilling zones.

Coastal drilling occurs in many waters that lie near or adjacent to large onshore oil fields, but deepwater production is a more specialized activity, occurring in far fewer locations. At present, such drilling is under way in several areas—the Gulf of Mexico, offshore Brazil, the Gulf of Guinea, and the South China Sea—and most of the big private firms have sought to be present in all of them. Of these, the U.S. Gulf of Mexico has attracted particularly avid attention, especially from BP, Chevron, and Shell.

The Gulf of Mexico has become such a powerful magnet for deepwater development because it is thoroughly served with support infrastructure and yet remains relatively undeveloped. Recent exploration activity suggest that it harbors large deposits of oil and natural gas in what is called the Lower Tertiary trend, a formation of ancient rocks buried beneath miles of water, sand, salt, and stone. Some analysts believe the Lower Tertiary could hold as much as 15 billion barrels of oil—

equivalent to half of America's proven reserves.[13] "This looks to be the biggest discovery in the United States in a generation, really since the discovery of Prudhoe Bay [in Alaska] 38 years ago," oil historian Daniel Yergin said of the Lower Tertiary formation. "What's really happening is the opening up of a whole new horizon in the ultra-deep waters of the Gulf of Mexico, and it looks like the upside is very significant."[14]

Eager to tap into this colossal treasure, the giant oil companies have dedicated enormous sums to acquiring and developing offshore blocks in the Gulf. (Governments often divide up their offshore production zones into rectangular plots, or "blocks," and auction off the exclusive right to explore and extract oil from each one.) Chevron, for example, has allocated $3.5 billion for the Tahiti deepwater prospect,[15] which it described in 2008 as "one of the largest discoveries to date in the deep-water U.S. Gulf of Mexico." Extracting oil from the Tahiti field, the company boasted, was a feat that was "pushing the limits of technology . . . in extremely high-temperature, high-pressure environments."[16] Other companies have made similarly massive commitments to the Gulf, buying up many exploration blocks and exploring them systematically. A 2006 investigation by the *New York Times* reported that BP was spending more than $2 billion on such endeavors every year.[17]

In pushing ahead with these costly and elaborate oil-extraction efforts, the oil companies have periodically encountered one of the Gulf's inescapable dangers: hurricanes. Many of the hurricanes that afflict the United States each summer and fall pass through the Gulf of Mexico before striking land, and typically these storms reach their greatest intensity over the Gulf's open waters—posing a potentially devastating threat to exposed drilling equipment. In July 2005, as BP's *Thunder Horse* rig was being readied for production, it was severely damaged by Hurricane Dennis; emergency repairs by company technicians saved the rig from sinking into the Gulf, but it took BP three years and some $5 billion to make it seaworthy and capable of undertaking full-scale production.[18] Hurricane Katrina, which swept through in August 2005, is mostly remembered today for its catastrophic impact on the city of New Orleans, but it also destroyed 47 drilling platforms in the Gulf of

Mexico. Hurricane Rita, coming one month later, destroyed another 66 platforms and badly damaged 32 more.[19]

Despite these dangers, the major firms have pushed into deeper and deeper waters, breaking one record after another. In December 2005, Chevron announced that it and its partners had dug the "deepest well ever drilled in the U.S. Gulf of Mexico." Called Knotty Head and located some 170 miles southeast of New Orleans, this well was dug in 3,500 feet of water and extended another 30,700 feet into the earth.[20] Just nine months later, Chevron announced another record-setting achievement: the Jack No. 2 well in Walker Ridge block 758, approximately 270 miles southwest of New Orleans. This well, the company reported, was located in 7,000 feet of water and was drilled to a depth of 28,175 feet.[21] More recently, the record passed to Shell, which announced in March 2010 that it had commenced operations at "the world's deepest offshore drilling and production facility." Located in Alaminos Canyon block 857, some 200 miles east of the Texas coast, Shell's Perdido development sits in 8,000 feet of water—which is, as the company put it, "roughly equivalent to six Empire State Buildings stacked one atop the other."[22]

Determined to compete with Shell and Chevron as a major player in the deepwater Gulf, BP was especially aggressive in acquiring promising exploration blocks and drilling in ever-deeper waters. In its unrelenting hunt for new fields to exploit, BP leased a number of rigs from various oil-service firms, deploying them throughout the region and moving them from one promising site to another. These giant vessels, capable of drilling in thousands of feet of water, are costly to operate: the *Deepwater Horizon*, for example, was costing BP $1 million per day in rental and staffing fees. When BP first deployed the rig at the Macondo prospect in January 2010, it set a target date of March 7 for completion of that well. However, due to a series of geological obstacles and technical mishaps, drilling was not completed until April 19, producing a cost overrun on the project of approximately $58 million.[23] It is not surprising, then, that BP's site managers felt particular pressure to seal the well and move the *Deepwater Horizon* to its next scheduled location.

In their rush, the site managers made several last-minute decisions

DEEPWATER HORIZON DISASTER

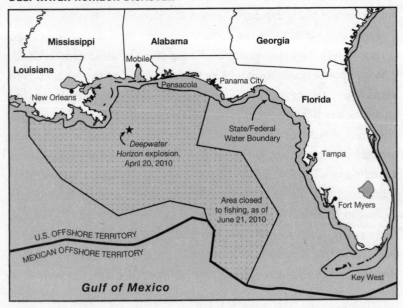

that, in the opinion of many analysts, contributed to the risk of a blow-out—an explosive release of oil and gas from the well into the riser, a connecting tube leading to the drillship itself. When preparing for the final cementing that would prevent natural gas from leaking into the wellbore, for instance, they decided to use only six "centralizers" to position the well's steel casing, whereas the original design had called for twenty-one centralizers. They also went ahead with the sealing of the well even though several "negative-pressure" tests suggested a dangerous buildup of gas in the wellbore. These were not the only factors behind the disaster: faulty equipment, imperfections in the sealing cement, miscommunication between key actors aboard the ship, and other issues also played a role. But the desire to complete the job swiftly and move the expensive drillship to its next assignment certainly contributed to the disaster.[24]

In the aftermath of the April 20, 2010, tragedy, some observers tried to portray BP as an outlier in the industry, an exceptionally risky operator. But BP was hardly the only company to overlook substantial risks to human and environmental safety as it pushed the limits of deepwater drilling. Indeed, fires and other accidents have occurred at many other firms' deepwater facilities, and a major disaster could have taken place on any of them.[25] "In the years before the Macondo blowout, neither industry nor government adequately addressed these risks," observed the national commission established by President Obama to investigate the BP explosion. "Absent major crises, and given the remarkable financial returns available from deepwater reserves, the business culture succumbed to a false sense of security. The *Deepwater Horizon* disaster exhibits the costs of a culture of complacency."[26]

GOVERNMENTAL COLLUSION

As the national commission noted, oil and gas companies were not solely to blame for the perilous state of drilling in the U.S. Gulf of Mexico. Government action—and inaction—also played a crucial part. Indeed, it is important to recognize that giant energy firms were not the only ones eager to boost energy output from the deepwater Gulf to replace the reserves being depleted on land and in shallower waters: from the mid-1990s onward, key figures in the American government were equally interested in promoting such an increase. Hoping both to reduce U.S. reliance on imported oil and to spur economic growth in the Gulf Coast region, a succession of presidents and influential lawmakers took a number of significant steps to encourage offshore drilling in federally controlled waters.

Initially, the primary focus of those efforts was the central and western area of the Gulf of Mexico, off Alabama, Louisiana, Mississippi, and Texas. In 1995, Congress and the executive branch authorized the Interior Department's Minerals Management Service (MMS) to waive or reduce royalty payments owed to the federal government by energy firms that produced oil and natural gas in the Gulf's deep waters. When the original bill expired in 2000, Congress authorized the MMS to continue providing such "royalty relief" under other legislation. The oil companies eagerly responded, snapping up drilling leases in the deepwater Gulf and substantially expanding their operations there.[27]

The Interior Department's Minerals Management Service also facilitated drilling in the deepwater Gulf by taking a lax approach to environmental and safety regulations. Until the tragic events of 2010, the MMS was officially responsible for enforcing the National Environmental Policy Act, the Endangered Species Act, and other environmental legislation as it pertained to offshore drilling; the agency was also responsible for ensuring that offshore operators complied with federal safety rules. If they had been so inclined, therefore, MMS officials could have employed these regulatory tools to exert significant control over offshore operations, possibly slowing the rush into the Gulf's deep waters. However, it is clear that the MMS often waived compliance with these measures, or simply rubber-stamped promises by the operating firms that they would follow the requirements.[28] As the investigators of the *Deepwater Horizon* disaster later put it, "many critical aspects of drilling operations were left to industry to decide without agency review." The MMS, for instance, never established any minimum criteria for negative-pressure tests, one of the key factors in the Macondo blowout.[29]

In 2008, with drilling in the central and western Gulf already going at full tilt and oil prices headed toward record highs, many Republicans and some Democrats began calling for offshore production to be expanded even further—into the eastern Gulf (off Florida) and areas off the Atlantic and Pacific coasts, where drilling had been banned for several decades due to fears of environmental damage. Chants of "drill, baby, drill" were heard at many Republican rallies during the presidential campaign, and even the Democratic candidate Senator Barack Obama refused to rule out such steps. After assuming the presidency, Obama initially took a go-slow approach on the issue, but on March 31, 2010, he made a pro-drilling announcement whose scope astonished many observers. Obama had decided to open up to drilling not only a large area of the eastern Gulf of Mexico, but also a long stretch of the Atlantic coast as well as portions of the Beaufort and Chukchi Seas abutting Alaska, all of which had previously been off-limits. In his speech, the president suggested that investing in renewable forms of energy was a better long-term plan for America, but he argued that increased drilling was necessary "to maintain our economic growth and our security" while work on renewables got under way.[30]

The explosion of the *Deepwater Horizon* just nineteen days after this announcement did not alter Obama's permissive attitude toward offshore drilling. On April 23, 2010, three days after the explosion, a White House spokesperson affirmed that President Obama still wanted to increase offshore oil production and still believed that "the great majority of that can be done safely, securely, and without harm to the environment."[31] Only after the vast scale of the disaster became evident, with BP repeatedly failing in its initial attempts to plug the undersea leak, did the president adopt a more cautious stance. In May, Obama suspended all plans for further leasing of offshore blocks in the areas covered by his March 31 announcement, and imposed a six-month ban on drilling in the deepwater Gulf of Mexico to allow the Department of the Interior to improve safety procedures on offshore rigs. The dysfunctional Minerals Management Service was disbanded, and its regulatory functions were assigned to a new agency, the Bureau of Ocean Energy Management, Regulation, and Enforcement (BOEMRE). Finally, President Obama established a bipartisan commission to investigate the *Deepwater Horizon* explosion and suggest reforms to prevent such a disaster from occurring again.

The commission's key findings about the disaster itself have already been summarized here: the *Deepwater Horizon* explosion was largely the result of faulty decisions made by BP and by some of its contractors in the last days of work on the Macondo well, which were, in turn, shaped by the overall "culture of complacency" that pervaded both industry and government. As far as future offshore drilling is concerned, the commission took a somewhat ambivalent stance. It did not ask for deep offshore drilling to be banned altogether, acknowledging that such endeavors can contribute to America's energy needs and to the economy of the Gulf Coast region. But the commission was emphatic that the drilling needed to be more closely regulated. "To assure human safety and environmental protection, regulatory oversight of leasing, energy exploration, and production require reforms even beyond those significant reforms already initiated since the *Deepwater Horizon*," it declared.[32]

By the time the commission's final report came out in January 2011, however, the pendulum had already begun to swing back in the other direction. Furious that no new permits for deepwater drilling in the Gulf were being given out even after the six-month moratorium had ended in October 2010, oil companies took to the courts to force the issue.[33] In February 2011, a federal judge in New Orleans ruled that the delay was "inexcusable" and ordered the Interior Department to begin processing permits "within a reasonable period of time."[34] A few weeks later, the new Bureau of Ocean Energy Management, Regulation, and Enforcement issued its first deepwater permit under a set of revised safety rules; by April 2011, BOEMRE was issuing permits on a regular basis,[35] and by summer drilling in the deepwater Gulf resumed its predisaster tempo.

Even BP, the party widely deemed most responsible for the *Deepwater Horizon* disaster, has now announced plans to resume drilling in the Gulf of Mexico. The company will be "back and actively drilling during the second half of the year," BP chief financial officer Byron Grote proclaimed in April 2011, one year after the explosion.[36] In October 2011, after examining the company's proposal for renewed drilling, BOEMRE gave BP the go-ahead to drill four new exploratory wells. And while the Macondo field was not included in the proposal, BP executives now say that it will someday be unsealed and brought into production. "Clearly it was a discovery," said BP senior vice president Kent Wells of Macondo. "There is a good reservoir there." Given that someone is bound to exploit the site eventually, Wells insisted, there is no reason to rule out BP as the company that will do so.[37]

At present, the Obama administration's plan to expand drilling into the Atlantic coastal area has been put on hold, but the notion hardly has been abandoned. The political leaders of Virginia, for example, are particularly keen to promote offshore drilling in their state's offshore waters. Among other initiatives, they have been encouraging the federal government to go ahead with an auction for Lease Sale 220, a 2.9-million-acre tract in the Atlantic Ocean some fifty miles off Virginia's coast that is said to contain approximately 130 million barrels of oil and 1.1 trillion cubic feet of gas.[38] The planned sale was suspended in May 2010, but a year later the U.S. House of Representatives passed a measure meant to force the administration to reschedule it. Although the Senate has not approved a similar bill, and Obama is thus not legally bound by the House vote, he has promised to speed up the administration's reassessment of potential Atlantic drilling.[39]

DRILLING IN "ICEBERG ALLEY"

While the future of offshore drilling in America's Atlantic waters remains uncertain, there is no such doubt in Canada's Atlantic provinces. There, offshore production has been under way for several decades already and now appears to be headed for a significant increase.

Most of the offshore energy production in Atlantic Canada is concentrated in two main areas: oil in the Jeanne d'Arc basin southeast of St. John's, Newfoundland, and natural gas in the Scotian basin south of Halifax, Nova Scotia. In 2009, the three main fields in the Newfoundland area were jointly producing approximately 370,000 barrels of oil per day, while the main field off Nova Scotia was producing some 400 million cubic feet of natural gas (equivalent to 76,000 barrels of oil) per day. If new projects currently being discussed for the region—including deep-sea operations in the North Atlantic—reach fruition, these figures could rise significantly.[40]

Deep offshore drilling can be hazardous at the best of times, but getting oil from beneath Canada's Atlantic waters is particularly dangerous. Winter storms are fierce and frequent, producing strong winds and giant waves. For anyone unlucky enough to fall from a boat or drilling rig, immersion in the frigid waters of the North Atlantic for more than a few minutes is almost certain to prove fatal. Even the giant rigs themselves are at significant risk from the elements: most of the oil platforms in the Jeanne d'Arc basin are planted in what locals call "Iceberg Alley,"

OFFSHORE DRILLING IN "ICEBERG ALLEY"

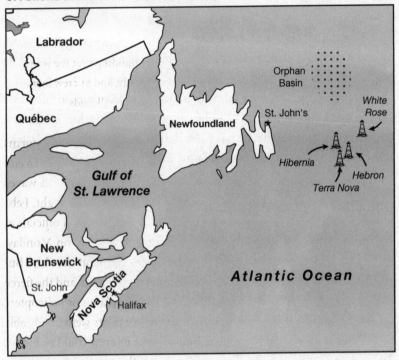

the treacherous stretch of ocean that sealed the fate of the *Titanic* on April 14, 1912.[41]

These sorts of hazards have slowed and complicated work on all of the major offshore operations in Atlantic Canada, particularly Hibernia, the region's biggest and most expensive project. Hibernia was first conceived in 1979, when a test well in the Jeanne d'Arc basin suggested the presence of a major oil deposit. To gauge the extent of the field, Mobil Oil, the lead company involved, rented a mobile drill rig called the *Ocean Ranger* and moved it to the Hibernia site. A reporter for the *New York Times* visited the drillship while it was stationed off Newfoundland in March 1981, and filed this dramatic report:

A fuzzy dawn is breaking in the foggiest part of the North Atlantic, where four men cling to a basket dangling 160 feet above a choppy, cobalt-blue sea. By stomach-churning tugs, they are being hoisted to their jobs on the world's largest drilling rig, the 15,000-ton *Ocean Ranger*. . . . The mist-shrouded rig, nicknamed the Ocean Danger, looms over them. Its derrick stands as tall as a 35-story building over the water, 14,400 horsepower of machinery pounds relentlessly, and 81 crew members scurry about a surface area bigger than two football fields.[42]

Eleven months after this article appeared, one of the mighty storms that regularly sweep through the North Atlantic assaulted the *Ocean Ranger*. Battered by winds of up to ninety miles per hour and waves more than fifty feet high, the ship began to list. On Sunday night, February 14, 1982, officers aboard the vessel spoke by radio with officials at Mobil Oil about the worsening situation and, at 2:54 a.m. on Monday, Mobil ordered all eighty-four crew members to abandon the ship. But radio communications with the stricken vessel then ceased, and the fierce storm conditions made it impossible to send rescue planes or helicopters to the site. The next day, when Canadian Air Force pilots were finally able to search the area, no sign of the *Ocean Ranger* or its crew could be found. Eventually, twenty-two bodies were recovered; the remaining sixty-two crew members are assumed to have disappeared in the icy Atlantic.[43]

Despite the *Ocean Ranger* disaster, Mobil and its partners did not give up on the Hibernia prospect. In 1988, the Canadian government—eager to generate economic activity and boost employment in perennially depressed Newfoundland—offered $2 billion in grants and loan guarantees to the beleaguered venture, and the government eventually also acquired a significant number of shares in the enterprise. The consortium then spent several years and $5 billion building the world's largest, heaviest, and costliest oil-drilling platform, a 1.2-million-ton Leviathan that sits in 300 feet of water and is armored with sixteen protecting "teeth" designed to absorb the impact of any icebergs that might drift into its path.[44] The *Hibernia* platform finally began producing oil in 1997, and currently supplies approximately 135,000 barrels per day.

Two other drilling platforms—*White Rose* and *Terra Nova*—are also currently active in the Jeanne d'Arc basin, and plans are under way for more operations to join them in the region. ExxonMobil, for example, has begun work on the *Hebron* platform, an armored monster like *Hibernia* to be deployed in an adjacent Jeanne d'Arc sector. Production is slated to begin at Hebron in 2017 and could reach 180,000 barrels per day.[45] Statoil of Norway has also announced plans to drill in this area, while several other companies have acquired leases in the Orphan basin, which is even deeper and farther north than Jeanne d'Arc.[46]

One month after the *Deepwater Horizon* explosion in the Gulf of Mexico—at a time when all deep-offshore drilling in the United States was halted pending a review of safety regulations—Chevron began work on Canada's deepest well to date: the Lona O-55 prospect in the Orphan basin, located in about 1.7 miles of water some 260 miles northeast of St. John's.[47] Despite the environmental damage then being inflicted on the Gulf of Mexico, Canadian government officials expressed complete confidence that drilling in the Orphan basin was "safe and prudent."[48] Still, given that the Lona O-55 well is located in the very heart of Iceberg Alley, many critics worry that the project is especially likely to result in catastrophe.

BRAZIL'S "PRE-SALT" DISCOVERIES

While numerous drilling platforms are already operating in the Gulf of Mexico and in Canada's Atlantic waters, no area of the deep Atlantic currently being explored for new sources of oil and gas surpasses the promise of deep-offshore Brazil. In November 2007, Brazil's state-run oil company Petróleo Brasileiro S.A. (Petrobras) announced that it had discovered a giant supply of petroleum under the ocean some 180 miles east of Rio de Janeiro. The new reservoir, called Tupi, lies beneath 1.5 miles of water and another 2.5 miles of rock, salt, and sand. According to preliminary estimates, Tupi harbors some 8 billion barrels of oil, making this the largest oil discovery since the Kashagan field was found in the Caspian Sea in 2000. Even more significant, Tupi was found to lie near several other "pre-salt" fields, swelling Brazil's deep-offshore bonanza to mammoth proportions—perhaps exceeding 50 billion barrels altogether.[49]

BRAZIL'S "PRE-SALT" FIELDS

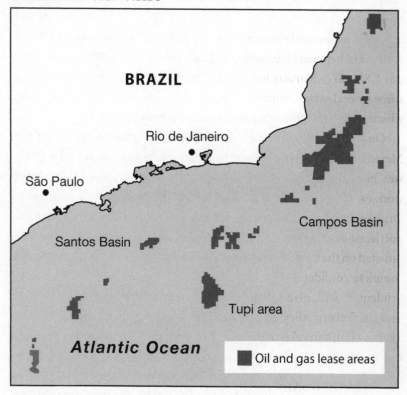

The discovery of Tupi and other pre-salt fields "could make Brazil jump from an intermediate producer to among the world's largest producers," exulted Dilma Rousseff, who at the time was serving as chief of staff to President Luiz Inácio Lula da Silva (known as Lula) and has now succeeded him in the presidency.[50] (In 2010, Tupi was officially renamed Lula in honor of the president.) Although it will take several years to determine the true extent of these reservoirs and to initiate full-scale production, Petrobras predicts that its net output will jump from 2.7 million barrels per day in 2011 to 6.4 million barrels in 2020, with much of the increase coming from the pre-salt fields. As its output grows, Brazil eventually will eclipse Venezuela, the current top oil producer in South America. But achieving this increase will require overcoming enormous challenges, both technological and political.[51]

From a practical standpoint, extracting oil from the pre-salt basins will require even greater technological virtuosity than that employed in the Gulf of Mexico. As in the Gulf, the offshore rigs will be operating in waters well over one mile in depth, and they will have to penetrate through several additional miles of earth and salt to reach the oil. The undersea layers of rock and sand also contain immense pockets of natural gas, which somehow must be separated from whatever oil is recovered from the field. All of this will require the use of advanced technologies at the cutting edge of the industry's capacity. Petrobras has long been a leader in offshore production, but the challenge of developing the pre-salt basins is so great that it is being forced to participate in joint ventures with major private companies, including Chevron, ExxonMobil, and Shell.

Brazilian government officials are aware of the need to draw on the technical expertise of the private firms, known as international oil companies (IOCs); at the same time, however, they are reluctant to award too much control to the IOCs, lest the profits from the pre-salt fields be used to enrich foreign corporate interests rather than the Brazilian people. For top officials like Lula and Rousseff, the offshore fields are part of Brazil's national inheritance, and should be used solely to promote the national interest. "We have to take advantage of this oil to develop the country," Lula proclaimed in a 2008 interview. "It's a chance for the Brazilian poor to use the money as opposed to having people with a lot of oil and three or four watches and a Rolex in their pockets. We want to take advantage of these riches to ensure that Brazil can take a great leap forward."[52]

To achieve this goal, Lula and Rousseff have devised strict controls for the development of the pre-salt fields. Under the government's plan, approved by the Brazilian Congress in December 2010, state-controlled Petrobras will be designated the sole operator of every partnership established to exploit the fields, and will be guaranteed a minimum 30 percent stake in these consortia. In addition, a new government agency, Petrosal, is being established to administer the state's share in the projects, and a new national fund will be created to manage and allocate the resulting revenues.[53] "The subsalt oil fields are a gift from God—wealth which, if properly managed, can drive major transformations in Brazil," Lula declared when announcing the measures.[54]

The ambitious plans for government involvement have generated considerable controversy in Brazil and beyond. Some energy experts warn that the new regulations might discourage participation by the IOCs. "The emphasis upon Petrobras as the sole operator in the pre-salt basin would surely slow the pace of development of new projects," the U.S. Department of Energy warned in 2009. "The rules would also increase the government take of profits from oil production, possibly reducing the incentive for private companies to participate."[55] The creation of the new government social fund has also raised concerns about potential cronyism and corruption.[56]

In response, Lula, Rousseff, and their allies argue that Petrobras and Petrosal are fully capable of managing the pre-salt fields. They also insist that Brazil's political and economic system is sufficiently robust to escape the "resource curse" that has afflicted other developing nations, where a sudden infusion of oil wealth has often resulted in widespread corruption and authoritarianism. "This model is right for the amount of oil we have, for the low level of exploratory risk and because of the high levels of returns," Rousseff declared in 2009.[57] As for the "resource curse," she said, it is not a worry, given "the hard-earned fact that the oil bonanza arrives in a diverse economy and a land rich in many natural resources."[58]

Brazil's efforts to develop its offshore reserves have received strong support from President Obama, who believes that Brazilian oil exports will someday enable the United States to reduce its reliance on the ever-turbulent Middle East. In 2009, the U.S. Export-Import Bank awarded Petrobras a loan of up to $2 billion for developing the pre-salt fields, while Obama promised Brazil other forms of assistance. "We want to work with you," he told a group of Brazilian business leaders in March 2011. "We want to help with technology and support to develop these oil reserves safely, and when you're ready to start selling, we want to be one of your best customers."[59]

How all of this will play out in the years ahead remains to be seen. Production in the pre-salt basins is just beginning; it is still too early to tell whether they are indeed as vast as advertised, and whether Petrobras is capable of managing the sophisticated technologies needed to exploit them. The *Deepwater Horizon* disaster suggests that drilling in such complex deep-offshore formations always entails considerable risk, and it is not yet clear whether the new regulatory framework devised by Rousseff will work as intended. But whatever the exact details, it is already evident that the pre-salt reservoirs in Brazil's deep-Atlantic waters represent one of the great oil finds of the twenty-first century and will play a significant role in the global energy equation.

JUBILEE AND VENUS

Brazil is not the only country trying to figure out how to manage a sudden influx of oil income. Across the Atlantic, petroleum companies are finding new fields in waters off Ghana, Liberia, Ivory Coast, and Sierra Leone—impoverished African nations with little previous exposure to the international oil industry. These discoveries could potentially provide a vast new revenue stream to the countries involved, in some cases far exceeding their current GDPs. At the same time, they raise the specter of corruption, crony capitalism, distorted development, and other features of the "resource curse." African leaders insist that they are aware of the dangers—"We're not going to have the so-called oil curse," said Liberian president Ellen Johnson Sirleaf[60]—but they have no experience in negotiating with major oil companies and their countries' economies could easily be distorted by such massive transfers of wealth.

Of the four neighboring countries, Ghana has been the first to experience the benefits and difficulties of actual oil production. The area had long been ignored by the major oil companies, but Tullow Oil, a scrappy midsized firm based in London, has been exploring Ghana's offshore fields and in 2007 it discovered a substantial oil deposit in the

JUBILEE AND VENUS FIELDS, WEST AFRICA

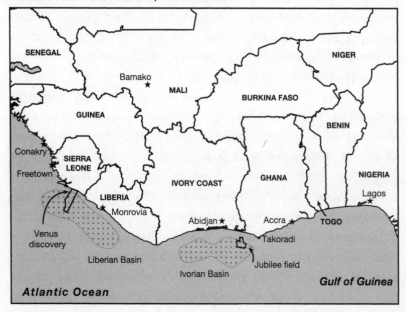

Gulf of Guinea. This oil field, named Jubilee, is located about forty miles from the shore and is estimated to hold as much as 1.8 billion barrels of oil—ranking it with some of the largest offshore fields in Angola and Nigeria. Subsequent exploration around Jubilee revealed the existence of additional deposits in the nearby Owo and Tano blocks, suggesting the existence of a vast undersea reservoir.[61] Suddenly, Ghana had the potential to become one of Africa's top producers.[62]

Extracting oil from Jubilee has proved particularly difficult, however, due to the almost total lack of infrastructure in the country. To overcome the absence of established aviation services, for instance, Tullow had to create its own air transport branch, with a full suite of helicopters and fixed-wing aircraft.[63] The Ghanaian government has helped out by converting a small fishing port, Takoradi, into a major oil services center, but even so Jubilee remains highly isolated: it's a nine-hour boat ride from the oil field to Takoradi, and another four to five hours by car or truck to the nearest international airport, at Accra.[64] Still, by using a floating production, storage, and offloading (FSPO) system—a mammoth vessel combining the functions of a drilling platform, storage container, and loading wharf—Tullow was able to begin commercial extraction at the Jubilee field in January 2011. By the end of the year, production was expected to reach 120,000 barrels per day.[65]

As in Brazil, the technical and logistical difficulties have been accompanied by political challenges—in this case, by the Ghanaian government's efforts to control ownership of the offshore fields and ensure significant participation by the state-owned Ghana National Petroleum Corporation (GNPC). In 2009, Kosmos Energy, one of Tullow's partners in Ghana, sought to sell its 23.5 percent share in Jubilee to ExxonMobil for $4 billion. The government, however, stepped in and blocked the deal, claiming that Kosmos had not included the GNPC in the negotiations as required and had provided oil field data to Exxon without government approval.[66] The following year, GNPC teamed up with the China National Offshore Oil Corporation to offer Kosmos $5 billion for its Jubilee stake, but Kosmos, in turn, rebuffed this offer, claiming that the field was now worth much more than previously assumed.[67] (At last report, the government has cleared Kosmos of any wrongdoing in the earlier Exxon discussions and has invited it to consider a new partnership with GNPC.)

The rapid inflation in the estimated value of the Jubilee field and the fumbling Ghanaian effort to control its ownership has led some observers to fear that the government is not capable of overseeing a project of this magnitude and complexity.[68] "Those petrodollars are an open invitation to people to get involved in politics and steal money, an incentive for keeping the state apparatus inefficient and developing a system that permits fraud," warned Kofi Bentil of IMANI, a liberal think tank in Accra.[69] The government, for its part, maintains that it is fully capable of addressing the daunting issues of sudden oil wealth. "We have discovered oil at a good time in the country's history," said Kwaku Boateng of the Ghanaian Ministry for Energy. "We have democracy, government is functioning very well, and we have a very active civil society. . . . I think we can succeed with the help of God."[70]

Ghana, with a relatively stable political system and a GDP of $16 billion in 2008, may prove capable of avoiding the worst of the resource curse. But Ghana's neighbors, which have less robust economies and weaker political institutions, are likely to be in greater danger. Already, a host of international firms have descended on Liberia, Sierra Leone, and Ivory Coast in search of discoveries akin to Jubilee. This effort paid off in September 2009, when Anadarko Petroleum found a major field, dubbed Venus, in waters off the coast of Sierra Leone. Anadarko officials expressed optimism that the Venus find is part of a larger reservoir stretching eastward into Liberia, and predicted that further exploration of the area would reveal geologically related fields in Ivory Coast.[71]

The production of oil in these countries' offshore territories could provide much-needed revenues to help spur development and heal the scars of war. All three have experienced brutal civil conflicts in recent years and desperately need fresh income to repair infrastructure and generate employment. None of them have ever had to deal with giant international corporations such as Chevron, Exxon, or Total, however, and they clearly risk being victimized in one way or another by the corrosive effects of sudden oil wealth.[72] Nonetheless, it is hard to imagine that any of these nations will be able to resist the powerful allure of instant riches, no matter the cost.

THE FALKLANDS: BACK TO THE FUTURE?

Yet another promising sector of the deep Atlantic lies some 2,300 miles south of Rio de Janeiro, in the waters surrounding the British-controlled Falkland Islands. Some experts believe the Falklands region could hold as much as 18 billion barrels of oil, and early test drilling has produced some positive results.[73] But these waters are claimed by Argentina as well as by the United Kingdom, raising questions about the legitimacy of any exploration and production leases awarded to energy firms by either nation. The two countries fought a brief but bloody war for control of the islands in 1982, and to this day the issue of sovereignty remains unresolved.

Both sides are pressing their claims before various international bodies, and the situation is complicated by the fact that the relevant international treaty—the United Nations Convention on the Law of the Sea, or UNCLOS—offers contradictory criteria for determining national boundaries in contested maritime areas. One of the provisions of UNCLOS allows every coastal nation to establish an exclusive economic zone (EEZ) extending for 200 nautical miles from its shoreline; another clause in the treaty, however, gives a coastal state the right to claim development rights to its outer continental shelf, even if it stretches beyond 200 miles. (This latter clause is the basis upon which Russia is attempting to claim control over the North Pole.) To make matters worse, there is no international court or tribunal empowered to adjudicate disputes that arise from the conflicting provisions of UNCLOS.

The Falklands—or the Malvinas, as they are called by Argentineans—consist of two large islands and approximately 200 small ones and are located off the southern tip of Argentina, about 300 miles east of the Strait of Magellan. At various times in their history, they have been claimed by France, Spain, Argentina, and Great Britain. The Argentineans occupied them between 1829 and 1833, and insist that they inherited sovereignty to the Malvinas from Spain; since 1833, the islands have been occupied and administered by the British. One hundred and fifty years after this changeover, on April 2, 1982, Argentinean forces invaded the islands in an apparent bid to generate popular support for the military junta then governing the country. Britain, under Margaret Thatcher, launched a surprisingly vigorous counterinvasion, eventually overpowering the Argentinean garrison. The war lasted seventy-four days and took the lives of 906 combatants (649 Argentineans and 257 British) plus three Falkland Islands civilians.

At the time of the war, the only issues at stake in the fighting were sovereignty and national pride, plus the political careers of the key figures involved. The islands themselves were thought to possess little of economic value save for vast herds of sheep owned by the few thousand permanent residents. In recent years, however, seismographic research has indicated that undersea areas both north and south of the main islands may harbor large deposits of oil and natural gas.[74] A British company, Desire Petroleum, reported the discovery of several promising natural gas deposits in April 2010, while another British firm, Rockhopper Exploration, has announced a major oil find in the Sea Lion prospect in the North Falklands basin.[75] Drilling efforts by other companies have proven less successful, but Desire and Rockhopper are confident of finding additional oil and gas deposits in these areas.[76]

The leases held by Desire Petroleum, Rockhopper, and other firms operating in the Falklands area were all awarded by British authorities in accordance with UK claims that the seabed around the islands falls within a 200-mile-wide British EEZ. As per UNCLOS protocol, the UK government has submitted a formal statement of these territorial rights to the United Nations Commission on the Limits of the Continental Shelf, which is responsible for recording and authenticating claims to offshore economic territories. The Argentineans, who argue that the region lies within Argentina's outer continental shelf, have also submitted a claim to the UN commission asserting their rights to the area.[77] Because the commission is not designed to resolve conflicting claims of this sort, the matter continues to fester, with both sides arguing for the justice of their position in various international settings.

Although officials from Argentina and Britain insist that another war over the Falklands is not in the offing, both countries have taken steps to demonstrate their determination to prevail. When Desire Petroleum began drilling in the area, the UK government dispatched a squadron of advanced Typhoon bombers to the islands and kept a four-ship naval force there on high alert.[78] Meanwhile, the Argentineans announced that any ships sailing to or from the Falklands through Argentinean waters must obtain a special permit—an obvious ploy to discourage offshore drilling, as no other supply ports are located in the vicinity.[79] The United States has called on Argentina and the United Kingdom to resolve the dispute through direct negotiations, but at this point neither side has shown any willingness to talk or to withdraw their competing claims.[80]

OFFSHORE ASIA

Maritime boundary disputes are also bedeviling the pursuit of oil and natural gas in the Pacific, where the competing claims between various countries are often even more tangled than in the Falklands. Some of the problems in the region, such as lingering feelings of hostility toward Japan as a result of its aggressive actions before and during World War II, are particular to the Pacific; others, such as the risk of environmental disaster, are more universal. But as all these various concerns intersect, offshore drilling in the Pacific is proving to be as problematic as in the Atlantic.

Asia is now the fastest-growing market for oil and natural gas, accounting for an estimated 64 percent of the anticipated increase in global energy demand between 2008 and 2035.[81] A lot of this energy will have to be imported, but Asian nations, like others, have long sought to rely as much as possible on local sources of supply. And while Asia does possess some large onshore oil and gas fields, most of these reservoirs have been substantially depleted, meaning that most future growth in Asian hydrocarbon output is likely to occur offshore—in disputed areas of the East and South China Seas, the Gulf of Thailand, and waters off Indonesia. Exploration in those areas suggests that they harbor significant reserves of gas and oil, but the political challenges are not going to be easy to overcome. As difficult as it can be to resolve border disputes on land, it is even harder to do so at sea—where there are few, if any, natural markers; where both history and geography often prove inconclusive; and where shifting a border line by as little as ten or twenty miles could mean the gain or loss of a multibillion-dollar hydrocarbon field.

Malaysia and Indonesia, for example, have been engaged in a long-running dispute over the Ambalat block in the Celebes Sea, a potentially rich source of oil and natural gas off Borneo, where Malaysia's easternmost Sabah region meets Indonesia's province of East Kalimantan. Malaysia's state oil company Petronas insists that the block falls within Malaysian territory, and in 2005 it gave Royal Dutch Shell a license to develop the area. Indonesia, asserting an identical claim, has awarded development rights to Chevron and Eni, an Italian company. Both countries have deployed naval forces in the area and issued a series of increasingly threatening statements, including a 2009 pledge by Indonesia's incoming defense minister that his country "will fight to the end" to retain control of the territory.[82] Given the risk of violence, none of the companies involved have so far chosen to exercise their rights to drill.[83]

The risk of armed conflict also hovers over oil and gas development in the East and South China Seas—two relatively large bodies of water potentially containing many rich hydrocarbon deposits. The East China Sea is believed to sit atop a large natural gas field off eastern China; the South China Sea possesses valuable oil fields in areas off the Paracel and Spratly Islands, which lie between China, the Philippines, Vietnam, and the island of Borneo. Because so many countries have advanced overlapping claims to all or part of these maritime regions—China, Japan, and Taiwan in the East China Sea; Brunei, China, Malaysia, the Philippines, Taiwan, and Vietnam in the South China Sea—it has proven nearly impossible to establish definitive offshore boundaries and award production licenses to interested energy firms.[84] None of the parties to these disputes have demonstrated any inclination to compromise, and all have paraded military forces through the region on one occasion or another to showcase their resolve.[85]

The struggle over a large natural gas field in the East China Sea—an area called Chunxiao by the Chinese and Shirakaba by the Japanese—echoes other disputes that have arisen under the contradictory provisions of the UNCLOS treaty. The Chinese claim that the field, which is located roughly halfway between the two countries, lies on China's outer continental shelf, and so is theirs alone to exploit; the Japanese say that it falls within their 200-nautical-mile exclusive economic zone, and so it largely belongs to them. Powerful nationalistic sentiments on both sides further complicate the issue. Many Chinese resent Japan's invasion and occupation of China during World War II, and so oppose any territorial concessions to Tokyo; many Japanese are fearful of China's rise, and so oppose any concessions to Beijing.[86]

As the dispute drags on, both China and Japan have regularly sent their air and naval forces to the region. On at least one occasion, a violent confrontation has nearly resulted, with crews of both sides aiming their weapons at each other or engaging in other threatening actions.[87] Officials from the two countries have met several times in search of a solution to the impasse; at one meeting, in June 2008, they agreed on a formula whereby Japanese firms would participate in a Chinese effort to exploit the undersea field.[88] But neither side has surrendered its claim to the disputed area, and both continue to station warships in the general area. There is every risk, therefore, that a future naval incident could lead to something far more serious.[89]

A similar scenario could easily unfold in the disputed territory of the South China Sea, where more than half a dozen different countries claim all or part of a region that is believed to contain large undersea hydrocarbon deposits. China, citing historical ties to the small islands that dot the area, insists that the entire region is part of its national maritime territory; Taiwan echoes China's position, while Brunei, Malaysia, the Philippines, and Vietnam all say that their EEZs extend deep into the Chinese zone. All of the Southeast Asian countries involved have made efforts to search for oil in these EEZs, but China has used force on several occasions to chase off survey ships from what it declares to be its own waters.[90] As with the East China Sea, then, this is another area where offshore oil and gas exploration has led to increasing tensions, and a small incident could have very dangerous repercussions.

Despite all the hazards described above, drilling for oil and natural gas in the deep waters of the Gulf of Mexico, the Atlantic, and the Pacific is likely to accelerate in the years ahead, as other prospects diminish and the struggle to secure energy supplies intensifies. Even the ecological damage wreaked by the *Deepwater Horizon* disaster of April 2010 is not likely to slow this drive. With onshore and shallow-water reservoirs becoming increasingly exhausted, deepwater exploration provides one of the few remaining options for corporations and governments that seek new hydrocarbon sources. As suggested by Lamar McKay, chairman and president of BP America, "the deepwater is indispensable to the world's energy future."[91]

But no matter how "indispensable" it might seem, an increase in deepwater drilling will bring with it much greater risk of environmental and political calamity. Thousands of feet under the sea, drilling equipment is exposed to exponentially greater underground pressures, increasing the risk of a catastrophic accident. As global temperatures rise, meanwhile, hurricanes and typhoons will become more frequent and severe, posing a growing threat to rigs in the Gulf of Mexico and offshore Asia. Disputes over contested offshore boundaries are also likely to become more contentious, especially among fiercely nationalistic countries such as China, Japan, and Vietnam. The giant oil firms will, no doubt, persevere despite these problems, but they will not be able to escape them altogether.

3 ► INVADING THE ARCTIC

In July 2010, the intrepid fishermen who ply the ice-strewn waters off Greenland's west coast witnessed a strange and unaccustomed sight: the *Stena Forth*, a mammoth drillship leased by Edinburgh-based Cairn Energy to search for oil. Described as "the largest dual-mast ultra-deepwater drillship in the world," the *Stena Forth* carries a drilling rig some twenty stories high, which can bore to depths of 35,000 feet in water more than a mile deep.[1] Easily the largest man-made contrivance ever seen in the region, the ship was stationed off Disko Island in the Davis Strait, some 100 miles offshore. Cairn, a small company that takes big gambles on unproven reserves in remote parts of the world, had acquired several large exploration blocks in the area and was now probing beneath the ocean's floor. After sinking three exploratory wells, the *Stena Forth* and a second drillship, the *Stena Don*, found evidence of oil at a site called Alpha-1S1.[2] Encouraged by this first round of drilling, Cairn proceeded to acquire additional exploration blocks in the region and announced plans for an expanded drilling program in the summers of 2011 and 2012.[3]

At present Cairn is the only company exploring for oil in Greenland's offshore areas, but many other energy producers are closely watching its activities. In a May 2010 auction, an array of prominent firms, including ConocoPhillips, Shell, and Statoil of Norway, bid for exploration blocks adjoining Cairn's operations; other companies, including Chevron and ExxonMobil, had acquired several such blocks in previous auctions. All told, more than 77,000 square miles—an area the size of Nebraska—have now been leased for exploratory drilling in Greenland's western and southern waters.[4] "The rush is on," declared *Bloomberg News*, noting that Greenland is becoming increasingly attractive to major oil firms as petroleum supplies dwindle elsewhere.[5]

GREENLAND'S OFFSHORE OIL FIELDS

At present, these companies are mostly focusing their attention on the Davis Strait and other areas off Greenland's west coast, which are thought to harbor some 7.3 billion barrels of oil (about as much as Sudan) and 1.4 billion cubic meters of natural gas (equivalent to the entire reserves of the Netherlands). But that western region is not the area's only potential hydrocarbon treasure trove. Many geologists believe that an even larger energy reserve lies off Greenland's east coast, in the East Greenland Rift basin—a reservoir containing as much as 8.9 billion barrels of oil and 2.4 billion cubic meters of gas.[6] Because the East Greenland Rift basin is farther north than Disko Island, exploration and production there is likely to prove even more challenging than Cairn's current efforts: sea ice covers the area for a longer stretch of the year, and weather conditions are often severe. Still, a consortium of major firms—including BP, Chevron, ExxonMobil, Shell, and Statoil—is preparing to start bidding on East Greenland Rift basin exploration blocks in January 2012, and other oil companies are likely to follow in 2013.[7]

The development of oil and gas fields off the country's eastern and western coasts could do much to improve living standards for the 57,000 permanent residents of Greenland, a self-governing territory under Danish authority. Greenland's GDP is only $2 billion per year, one-third of which comes from subsidies provided by Denmark; at present, the island's biggest industry is fishing, a low-paying and seasonal occupation at best. Many Greenlanders—a majority of whom are descendants of the Inuit peoples who first settled the area some 800 years ago—hope that the discovery of oil will generate high-paying skilled jobs and eliminate the territory's economic reliance on Denmark, widely considered a relic of the colonial era.[8] A *Wall Street Journal* dispatch from Nuuk, the island's capital, noted that "hitting an oil jackpot would raise hopes here of eventually breaking that financial dependence and putting Greenland on a path toward full independence."[9]

But while most Greenlanders seem to favor development of the island's hydrocarbon resources, some residents feel that the environmental risks of offshore drilling are too high. "Every night I pray they don't find oil and gas in the Greenland area because that will end the

peace and calm heaven here," said Aqqaluk Lynge, president of Greenland's Inuit Circumpolar Conference.[10] Lynge and other activists are
worried that a major oil spill like that triggered by the *Deepwater Horizon*
explosion in the Gulf of Mexico would severely damage Greenland's
fragile coastal zones and threaten the survival of many fish species and
marine mammals, including some considered vital to Inuit culture.[11]

Greenland's native environmental advocates have been reinforced
by activists from Greenpeace, who fear that the planned oil production
will not only endanger the country's coastlines but also contribute to
global warming.[12] In August 2010, four Greenpeace members attached
themselves to the hull of the *Stena Don*, making its crew suspend
operations for thirty hours—until bad weather forced the protesters to
abandon their perch seventy-five feet above the Arctic Ocean.[13] The following year, eleven Greenpeace activists hauled themselves aboard the
drillship *Leiv Eiriksson* while it was heading to Greenland to conduct
test drilling for Cairn. (Once again, the protesters were eventually forced
off by bad weather.) Despite the obvious risks of boarding oil-company
vessels on the high seas, Greenpeace insists it will continue its protests.[14]

Canadian officials, too, have raised concerns about oil drilling in
waters off Greenland's western shores. Many islands in Canada's northern territory of Nunavut are near Cairn's development blocks in the
Davis Strait, the body of water that separates eastern Canada from
Greenland, and so could suffer coastal damage in the event of a major
oil spill. "The clear and present danger is Greenland," said Larry Bagnell, the Liberal Party critic for northern affairs. If a spill occurred in
the winter, when ice covers the area, it would be impossible to dig a
relief well like the one used to seal BP's Macondo well in the Gulf of
Mexico. In such a scenario, Bagnell noted, oil would continue "to spew
beneath the ice, all over the Arctic, for months and months."[15]

But despite these concerns, the drive to find and exploit Greenland's offshore hydrocarbon reserves is bound to gain momentum in
the years ahead, as the major energy firms seek to replace fields being
depleted elsewhere. And in a kind of perverse self-reinforcing loop,
global warming—driven largely by hydrocarbon emissions—will make

it easier over time to ramp up the production of oil and natural gas in Greenland's waters. As temperatures rise, sea ice will melt sooner in the spring and form later in the fall, extending the drilling season by one or two months.[16] Warming temperatures will also shrink the Arctic ice-cap, making it possible to operate in more northerly waters. Of course, as global warming accelerates the melting of Greenland's mighty glaciers, it will also produce an increasing number of menacing ice-bergs and lead to a dangerous rise in the sea level around the world, but such considerations don't seem to deter Cairn and the other companies seeking to develop Greenland's reserves.

With oil companies bidding on more and more exploration blocks and sending additional drillships to the area, Greenland is coming to encapsulate many features of what is being called the Arctic oil rush. Long neglected because of its harsh operating environment, the Arctic is now attracting widespread interest from oil producers. As the Green-land experience suggests, exploiting the Arctic will not be easy: extremely low temperatures, frequent storms, ubiquitous sea ice, and growing concern over endangered species and a fragile environment all pose significant obstacles. But with oil prices above $80 per barrel and with few other areas to rely on, many of the world's leading energy compa-nies increasingly view production in the Arctic as one of their best remaining options.

THE ARCTIC'S POWERFUL LURE

Obviously, energy companies would not be spending billions of dollars to prospect for oil and natural gas in the frozen wastes of the Arctic if they were not convinced that the area contains large reserves of untapped hydrocarbons—a conviction that has come about only in the last few years. During the twentieth century, some hints of the Arctic's hydrocarbon potential could be deduced from the discoveries of oil at Prudhoe Bay in Alaska and natural gas fields in northern Siberia. But these deposits, all on land, provided little hint of what might be found in more northerly producing areas, many of which are located offshore.

A more reliable appraisal of the Arctic's potential resource base had to wait until July 2008, when the U.S. Geological Survey (USGS) published the results of its systematic assessment of all available seismic and geological information on Arctic hydrocarbon resources.

The headline finding of the USGS survey, known as the Circum-Arctic Resource Appraisal, was that the area above the Arctic Circle possesses roughly one-fifth of the world's undiscovered oil and natural gas reserves. The largest share of this energy cornucopia was said to consist of natural gas: roughly 1,689 trillion cubic feet of it, representing an estimated 30 percent of the world's total undiscovered supply. In addition, the Arctic was said to hold 90 billion barrels of oil (13 percent of the world's undiscovered supply) plus 44 billion barrels of natural gas liquids.[17]

Because the USGS study was based on geologic evidence rather than exploratory drilling, it could not state with absolute certainty that the Arctic contains hydrocarbon deposits on the indicated scale. But the report did note that rocks and sediment in the areas under investigation are of the kind typically associated with the recovery of oil and natural gas in other energy-producing regions. What's more, the appraisal tallied only oil and gas reserves that are "recoverable using existing technology,"[18] leaving open the possibility that technological advances will result in even greater yields. And although the USGS did not comment on the likely costs of operating in the Arctic—an obvious issue of concern for companies thinking of exploring there—it gave the impression that the Arctic's hydrocarbon deposits will become increasingly accessible in the years ahead. "For a variety of reasons, the possibility of oil and gas exploration in the Arctic has become much less hypothetical than it once was," said Donald L. Gautier, the chief geologist for the study.[19]

As part of its report, the USGS divided the Arctic into a patchwork of thirty-three separate energy-bearing "provinces," and provided estimates of the oil and gas potential of each. Half of those provinces are located in Russia and its adjacent waters; the other half are scattered among Norway, Greenland, Canada, and Alaska. All thirty-three of these subregions were said to possess some oil and natural gas potential, but

TABLE 3.1: MAJOR HYDROCARBON PROVINCES IN THE ARCTIC REGION

PROVINCE (in rank order by combined resources)	LOCATION	ESTIMATED HYDROCARBON RESOURCES			
		Oil (Gbl)	Natural Gas (tcf)	Natural Gas Liquids (Gbl)	Combined Resources (Gbl boe)
West Siberian Basin	Russia	3.7	651.5	20.3	132.6
Arctic Alaska	Northern Alaska and adjacent waters	30.0	221.4	5.9	72.8
East Barents Sea	Russia's share of the Barents Sea, above the Kola Peninsula	7.4	317.6	1.4	61.8
East Greenland Rift Basin	Waters off Greenland's northeastern coast	8.9	86.2	8.1	31.4
Yenisey-Khatanga Basin	Arctic Ocean waters above northern Siberia	5.6	100.0	2.7	24.9
Amerasia Basin	Waters above northeastern Alaska and northern Canada	9.7	56.9	0.5	19.7
West Greenland and East Canada	Baffin Bay and the Davis Strait area	7.2	51.8	1.1	17.1
Norwegian Margin and Barents Platform	Waters off northern and northwestern Norway	3.5	58.5	0.8	14.0
Total, 8 Provinces Above		76.0	1,543.9	40.8	374.3
Total, All Arctic Regions		90.0	1,668.7	44.1	412.2

Source: U.S. Geological Society, "Circum-Arctic Resource Appraisal," Fact Sheet 2008-3049.
boe = barrels of oil equivalent
Gbl = billions of barrels
tcf = trillion cubic feet

about 90 percent of the reserves are thought to be held in just eight of the provinces, including West Siberia, Arctic Alaska, East and West Greenland, the Barents Sea, and the Amerasia basin (see Table 3.1).

For the most part, these are the Arctic areas that are attracting the strongest interest from the major energy firms. Step by step, the companies are migrating ever farther northward: from established fields in Alaska and northern Canada to the adjacent Chukchi and Beaufort Seas; from the Norwegian Sea to offshore Greenland and the Barents Sea; and from West Siberia to the Yenisey-Khatanga basin lying above it. Some of these efforts have achieved greater progress than others, but all of them are a major priority for the big corporate players.

NORTH FROM ALASKA

As previously noted, the global hunt for oil first streaked past the Arctic Circle in the 1960s, when geologists exploring the North Slope of Alaska discovered the Prudhoe Bay field—the largest petroleum reservoir ever found in North America. Once the Trans-Alaska Pipeline System (TAPS) was completed in 1977, crude oil from Prudhoe Bay began to flow southward to an ice-free port at Valdez, on Alaska's southern coast. For two decades, Prudhoe Bay provided a significant share of America's domestically produced crude, bringing sizable profits to the major firms operating there, especially BP, ExxonMobil, and ConocoPhillips. Now, however, the field is in undeniable decline. Total Alaskan output peaked at 2 million barrels per day in 1988 and has been shrinking ever since, with yields dropping below 1 million barrels per day in 2000 and continuing to fall.[20] Needless to say, this has prompted the oil companies and the state of Alaska—which derives much of its operating budget from oil revenues—to aggressively seek out new petroleum deposits.

At first, the corporations and the state pinned their hopes on eventual exploitation of the Arctic National Wildlife Refuge (ANWR), a vast wilderness area on Alaska's North Slope located just to the east of Prudhoe Bay. When Congress established ANWR in 1980, it included a special measure—Section 1002—designating a 1.5-million-acre segment of the reserve for possible oil extraction, pending the outcome of geological and environmental studies to be conducted by federal agencies. Section 1002 clearly envisioned the possibility of drilling in ANWR, but only if seismic research indicated the presence of significant quantities of oil and if Congress explicitly approved such drilling in a separate, follow-up vote.

The statute's first requirement was satisfied in 1998, when the USGS reported that the "Section 1002 Area" contained oil reserves of between 5.7 and 16.0 billion barrels of oil, with a mean estimate of 10.4 billion barrels.[21] If the mean figure was accurate, the oil at ANWR represented a 37 percent increase in total identified U.S. petroleum reserves—a powerful lure by any reckoning. The political hurdle set up by Section 1002, though, has proved more difficult to overcome. President George W. Bush often voiced his support for ANWR drilling, and on several occasions during his administration the House or the Senate voted to pass the necessary legislation. Each time, however, a majority of Democrats managed to block approval of such a measure, claiming that oil drilling would befoul a pristine wilderness area and jeopardize the survival of various endangered species, including the porcupine caribou. By the end of Bush's two terms in office, public opinion seemed to turn against ANWR drilling, and during the 2008 presidential campaign Barack Obama was among several candidates who strongly rejected the possibility of opening the wildlife refuge to oil exploration.[22]

With drilling in ANWR appearing less likely, energy companies and their allies in Congress have looked toward other options for expanding Alaskan oil production. One such possibility involves exploitation of the National Petroleum Reserve in Alaska (NPRA)—a vast area of land on Alaska's North Slope located to the west of Prudhoe Bay. Originally known as Naval Petroleum Reserve Number 4, the NPRA was set aside in 1923 by President Warren G. Harding as a future source of fuel for the U.S. Navy, which was then converting from coal to oil propulsion. As a result of subsequent discoveries of oil in Texas, Louisiana, and other states, however, the NPRA was largely ignored until fairly recently; indeed, the 23.5-million-acre territory (nearly 25 percent big-

ALASKA AREA OIL FIELDS

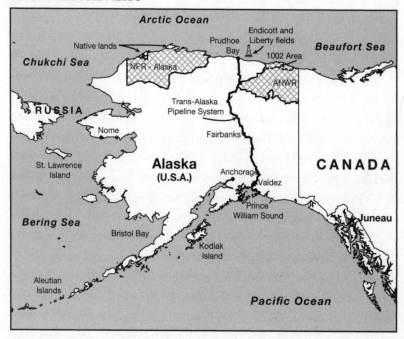

ger than ANWR) has been described as "the largest tract of undisturbed public land in the United States."[23] Some environmentalists have sought to designate the NPRA as a wilderness area and thereby protect it from future development, but oil companies and Alaskan politicians would like to open the area to commercial drilling, and their lobbying has paid off. President Obama, coming under increasing pressure to raise domestic oil output and thereby reduce reliance on imports, announced in May 2011 that his administration would begin holding annual auctions for exploration blocks in the national reserve.[24]

Oil companies and their supporters have also focused on the undersea plain extending into the Beaufort and Chukchi Seas beyond northern and northwestern Alaska. These coastal areas are believed to possess the same geological characteristics as those found in Prudhoe Bay and ANWR, which makes them likely to contain considerable reserves of oil and natural gas. What's more, they are relatively close to the existing transportation infrastructure in the North Slope, and so can funnel additional crude into the TAPS pipeline—a major objective of Alaskan state officials.

The Beaufort and the Chukchi Seas are, in essence, extensions of the Arctic Ocean, with the Beaufort Sea stretching above northern Alaska and the Chukchi Sea wedged between northwestern Alaska and the easternmost reach of Siberia. Together with Alaska's other offshore regions, these two bodies of water are thought to hold 26.7 billion barrels of oil equivalent[25]—an amount roughly equal to the original reserves of the Prudhoe Bay field, and several times greater than the estimated reserves of the Arctic National Wildlife Refuge. During the Clinton and Bush administrations, the U.S. government conducted several auctions for exploration blocks in these waters, and the major energy companies wagered substantial sums on the prospects for future drilling there. A 2008 auction for leases in the Chukchi Sea, for instance, saw several firms, including Shell, ConocoPhillips, Eni, and Statoil, jointly bid $3.4 billion for the right to explore several promising blocks in the area.[26]

Extracting oil from the Beaufort and Chukchi Seas will not be easy. In winter, the waters are covered with thick pack ice; at other times, large ice floes stream through the ocean, posing a grave risk to ships and drilling structures. Winter temperatures routinely fall below minus 40 degrees Fahrenheit, and severe storms with gale-force winds are common. Deploying ordinary drilling rigs, like those used in the Gulf of Mexico and other temperate regions, is not an option for much of the year, since any collision with ice floes would likely prove catastrophic. To operate in the Arctic waters, energy firms must sheathe drilling rigs in armor against ice contact, or deploy them during summer months only. The fact that so many firms are prepared to employ such measures, at immense cost, is a testament to their craving for new energy reserves.

One of the most aggressive players in the hunt for offshore Alaskan oil has been BP. As lead producer of the Prudhoe Bay field and the principal owner of the Trans-Alaska Pipeline System, BP is naturally interested in securing additional supplies of crude that can be funneled into its existing infrastructure. With its onshore rigs in the area producing less and less oil, the company has sought to make up for the decline by moving north into the waters of the Beaufort Sea, which abuts its existing fields in Prudhoe Bay. BP's preferred approach for dealing with the Arctic engineering challenges has been to build artificial islands in shallow coastal areas and use them as platforms for erecting conventional drilling rigs. Rising above the level of sea ice, the islands are reinforced with concrete barriers, protecting drilling equipment from the dangers of pack ice and large ice floes. They also allow more space for company personnel than the comparatively cramped quarters of a drillship.

The first endeavor of this sort was BP's Endicott project, which came on line in 1987. Located in shallow water about two and a half miles from shore, the complex consists of two man-made islands connected to land by a gravel causeway. The company describes Endicott as "the first Arctic offshore production facility in the world," and virtually a world unto itself. "Endicott was built as a self-contained community," BP explains, "with its own production and living facilities, including a power generation facility, a desalination plant for making drinking water, a sewage treatment plant, oil processing facilities, fire-fighting equipment, a medical facility, and fitness and recreation center."[27]

A second BP project in the Beaufort Sea, Northstar, is even more ambitious. Located on an artificial island that sits in thirty-nine feet of water, Northstar is six miles from the nearest shore—a distance deemed too great to be connected to land via a causeway, as was done with Endicott. Instead, the island was built by carrying more than 700,000 cubic yards of gravel from the mainland to the project site during the winter, over roads built on top of sea ice. In the summer months, when the sea was relatively ice-free, drilling equipment and living modules were carried to the site by a giant barge.[28] To funnel Northstar's crude into the Trans-Alaska Pipeline System, BP also built an underwater pipeline leading from the island to the mainland, where it then connects to existing infrastructure at Prudhoe Bay.

In addition to facing many daunting logistical challenges, Endicott, Northstar, and other BP-operated projects on the edge of the Beaufort Sea have aroused significant opposition from environmental groups. Some activists fear that drilling operations will accelerate global warming while interfering with the feeding and mating behavior of endangered marine mammals, including polar bears, walruses, and bowhead whales; these concerns prompted several members of Greenpeace to occupy a BP barge that was en route to the Northstar construction site, halting its journey until they were removed by Alaska state troopers.[29] The Endicott operation, meanwhile, has come under scrutiny because its pipeline to the mainland is apparently suffering from a dangerous level of corrosion, raising the possibility of a catastrophic oil leak. On April 20, 2010—the same day that the *Deepwater Horizon* exploded in the Gulf of Mexico—federal regulators sent a letter to BP officials in Alaska indicating that safety inspections had found damaged insulation, torn seals, and a substantial reduction in the thickness of the Endicott pipeline's walls. BP officials insisted that they were taking all necessary steps to protect against corrosion in the pipeline, but nonetheless promised to step up their vigilance.[30]

Worries about the safety of the Endicott pipeline are particularly significant because BP intends to use the Endicott facilities as the base for an even more daring venture in the Beaufort Sea: the Liberty project. The subsea Liberty field, which holds an estimated 100 million barrels of oil, is located five miles offshore and some eight miles from the Endicott platform. Instead of building yet another artificial island to exploit the field, however, BP has decided to reach out to it from the existing Endicott infrastructure. To this end, the company has installed on Endicott the most powerful drilling rig ever built, a 7,000-ton behemoth that stands twenty stories tall and cost $215 million to construct. Once in operation, the Liberty rig will dig a vertical well beneath one of Endicott's islands; then, using a steerable drill bit, it will bore a horizontal conduit beneath the ocean floor to the offshore reservoir, where it will again turn downward into the oil-bearing deposit. Such a technique, called "ultra-extended-reach drilling," has never been employed in the Arctic before.[31]

In seeking government approval for the Liberty project, BP has argued that the extended-reach drilling technology reduces the danger to the environment by making it unnecessary to build any new offshore facilities.[32] Critics contend, however, that a wellbore of this type will be more prone to "gas kicks"—the same type of sudden natural gas eruptions that triggered the *Deepwater Horizon* blowout and explosion.[33] What's more, if a blowout did occur in the Liberty field, the damage to the region would be greatly magnified by the Arctic's fragile environment and its remoteness from major ports and protection services. Unlike the Gulf of Mexico, the Beaufort Sea has very few service vessels and no skimmers or booms stockpiled nearby to protect vulnerable coastal areas. Any rescue effort would have to be mounted from thousands of miles away and would be almost impossible to undertake in the winter.[34]

Despite such concerns, when the Obama administration suspended all new offshore drilling for six months in the aftermath of the *Deepwater Horizon* disaster, the Liberty project was given an exemption from the moratorium—on the somewhat questionable grounds that Liberty was to be drilled from Endicott, which in turn is connected to land by a man-made causeway, and thus officially counts as an "onshore" project rather than an "offshore" one. Even with this exemption, however, BP has several times pushed back the start of drilling at Liberty; as of this writing, production at the site is not expected to begin before 2013.[35] Environmental activists, who believe that the company has shown itself incapable of coping with a major blowout, hope that these delays will help convince federal regulators to deny BP an operating permit for the Liberty field altogether.[36]

Opponents of Alaskan offshore drilling have also been trying to prevent Royal Dutch Shell, another key player in the region, from carrying out its own plans for northward expansion. But Shell—which spent several billion dollars between 2005 and 2008 to acquire exploration blocks in the Beaufort and Chukchi Seas—has shown no signs of backing down, despite years of postponements and delays. Test drilling was supposed to start in the summer of 2009, but those plans had to be scrapped when a coalition of environmental and Native American organizations initiated legal action, claiming that Shell had failed to conduct all required environmental assessments. A federal court ruled in early 2010 that Shell could proceed, but the drilling had to be postponed again due to the six-month moratorium on new offshore projects that followed the *Deepwater Horizon* explosion.[37] And in early 2011, just when it appeared that Shell had cleared all obstacles to drilling in the Beaufort Sea (drilling in the Chukchi Sea remained tangled in environmental lawsuits), an appeals panel of the Environmental Protection Agency ruled that it needed more time to assess the potential impact of diesel emissions from Shell's offshore facilities on coastal Native American communities. Concluding that the issue would not be resolved by the onset of the summer 2011 drilling season, Shell announced that it would be forced, yet again, to postpone its operations.[38]

Notwithstanding these setbacks, Shell has worked tirelessly to win public support for its Arctic plans. Acknowledging the concerns of environmentalists and federal officials, the company has expanded its fleet of cleanup vessels; at the same time, it has emphasized the economic benefits of drilling in the northern seas. "Every day we're delayed," said Peter Slaiby, Shell's vice president for Alaska operations, "we're delaying jobs and energy development."[39] Bolstered by such arguments and strong support from Alaska's congressional delegation, Shell finally received federal approval for its plans in August 2011; although the company must still obtain additional operating permits, it now expects to begin drilling in the Beaufort Sea in the summer of 2012.[40]

Whatever happens with Shell and BP over the next few years, Alaska's offshore areas are likely to remain a major battleground in the struggle over American domestic drilling. On one hand, many believe the region should be fully exploited in the interests of enhanced U.S. energy security. "Companies demonstrating solid exploration and development plans and oil-spill response plans should be able to develop our nation's abundant oil," Senator Mark Begich of Alaska proclaimed in June 2010,[41] reiterating a point of view common to many Alaskan officials. But environmental activists maintain that drilling in the Arctic is inherently risky, given the heightened vulnerability of plant and animal life to oil-spill damage and the difficulty of conducting cleanup operations. "A spill would be the nail in the coffin for Arctic communities and wildlife like polar bears, which are already struggling to survive," said Michael Brune of the Sierra Club.[42] It remains to be seen which of these views will prevail—but with onshore reserves at Prudhoe Bay and elsewhere in Alaska continuing to decline, it is certain that the struggle over Alaska's offshore energy will become only more intense in the years to come.

NORWAY'S ARCTIC AMBITIONS

Like the state of Alaska, Norway has long been a pioneer in the development of Arctic energy resources. Norway's oil and natural gas assets are relatively modest when compared to those of the top hydrocarbon-producing nations—the Norwegian oil fields contain an estimated 6.7 billion barrels, less than a tenth of the oil found in Russia and a mere 3 percent of Saudi reserves—but the Norwegians have been very effective in developing their resources and bringing them to market. In 2010, Norway extracted 2.1 million barrels of oil per day and 3.8 trillion cubic feet of gas per year, making it the world's thirteenth leading oil and sixth leading gas producer—a remarkable showing for a country that ranks number 117 in terms of population.[43] However, most of this oil and gas was extracted from fields in the North Sea and lower Norwegian Sea that have been in production for many years and are now facing inescapable decline. If Norway is to sustain its level of output in the future, therefore, it will have to shift its production activity northward, to new fields located above the Arctic Circle.[44]

The most significant expression of this northern strategy so far has been the construction of the Snøhvit natural gas facility at Hammerfest,

NORWAY'S OFFSHORE OIL AND GAS FIELDS

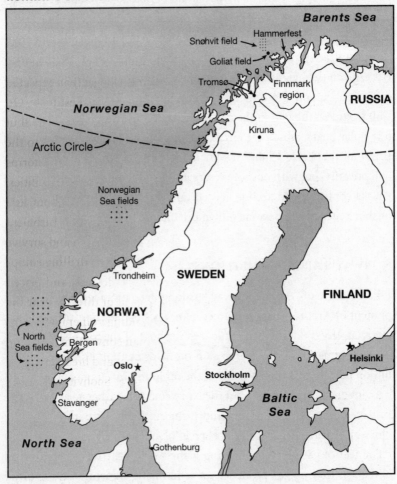

Norway. Completed by Norway's state-controlled energy firm Statoil in 2007 at an estimated cost of $7.7 billion, the Snøhvit operation is centered on an undersea well system located some ninety miles offshore in the Barents Sea, an extension of the Arctic Ocean. A pipeline connects the field to processing facilities on the island of Melkøya in Hammerfest harbor, where the gas is cooled to minus 260 degrees Fahrenheit and converted into liquefied natural gas (LNG) for export abroad. When

everything works according to plan, the Hammerfest plant can produce 200 billion cubic feet of LNG per year, the equivalent of about
100,000 barrels of oil per day.[45]

The installation and operation of the Snøhvit complex has hardly
been trouble-free, however. Construction took much longer than expected
and cost approximately 50 percent more than the original estimate. On
several occasions since 2007, moreover, the facility has had to be shut
down for costly repairs.[46] Many of these problems can be traced to the
harsh weather conditions that prevail in the Barents Sea, where storms
are frequent and giant waves pose a constant threat to offshore facilities.
The Gulf Stream keeps the area free of ice throughout the year, but, as a
Statoil Web site notes, "Winds, freezing temperatures, and turbulent
seas make extreme demands of those intending to function and survive
here."[47] To overcome these perils, Statoil installed all its drilling equipment on the ocean floor using remote-controlled devices, and placed
its processing facilities on Melkøya Island instead of directly near the
wells. This setup has allowed Statoil to avoid building vulnerable ocean-
surface installations, but it is far more costly than conventional drilling
technology and significantly more prone to glitches and breakdowns.

Still, despite all the delays and cost overruns at Snøhvit, officials at
Statoil find tremendous value in having gained so much experience in
operating natural gas facilities in far northern waters.[48] Faced with unrelenting pressure to replace its declining oil and gas fields in more southerly
waters, the company now sees no choice but to look to Norway's "Far
North"—well beyond the Arctic Circle, and in even higher latitudes than
Snøhvit. As part of this drive, Statoil has acquired a substantial number of
exploration blocks in areas of the Barents Sea above Norway's northern
rim, a territory often visited by fierce Arctic storms. Seismic testing and
exploratory drilling are already under way in some of these blocks, and
Statoil plans to develop any of them that exhibit commercial potential.[49]

Other companies, too, are eager to establish a presence in Norway's
northern waters. In May 2009, the Norwegian government gave approval
to Eni of Italy to proceed with development of the Goliat (Goliath) field,
the first petroleum deposit to be exploited in the Barents Sea. Located

to the east of Snøhvit and some forty miles offshore, the Goliat field is believed to hold approximately 200 million barrels of oil. To extract these petroleum riches, Eni and Statoil (which holds a 35 percent stake in the field) are spending $1.6 billion on a floating production, storage, and offloading vessel. The mammoth FPSO ship will be serviced from Hammerfest, further contributing to the transformation of this once sleepy fishing village into a major oil and gas hub. Eni and Statoil have also discovered oil at a field called Skrugard, located 120 miles from the coast and well north of the Goliat and Snøhvit deposits.[50]

Just as in Alaska's offshore territories, the expansion of drilling in the Barents Sea has aroused fierce opposition from environmentalists. "Of all the Arctic seas, the Barents Sea sustains the highest seafloor biodiversity communities, including the world's largest deepwater coral reef, huge mussel banks, and large coastal kelp forests," the World Wildlife Fund noted in a report on threats to the region. The Barents Sea also supports some of the world's largest colonies of seabirds, including significant concentrations of puffins, razorbills, little auks, common guillemots, and black guillemots. The coral reefs, along with many species of birds and fish, would be highly vulnerable to any oil spill occurring in the area. In particular, the WWF pointed out, a spill from the Goliat field—located just off the northern Norwegian coast—"has a great potential to impact on some of the most vulnerable biodiversity" in the area.[51]

Norwegian activists have sought to block drilling at Goliat and other sites in the Barents, but the country's top officials are highly reluctant to risk the stream of revenue from oil and gas exports.[52] In June 2010, the Norwegian government included fifty-one new Barents Sea exploration blocks in an auction for offshore drilling site licenses. "The petroleum industry has created enormous wealth for Norwegian society," said Terje Riis-Johansen, the minister of petroleum and energy, when announcing the auction, and he was confident that the new licenses would "contribute to prolonging this value creation."[53] At the moment, then, Norway appears fully committed to plans for further drilling in its Far North—no matter what the costs.

THE RUSSIAN ARCTIC

Like Norway, Russia has long relied on the proceeds of hydrocarbon production to fuel economic growth and finance government activity. Much of its oil and natural gas comes from the western Siberia region, a vast, desolate area that straddles the Arctic Circle. Many of Russia's most prolific oil and gas fields—including Samotlor, Urengoy, and Yamburg— are located here, and their development since the 1960s has helped make Russia the world's top oil and gas producer. But with many of these fields now substantially depleted, Russian energy companies—like their Western counterparts—are increasingly being forced to look northward as they hunt for new reserves.[54]

According to the USGS's 2008 "Circum-Arctic Resource Appraisal," northern Siberia and the frozen seas above it hold the largest share of the Arctic's untapped hydrocarbons. No less than 53 percent of the Arctic's total hydrocarbon potential—219 billion barrels of oil equivalent—is thought to lie in just three of the major producing regions in Arctic Russia.[55] (See Table 3.1 on page 76.) The Russian energy areas are particularly rich in natural gas, noted Donald L. Gautier, the principal author of the USGS study. "Of course," he added, "the Russians are already the world's biggest producer of gas." With this new data, it appears that Russia's "preeminence" in natural gas "is likely to be accentuated and extended."[56]

Maintaining this preeminent position through the development of Arctic hydrocarbon reserves has become one of Moscow's top priorities. "Our first and main task is to turn the Arctic into Russia's resource base of the twenty-first century," President Dmitry Medvedev told a September 2008 meeting of the Russian Security Council.[57] In accordance with his dictum, the council adopted a long-term strategic plan for the region that calls for the Arctic to become Russia's main source of oil and natural gas by the year 2020.[58] Since most large Russian energy firms, such as Rosneft and Gazprom, are state controlled, their efforts invariably reflect the official Kremlin policy.

Achieving Medvedev's goal, however, will require the Russian companies to overcome mammoth obstacles. Most of the new oil and gas fields slated for development are located in remote, unpopulated areas with few if any links to major transportation hubs. Although some of the deposits are on land, and so do not face the particular problems of offshore production, the soil in the Arctic is often marshy and can turn into mud during the warm summer months—making travel and construction a nightmare. During the winter, meanwhile, frigid temperatures and frequent storms pose a severe threat to workers and equipment. Moreover, as in Alaska and Greenland, the Siberian territories are inhabited by indigenous peoples and endangered species whose survival is often jeopardized by oil company operations. Coping with all of these difficulties naturally increases the costs of operating in such areas, raising significant questions about the commercial viability of many of the Siberian projects.[59]

Still, despite these challenges, Gazprom and Rosneft are determined to proceed with their northward march. Both companies are engaged in many Siberian endeavors simultaneously, but three giant projects are

RUSSIA'S ARCTIC OIL AND GAS FIELDS

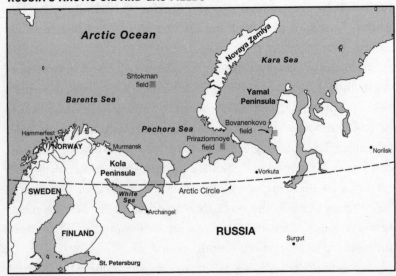

currently absorbing much of their attention: the Prirazlomnoye oil field and the Bovanenkovo and Shtokman natural gas fields. Each of these hydrocarbon reservoirs possesses great potential, making the enormous difficulties that are involved in the work apparently worthwhile for the Russian firms.

The Prirazlomnoye oil field, which was discovered in 1989, lies in the eastern portion of the Barents Sea—an area that is covered by ice for some 250 days a year, from November until June, with winter temperatures routinely falling below minus 40 degrees Fahrenheit. To exploit the field, Gazprom (through one of its subsidiaries) is building a fixed platform at the site, consisting of an underwater caisson resting on the ocean floor plus a topside drilling structure derived from a former North Sea oil rig; eventually, a protective berm will be built around the entire structure to ward off floating sea ice. But even once the drilling rig is set up and properly armored, the company will still have to deal with the problem of transporting the field's oil to distant markets. Since there is absolutely no delivery infrastructure in the area, Gazprom intends to build a fleet of ice-breaking shuttle tankers, each capable of slicing through four feet of sea ice. These specialized vessels will carry the crude output to an ice-free port on Kola Bay, 700 miles to the west, where it will be transferred to conventional tanker ships.[60]

Even more extensive efforts will be needed to exploit the two large Arctic gas fields that Gazprom seeks to develop, Bovanenkovo on the Yamal Peninsula and Shtokman in the Barents Sea. Both of these are described as "mega projects" by Russian officials, requiring massive investments and extensive site preparation; even after years of concentrated work and billions of dollars in preliminary development, neither one has yet opened for production.

Bovanenkovo is one of the largest natural gas deposits ever discovered in Russia, with estimated reserves of 170 trillion cubic feet, and its exploitation—along with that of other fields on the Yamal Peninsula—is considered a top priority. When fully operational, Bovanenkovo is expected to produce 2.7 to 4.1 trillion cubic feet of gas per year, the equivalent of about one-sixth of Russia's current output. But establishing the necessary production and transport infrastructure has proved a monumental challenge. The Yamal region—the name means "End of the World" in the language of the indigenous Nenets people—is barely above sea level, and the soil in many areas is too sandy to support permanent structures.[61] To gain access to the area, the Russians have had to spend billions of dollars on new railroads, pipelines, and living accommodations that were erected using unconventional construction techniques. These efforts were nearing fruition in mid-2009, but at that point Gazprom's management committee decided to slow down work on Bovanenkovo and reduce spending on the project due to the weak economic climate. The company made it clear, however, that it sees the site as strategically vital, and in October 2011 Gazprom announced plans to accelerate development at Bovanenkovo once again.[62]

The Shtokman gas field, located approximately 350 miles north of the Kola Peninsula in the Russian portion of the Barents Sea, is believed to rival Bovanenkovo in size. If and when it is brought online, it is expected to yield some 2.5 trillion cubic feet per year, roughly equivalent to the total output of Indonesia. Unlike Bovanenkovo, however, the Shtokman field is located offshore, lying beneath 1,100 feet of water, and extracting those underwater resources has proven to be extraordinarily difficult. The original plan called for installing fixed drilling platforms in the production area, but Russian scientists have warned that any such structures would be vulnerable to collision with giant icebergs—a risk that will grow as global temperatures rise and the melting of Greenland's glaciers accelerates.[63] In response to this danger, Gazprom now plans to deploy movable floating platforms in the Shtokman field, allowing for their repositioning in the case of emergency.[64] This still leaves the problem of transporting the gas to international markets, an obstacle Gazprom has yet to overcome.[65] In recognition of all these issues, the field's developers recently agreed to postpone the onset of production by at least three years, pushing the startup date from 2013 to 2016 at the earliest.[66]

Other mega projects of this sort are likely to materialize in future decades. In 2010, for example, Rosneft was granted licenses to three blocks in the South Kara Sea, covering some 50,000 square miles—about the same size as Norway's entire North Sea production area. The three blocks are located just to the west of Rusanovskoye, a supergiant natural gas field that was discovered in 1989 (and, at this point, is still undeveloped).[67] Rosneft's South Kara project, although still in its infancy, sparked international headlines in early 2011 when the state-owned Russian firm agreed to form a strategic alliance with BP to jointly develop the area. The partnership was described as a great coup for both sides: BP gained access to vast Arctic energy reserves and Rosneft gained access to BP's advanced drilling technology.[68] Despite its appeal, the plan had to be abandoned when the directors of TNK-BP—an energy firm jointly owned by BP and a trio of Russian oligarchs—brought suit to block it on the grounds that BP was contractually obligated to conduct any Russian operations through that joint enterprise.[69] But Rosneft wasted no time in seeking another partner for its Arctic venture: in August 2011, it announced a deal with ExxonMobil giving that company access to the Kara Sea fields in return for a minority interest in Exxon assets elsewhere.[70]

Russia also possesses other untapped oil and gas fields in the Arctic region, and intends to exploit the vast majority of them. As the Bovanenkovo, Prirazlomnoye, and Shtokman experiences show, however, the development of Russia's Arctic resources will be far from easy: even where the immense logistical problems can be overcome, other obstacles often block the way. No doubt Moscow's determination to make full use of the Arctic hydrocarbon riches will continue to push the projects ahead, but each new venture is likely to involve great cost and significant environmental risk.

TERRITORIAL DISPUTES AND GEOPOLITICAL FRICTION

As the major energy corporations have moved deeper and deeper into the Arctic in their search for new reserves of oil and natural gas, national governments have also started paying more attention to this region, according it greater weight in their strategic calculations than ever before. This, in turn, has brought to the forefront several long-simmering boundary disputes in the Arctic and has raised new questions about the ownership of the polar region itself. Such boundary disputes were considered of only minor importance when the Arctic was thought to possess little of economic value, but now that the region is believed to hold nearly one-fifth of the world's remaining untapped hydrocarbon resources they have acquired far greater significance. All of the five countries with a presence in the Arctic—Canada, Denmark (through its control of Greenland), Norway, Russia, and the United States—are reaffirming their historic claims in the area and taking fresh action to protect their interests there. In this manner the Arctic, long ignored by most major political actors, has become a new hotspot of geopolitical friction.[71]

As we have seen, Artur Chilingarov's planting of the titanium Russian flag on the North Pole seabed in 2007 provoked a particularly sharp set of reactions from the regional powers. Chilingarov made clear that his expedition was not merely an attention-grabbing stunt, but part of an effort to gather evidence for Moscow's contention that the entire territory belongs to Russia.[72] Chilingarov's remarks led many foreign officials to strongly repudiate the Russian claim and reassert their own countries' interests in the area. Soon, every nation with an Arctic presence was hurrying to announce that it would protect its interests there by any means necessary.[73]

Such pugnacious statements have generated a flurry of alarmist headlines, suggesting the onset of a major arms race in the greater Arctic region. Although none of the more frightening scenarios have yet come to pass, both Canada and Russia have indeed continued to bolster their military capabilities in the Arctic. In August 2011, for example, Canada conducted elaborate military exercises at its new Arctic training base at Resolute Bay, and in the following month Prime Minister Vladimir Putin announced a subtantial buildup of Russia's border security in the Arctic region.[74] However, neither country has chosen to deploy armed forces to the region in any significant numbers—a reflection, no doubt, of the great cost of maintaining combat troops in the extreme northern latitudes. All of the regional powers have also been cooperating with one another in scientific and safety matters under the auspices of the Arctic Council, an intergovernmental forum established in 1996 to address matters of common concern.[75] Still, while armed conflict in the

POLAR REGION BOUNDARY DISPUTES

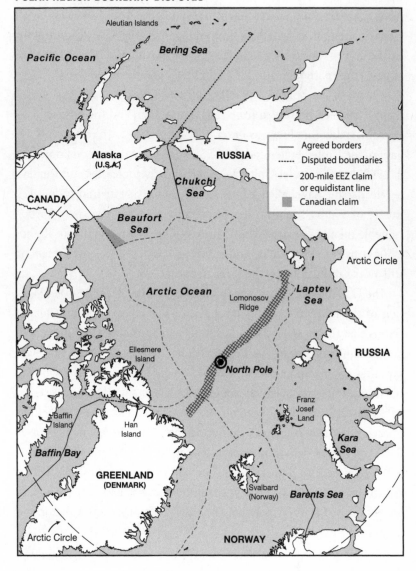

Arctic appears highly unlikely at present, none of the major Arctic countries have surrendered their claims to disputed territories.

To a considerable degree, then, the geopolitics of the Arctic region will be shaped by the outcome of disputes over contested international boundaries.[76] Some of these disputes are relatively straightforward disagreements over the exact borders of two adjoining Arctic states. Alaska, for example, shares maritime boundaries with Russia and with Canada, neither of which is entirely settled. The U.S. dispute with Russia can be traced back to the original acquisition of Alaska from the czarist empire: though the 1867 purchase agreement mentions a U.S.-Russia maritime border in the Bering and Chukchi Seas, no official maps have been preserved from that transaction, and the precise location of the dividing line was never fully determined. To rectify this situation, the United States and the USSR agreed on a common boundary in 1990, but the Soviet Union fell apart shortly thereafter and Russia's new leadership has challenged the accord, saying that it unfairly deprives Russia of 15,000 square miles of offshore territory that may harbor valuable oil and gas deposits. At present, the treaty remains in limbo: while considered legitimate and enforceable by the U.S. government, it still awaits ratification by the Russian parliament.[77]

The U.S. dispute with Canada, meanwhile, involves the exact location of the maritime boundary at Alaska's northeast corner. Canada claims that the boundary should simply extend the Alaska-Yukon border straight north into the Beaufort Sea; the United States, however, says that the maritime border should be perpendicular to the slanting coastline at that point, which would make it veer slightly to the east. (In either case, the line would extend 200 nautical miles to the outer extent of each country's exclusive economic zone.) The discrepancy between these two border definitions creates a wedge of about 8,300 square miles that is claimed by both nations. Because this wedge lies adjacent to known oil and natural gas deposits in both countries, neither Canada nor the United States has shown any willingness to compromise on the matter.[78]

Canada also faces a territorial dispute with Denmark regarding the

Nares Strait, which separates Canada's Ellesmere Island from the north-west coast of Greenland. In 1973, Canada and Denmark settled the location of almost their entire mutual boundary in the waters off Greenland—except for the question of Hans Island, a small speck of rock in the Nares Strait that is claimed by both nations. Although neither country has any interest in Hans Island itself, by owning it they would also gain control over a large body of surrounding water, which is thought to sit atop potentially valuable deposits of oil and natural gas.[79]

In addition to such bilateral disagreements, all five of the Arctic powers—Canada, Denmark, Norway, Russia, and the United States—are also party to a complex debate over ownership of the central Arctic Ocean and its seabed. This dispute arises from ambiguities in international law regarding rights to semi-enclosed bodies of water like the Arctic. In general, most legal experts have viewed the Arctic Ocean as an international waterway, open to navigation by all; various historical claims to portions of the Arctic—for instance, the 1926 declaration by Moscow that the entire area between the Soviet landmass and the North Pole belonged to the Soviet Union—are currently regarded as far-fetched. Under the United Nations Convention on the Law of the Sea, however, coastal nations may lay claim to the seabed on their outer continental shelf—and all of the Arctic states are in the process of doing so.[80]

The UNCLOS regulations, as we have seen, allow member states to claim ownership of the "natural prolongation" of their continental shelf, even if it extends beyond their EEZ; this is the clause that Argentina has cited in the Falklands/Malvinas dispute and that China wants to apply in the East China Sea. In the case of the Arctic Ocean, similarly, both Denmark (acting for Greenland) and Russia have declared that their respective continental shelves incorporate the Lomonosov Ridge, an undersea geological crease that transects the Arctic from northern Greenland to eastern Siberia. If either country were to prove that the ridge is, in fact, an extension of its landmass, it could theoretically monopolize the exploitation of valuable hydrocarbon resources in northern Arctic waters—especially as global warming makes polar drilling more feasible. Denmark has already conducted scientific surveys to establish that the Lomonosov Ridge stretches out from Greenland; Chilingarov's descent to the North Pole seabed, likewise, was intended in part to obtain geological evidence showing that the Lomonosov is an extension of Russian territory. Both countries have submitted the results of their investigations to the Commission on the Limits of the Continental Shelf, a body created by UNCLOS to verify such claims. However, it could be many years before the commission reaches a judgment—and even then, it is unclear whether the parties involved will accept the outcome if it goes against their perceived interests.[81]

At present, all of the Arctic powers insist that they are determined to settle these territorial disputes through peaceful means. One positive omen came in April 2010, when Russia and Norway resolved a long-running debate about the Barents Sea border between the two countries by agreeing to compromise on a line lying exactly halfway between their two competing claims. For the most part, however, the Arctic nations have shown little inclination to terminate outstanding disputes, so the risk of geopolitical conflict will persist. Indeed, as global temperatures rise and it becomes easier to extract hydrocarbons from northerly waters, international tensions are likely to grow. "It is no coincidence that our strategic interest in the Arctic warms with its climate," said Admiral James Stavridis, commander of the U.S. European Command, on the eve of a recent NATO workshop on Arctic security affairs. "For now, the disputes in the north have been dealt with peacefully, but climate change could alter the equilibrium over the coming years."[82] In its way, the risk of military conflict in the Arctic is yet another on the long list of dangers posed by global warming.

Stavridis's comments make it clear that the risk of international friction and conflict over Arctic resources cannot be entirely dismissed. For the near future, however, the greatest obstacles to resource exploitation in the region are likely to be geography, climate, cost, and the environment. As we have seen, all of the major projects currently under way or in the process of development above the Arctic Circle face enormous challenges of one sort or another and will require enormous investments to succeed. Global warming may improve the attractiveness of operating in the Arctic, by shrinking the polar icecap and lengthening drilling seasons, but it will also generate new problems of its own, such as an increased number of dangerous icebergs, that will slow the pace of development.

Despite these risks, however, there is every indication that the major energy companies will persist in their drive to exploit the alluring hydrocarbon resources of the Far North. With few other places to turn to, they are wagering ever greater sums in the development of these reserves. Progress may be gradual during the current decade, but the efforts are bound to gain momentum in the 2020s, as fields below the Arctic Circle become increasingly depleted. Political leaders may worry about the many environmental risks involved, yet feel compelled to allow increased Arctic drilling in order to satisfy national energy needs. The artificial islands now being built by BP in the Beaufort Sea will soon have company, as more and more human outposts appear above the Arctic Circle in a desperate drive for new supplies of oil and gas.

4 ► TAR SANDS, SHALE GAS, AND OTHER UNCONVENTIONAL HYDROCARBONS

Approximately 600 miles south of the Arctic Circle, in the boreal forest of northeastern Alberta, lies another hydrocarbon reserve of immense interest to energy companies: the Athabasca tar sands, a colossal deposit of sand and clay mixed with petroleum-rich bitumen. Geologists believe that the Albertan tar sands—often called "oil sands" by industry and government officials—may encompass as much as 1.7 trillion barrels of oil equivalent, of which an estimated 170 billion barrels are recoverable using existing technologies. If proved accurate, these figures would propel Canada into the second rank among the world's major oil powers, just after Saudi Arabia. But obtaining oil from the tar sands is not easy: even in warmer climates bitumen has the consistency of thick molasses, while in Canada's Far North it solidifies entirely, and so cannot be pumped from the earth like conventional petroleum. Instead, it must be mined like a mineral ore, or heated underground in order to make it fluid. Either approach is expensive, burns up tremendous amounts of energy, and involves multiple environmental risks. Yet even so, many of the major energy firms are flocking to Alberta in a desperate search for new hydrocarbon resources to exploit.[1]

Oil geologists had known for many decades that the Athabasca

ATHABASCA OIL SANDS

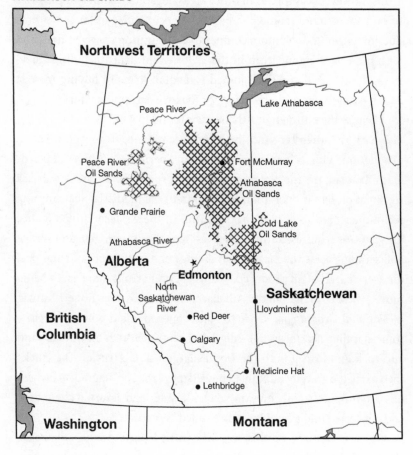

region (named after the Athabasca River, which snakes through northeastern Alberta) harbors large quantities of bitumen. Traces of the tarlike material can be found on the banks of the Athabasca and other local streams, and it has long been used by the Cree and Chipewyan peoples to caulk their canoes—until recently the only reliable means of transportation in this remote forested area. But extracting large quantities of bitumen from the Athabasca sands and converting them into a usable liquid proved far more costly than conventional oil drilling, so major energy firms generally paid little attention to the region. In the

1970s, however, as supplies in other areas began to shrink and the price of oil rose to more than $50 a barrel, the economics of tar sands production began to look more competitive. Beginning slowly at first, and with increasing momentum in the 1990s, giant firms including Chevron, ExxonMobil, and Shell joined Canadian firms in buying up vast Athabasca acreage and preparing for massive extraction efforts.[2]

Because the bitumen in Athabasca is found in solid form, the exploitation of Canadian tar sands bears no resemblance to conventional oil production, with its iconic drilling rigs and periodic "gushers" of petroleum. Instead, the most common form of production in the Athabasca region at present is open-pit mining, akin to the industrial-scale mining techniques used to obtain coal and iron in the western United States. This process requires cutting down vast forests of virgin pine and spruce and scraping aside the topsoil—an average of four tons of sand and peat for every barrel of oil produced. "Nowhere on Earth is more earth being moved these days than in the Athabasca Valley," observes Robert Kunzig of *National Geographic*.[3] Once the pit is opened, giant power shovels—some standing six stories tall—dig out the bitumen-rich mixture of sand and rock and load it onto the world's largest dump trucks. The trucks then carry the gravelly mixture to processing plants, or "upgraders," where it is ground into small chips, mixed with water and assorted chemicals, and converted into a liquid mixture called "syncrude."[4]

Open-pit mining of this sort has turned parts of the Athabasca region into a blackened moonscape, with enormous man-made craters sitting alongside vast piles of discarded rock and pools of poisonous wastewater.[5] The mammoth pits can be seen from space, darkening the otherwise uniformly green landscape of northern Alberta. The pools of spent water now cover some fifty square miles, and the "tailings" that they contain—leftover sand and clay particles mixed with the solvents used to convert the bitumen into a synthetic crude oil—are hazardous to wildlife: in April 2009, some 500 migrating birds perished after alighting in one of these ponds.[6] Canadian environmentalists also worry that the chemical-laced water from the ponds is leaking into the Athabasca River and endangering the health of downstream communities.[7]

The other possible form of bitumen exploitation causes less immediate damage to the surface but poses its own barrage of problems. This method, used when the bitumen deposits are too deep to be reached by open-pit mining, involves injecting steam into the buried tar sands; when heated in this manner, the bitumen turns into a liquid that seeps into underground pools, from where it can be pumped to the surface. Geologists believe that approximately 80 percent of Alberta's bitumen deposits will have to be extracted by this technique, known as steam-assisted gravity drainage (SAGD).[8] Although SAGD does not affect the landscape as much as open-pit mining, the construction of roads, pipelines, and other facilities slices up the forest, disrupting the survival patterns of many woodland creatures. "The land is dead," lamented Howard Lacorde, a Cree trapper whose trapline has been sundered by tar sands extraction. "There are no moose, no rabbits, no squirrels anymore."[9]

The SAGD process also poses a threat to the region's rivers and streams. Vast quantities of water are needed to produce the steam that is injected into the underground deposits, and even more is required to transport the liquefied bitumen to the upgraders and to process it there. Much of this water is recycled from prior use, but some of it is appropriated from the local rivers, reducing their flow and risking downstream environmental damage. And once water becomes mixed with sand, silt, and chemical solvents, it cannot be recycled or returned to the natural environment but must be stored indefinitely in tailings ponds, with all their attendant hazards.[10]

Along with water, the exploitation of Canadian tar sands consumes extraordinary quantities of energy. This is true of both methods of extraction, but especially of the SAGD technique, which usually produces the necessary steam by heating water in boilers powered by natural gas. Consuming so much natural gas in order to produce synthetic petroleum from bitumen is seen by some experts as a wasteful misapplication of a valuable commodity that might be better employed to heat homes or generate electric power. "What bugs me about oil sands is that it is a resource that is being inefficiently used," said Mario Raynolds of the Pembina Institute, a Canadian environmental policy organization.

"We're using natural gas, which is the cleanest fossil fuel, to wash sand and make a dirtier fuel. It's like using caviar to make fake crabmeat."[11]

Burning large quantities of fossil fuels to extract bitumen and convert it into usable crude also greatly increases the atmospheric emissions of carbon dioxide and other greenhouse gases (GHGs). All types of petroleum extraction, including conventional drilling, involve some expenditure of energy and so result in GHG emissions, but the exploitation of Canadian tar sands requires far more energy input than most such operations, and therefore releases a correspondingly greater amount of CO_2. According to the Pembina Institute, producing a barrel of oil from tar sands releases 188.5 pounds of carbon dioxide, compared to only 63 pounds for a barrel produced by conventional means.[12] Leveling vast stretches of boreal forest to permit bitumen extraction also reduces these forests' remarkable capacity to absorb atmospheric CO_2, further contributing to greenhouse warming. As the production of tar sands increases, therefore, Canada will have increasing difficulty reducing its GHG emissions as required by the Kyoto Protocol—which might explain why the country decided in late 2011 to officially withdraw from the treaty.[13]

Despite all these problems, however, major energy firms evidently believe that the Athabasca bitumen deposits represent an attractive investment as other sources of crude petroleum disappear and the demand for oil continues to grow. The Canadian company Suncor Energy, which already produces about 228,000 barrels of crude oil per day from a pair of open-pit bitumen mines, is spending an estimated $20 billion to develop the Voyageur project, which will employ SAGD technology.[14] The roster of international companies that have acquired a stake in tar sands production, meanwhile, includes Shell, Chevron, BP, Exxon, and numerous others (see Table 4.1). Several state-owned Chinese firms have also recently become active in Athabasca, possibly hoping that some of Alberta's oil will eventually find its way to China. In 2009, PetroChina (a subsidiary of the China National Petroleum Corporation) acquired a 60 percent share in the Athabasca Oil Sands Project, while the following year Sinopec bought a 9 percent share in Syncrude Canada—the biggest operator in the Athabasca region—for $4.65 billion.[15]

TABLE 4.1: MAJOR CANADIAN TAR SANDS PROJECTS

(As of April 2011)

PROJECT	COMPANY	PLANNED CAPACITY	START-UP DATE
Kearl	Imperial Oil (69.6% owned by ExxonMobil); Exxon Canada	110,000 bbl/d (Phase 1); 200,000 bbl/d (Phases 2–3)	2012–18
Mackay River	Athabasca Oil Sands Corp.; PetroChina	115,000 bbl/d (3 phases)	2014–19
Sunrise	Husky Energy; BP	210,000 bbl/d (4 phases)	2014–18
Fort Hills	Suncor; Total; Teck Resources	190,000 bbl/d	2015–16
Joslyn	Total; Suncor; Occidental Petroleum	200,000 bbl/d (2 phases)	2017
Narrows Lake	Cenovus Energy; ConocoPhillips	130,000 bbl/d	2017
Pierre River Mine	Shell Canada; Chevron Canada; Marathon Oil	200,000 bbl/d	2018–22

Source: U.S. Dept. of Energy, "Canada," Country Analysis Brief, April 2011.
bbl/d = barrels per day

The ultimate destination of Alberta's future bitumen output will depend, to some degree, on decisions made about new pipeline infrastructure. Most of the currently operating pipelines carry upgraded bitumen from Alberta to refineries in the American Midwest, but they are not large enough to handle all the syncrude expected to come from tar sands projects now in development. To add capacity, Canadian pipeline company TransCanada has been working to build a number of new conduits, including the proposed $7 billion Keystone XL pipeline that would carry syncrude as far south as Louisiana and Texas. However, work on the Keystone XL project has been criticized by some members of the U.S. Congress and others who oppose expanded tar sands production on environmental grounds. In November 2011, President Obama ordered a fresh review of the pipeline's route, delaying construction and raising doubts about its eventual installation. If Keystone XL does not get approved, new pipelines might be constructed instead from Alberta to Canada's east or west coasts, and oil from the tar sands might then flow to Europe or Asia.[16]

Whatever the eventual orientation of pipelines from Alberta, the development of its bitumen reserves will continue apace. A few years ago, Alberta's Energy and Utilities Board had predicted that corporate investments in various oil sands projects would add up to some $118 billion over the course of a decade.[17] Now, with the *Deepwater Horizon* disaster in the Gulf of Mexico having cast a pall over deep-offshore drilling, many experts believe that the drive to exploit Alberta's tar sands will acquire even greater momentum. "The uncertainty and the slowdown in drilling permits in the Gulf really underscores the growing importance of Canadian oil sands, which over the last decade have gone from being a fringe energy source to being one of strategic importance," says oil historian Daniel Yergin.[18]

THE "UNCONVENTIONALS ERA"

The accelerating development of Canada's bitumen deposits is part of a larger trend toward reliance on so-called unconventional fuels. As long as energy firms had access to adequate supplies of "conventional" hydrocarbons—easy-to-reach reservoirs of liquid crude oil and free-flowing natural gas—they did not need to seek out solid forms of petroleum such as bitumen and kerogen, or oil and gas trapped in challenging geological formations. As conventional deposits have become increasingly depleted, however, the companies see no choice but to increase their dependence on unconventional sources of supply. "The light crude undiscovered today is getting scarcer and scarcer," notes Jean-Luc Guiziou, the president of Canadian operations for French energy giant Total S.A. "We have to accept the reality of geoscience, which is that the next generation of oil resources will be heavier"[19]—that is, more viscous, dense, and difficult to extract. Much the same can be said of natural gas: with the depletion of conventional gas fields, more and more natural gas will be derived from unorthodox sources such as shale rock and coal-bed methane. Indeed, the shift is so pronounced that Chevron officials say that we have already entered a new energy epoch: the "Unconventionals Era."[20]

There is no question that the world's reliance on unconventional fuels is increasing. As noted earlier, the International Energy Agency predicts that the percentage of the world's total liquid fuel output supplied by unconventionals—tar sands, extra-heavy oil, coal to liquids, and shale oil—will triple over the course of three decades, going from 3 percent in 2008 to 9 percent in 2035.[21] Unconventional natural gas is likely to grow even faster than unconventional oil, especially in the United States. Technological advances in horizontal drilling and hydraulic fracturing (or "hydrofracking") are allowing energy firms to exploit many U.S. gas deposits that were once considered inaccessible. Overall, unconventional supplies derived from shale, other impermeable rock formations ("tight gas"), and coal-bed methane accounted for more than half of all U.S. gas production in 2008, and the U.S. Department of Energy projects that their share will climb to 75 percent by 2035. The new drilling techniques are also increasingly being applied in Canada, Europe, and China, and so reliance on unconventional gas supplies is expected to grow there as well.[22]

The growing use of unconventional oil and gas has dramatically altered the strategic outlook of the major energy companies, especially privately owned corporations such as Chevron, ExxonMobil, Shell, and Total. Historically, such firms—also known as international oil companies, or IOCs—have competed for access to hydrocarbon reserves in developing countries, setting up operations throughout Africa, Asia, and the Middle East. Increasingly, however, the reserves in many such countries are controlled by state-owned national oil companies (NOCs), narrowing the options for the IOCs. The private corporations have responded, in part, by increasing their production in the Arctic, in offshore areas, and in those few territories (such as West Africa and the Caspian Sea basin) where direct investment by IOCs is still permitted. But the large-scale embrace of unconventional fuels has given them another option: the ability to extract oil and gas in friendly, highly developed countries such as Canada and the United States. The higher cost of exotic production techniques in places like northern Alberta can be offset, in part, by proximity to the market; moreover, once the unconventional fuels are extracted and refined, they can be sold through the same well-established distribution and retail networks as conventional oil and gas. It is not surprising, then, that the IOCs are increasingly placing large bets on the development of unconventional hydrocarbons.

Although every one of the major energy firms is pursuing multiple paths in the search for unconventional resources, each has chosen to specialize in one or more particular technologies. Royal Dutch Shell, for example, is placing particular emphasis on novel techniques that might be used to obtain liquid fuels from Rocky Mountain shale rock. ExxonMobil, long a leader in the production of oil, is meanwhile diversifying by adding a focus on natural gas extracted from shale rock and tight sands. In 2009, it paid $41 billion to acquire XTO Energy, one of the nation's leading producers of natural gas and a pioneer in the development of drilling techniques to liberate gas from dense rock formations. By acquiring XTO, Exxon not only doubled its U.S. gas reserves but also gained access to the advanced technical skills needed to thrive in the Unconventionals Era.[23]

Assorted governments, too, are pushing for the development of unconventional energy resources, seeing a geopolitical advantage in developing energy reserves at home and in nearby countries.[24] In the United States, for example, senior officials have suggested that exploiting North America's unconventional oil and gas deposits will play a key role in diminishing U.S. reliance on energy acquired from less trustworthy partners elsewhere in the world. The construction of new pipelines to transport oil sands from Alberta to refineries in the United States would be particularly attractive, said David L. Goldwyn, the State Department's coordinator for international energy affairs. "It is undeniable that having a large supply of crude oil available by pipeline from a friendly neighbor is extremely valuable to the energy security of the United States."[25] Chinese officials, for their part, are similarly eager to promote the development of unconventional domestic hydrocarbon deposits as a way to reduce their country's reliance on imported energy.[26]

For both corporate and geopolitical reasons, therefore, the pursuit of unconventional oil and gas will acquire increasing momentum in the years ahead. As the Canadian experience with tar sands suggests, however, the production of unconventional fuels often places a heavy toll on the environment, and therefore it is bound to provoke opposition from activist groups. Such groups may not be able to halt the production of unconventionals altogether, but they might succeed in pushing through more stringent regulatory measures, impeding certain projects and slowing down the development of these hydrocarbon sources. Moreover, it is not inconceivable that the unconventionals could experience their own *Deepwater Horizon* moment, with a major accident in the Athabasca region, the shale gas fields, or other such areas, turning public opinion against the industry.

Still, such concerns have so far done little to prevent the major energy firms from pushing ahead with the development of unconventional oil and gas reserves. In addition to the Albertan tar sands, the three unconventional options currently attracting the greatest attention are Venezuelan extra-heavy oil, Rocky Mountain shale oil, and U.S. shale gas—all of which have recently seen billions of dollars in investments from the IOCs. Other possibilities, including such exotic approaches as converting coal to liquids, are also being actively pursued and could become increasingly prominent if the technological difficulties are worked out in the coming years.

HEAVY AND EXTRA-HEAVY OIL

Oil company officials who insist that the Petroleum Age is far from over usually point to the bitumen and heavy oil of Canada and Venezuela as evidence that the world still possesses enormous reserves of unconventional resources.[27] As already noted, the Albertan tar sands are believed to harbor as much as 1.7 trillion barrels of oil equivalent; the Orinoco Belt area of northeastern Venezuela, meanwhile, is thought to possess another trillion barrels of heavy and extra-heavy oil.[28] Not all of these resources are commercially recoverable using existing technology, but even a relatively small fraction of them would represent a substantial addition to the world's conventional oil reserves, currently estimated at 1.4 trillion barrels.[29]

In comparison to ordinary petroleum, heavy oil is denser and more resistant to flow, and contains more sulfur and other impurities; extra-heavy oil is more dense and more viscous yet. The difference between the various types of oil deposits is generally related to their geological history. "Most heavy oil, extra-heavy oil, and bitumen deposits are very shallow," explains a group of scientists associated with the National Petroleum Council. "They originated as conventional oil formed in deep depressions, but migrated to the surface region where they were degraded by bacteria and by weathering, and where the lightest hydrocarbons escaped."[30]

Converting heavy oil into usable petroleum liquids is not impossible, but the high viscosity and presence of impurities make the process significantly more difficult and expensive than standard drilling. As with Canadian tar sands, extracting heavy and extra-heavy oil from the ground almost always requires heating it or increasing its mobility in some other fashion—procedures that also, of course, result in increased greenhouse-gas emissions. What's more, after the heavy crude has been brought to the surface, it must be mixed with less viscous materials—usually natural gas liquids or light crude—before it can be shipped to refineries by pipeline. The necessary amount of such dilution can be quite substantial, with as much as one barrel of diluents required for every three or four barrels of extra-heavy oil produced.[31]

Despite such difficulties, major oil firms have increasingly been drawn to heavy and extra-heavy oil fields, and they have recently found an eager partner in the Venezuelan government. Venezuela has been a major oil supplier since the 1920s; at one time it produced well over 3 million barrels per day, but in recent years its output has declined, yield-ing about 2.5 million barrels of oil per day in 2010. Many of the coun-try's historic oil fields are substantially depleted, so the state-owned Petróleos de Venezuela S.A. (PdVSA) must actively develop new depos-its to prevent a decline in national output; since there are few conven-tional oil reservoirs remaining in Venezuela, the company has started looking to the Orinoco Belt—a broad band of unconventional oil lying between the Orinoco River and the Caribbean Sea—as a vital resource. A 2009 study by the U.S. Geological Survey revealed that of the roughly one trillion barrels of heavy and extra-heavy crude in the Orinoco Belt, as much as 652 billion barrels is "technically recoverable," making this one of the world's most promising reservoirs of unconventional petroleum.[32]

Initially, in line with the socialist ideals of his highly touted "Boli-varian Revolution," Venezuela's president Hugo Chávez had wanted the country to develop the Orinoco Belt on its own, and in 2007 he issued a decree requiring all foreign companies to surrender majority control of their Venezuelan oil operations to PdVSA. Many foreign companies, including ExxonMobil and ConocoPhillips, responded to this demand by abandoning the country altogether, leaving only a handful of firms to cooperate with PdVSA. It was not very long, however, before Chávez discovered that the technological expertise of the IOCs was necessary to help process the country's heavy-oil deposits and so reversed his stance.[33] "You need to be here," he told a group of Western oil officials in a 2010 speech aimed at attracting fresh investment in the country. "They say there's no type of judicial security here in Venezuela and stuff like that, but it's not true.... You have all your guarantees for your investments, your profits, and the capital that you want to repatriate."[34]

Among the foreign firms that have responded to Chávez's call is Chevron, a corporation more familiar than most with the vicissitudes of operating in Venezuela. Back in 1946, when it was known as the Stan-dard Oil Company of California, the firm had developed Venezuela's Boscan field, south of Maracaibo; three decades later, however, it lost all its holdings in the country when the Venezuelan government decided to nationalize petroleum production. Invited to resume operations in the country in 1993, Chevron suffered more losses when Chávez awarded control over all domestic oil projects to PdVSA (though Chevron was allowed to remain in Venezuela as a minority owner of the Boscan field and various smaller enterprises).[35] All these reversals apparently did little to dampen Chevron's enthusiasm for Venezuela's heavy oil: when the political pendulum swung back and Chávez started courting foreign oil investment once again, the company joined with PdVSA and several other firms to secure rights to the Carabobo 3 block in the eastern Orinoco Belt. Under the terms of its agreement with the Venezuelan government, the Chevron-led group will invest between $10 billion and $20 billion in the Carabobo project over the next ten years, with the goal of producing 400,000 barrels of oil per day.[36]

Chevron and its partners will be far from alone in seeking to develop the Orinoco heavy-oil riches. The same auction that led to Chevron's acquisition of the Carabobo 3 block also attracted a wide range of other oil companies from around the world, both private and state owned. A consortium that includes Repsol YPF of Spain, Petronas of Malaysia, Oil and Natural Gas Corporation of India, and several smaller Indian companies succeeded in winning rights to the Carabobo 1 block, another major tract in the area—again to be developed in conjunction with PdVSA. (The Venezuelan national company holds a 60 percent interest in all Carabobo projects.) Like the Chevron enterprise, the Carabobo 1 agreement will require the successful bidders to spend many billions of dollars on advanced drilling technologies and on the construction of an upgrader to convert the heavy oil into synthetic crude.[37]

Several major Chinese companies have also sought to establish themselves in the Orinoco region, with the enthusiastic support of the Chávez administration. "All the oil that China needs for its growth and consolidation as a power is here," President Chávez declared in April 2010 at a Caracas ceremony, which also celebrated a $20 billion Chinese loan for economic development in Venezuela.[38] So far, both the China National Offshore Oil Corporation (CNOOC) and the China National Petroleum Corporation (CNPC) have signed agreements with PdVSA for jointly developing portions of the Orinoco Belt, though it is not yet clear when—or whether—these ventures will move toward full-scale production.[39]

The risks inherent in trying to run an oil business under the mercurial rule of Hugo Chávez did lead some big firms to shun the country altogether, while other major companies have decided to hedge their unconventional petroleum bets by starting operations in Canada as well. From a technical viewpoint, however, Orinoco heavy oil is a distinctly more attractive source of unconventional petroleum than the bitumen in Athabascan tar sands: it is usually fluid enough to be pumped directly from oil wells, instead of having to be mined like coal or heated with injected steam. Despite Canada's business-friendly appeal, therefore, the heavy and extra-heavy oil deposits in Venezuela will remain a major source of unconventional petroleum for the foreseeable future.

OIL SHALE

Many questions still remain about the prospects for tar sands and heavy oil, but the technology for developing such deposits is already well established and so they are likely to become increasingly popular in the years ahead. No such technological assurance, on the other hand, currently exists for another potential source of petroleum: Rocky Mountain oil shale. Despite a long history of attempts to make use of this hydrocarbon resource, and a variety of ambitious new development programs, it is not yet clear whether there is any way to exploit oil shale in an economically viable, environmentally friendly fashion.[40] Nonetheless, the craving for new sources of energy is so strong that many firms are investing significant sums in oil shale research, hoping to speed up the development of this unconventional option.

Oil shale is particularly attractive to private energy firms because the largest reserves of it are located in the United States. According to the U.S. Geological Survey, the Piceance basin in western Colorado and the neighboring Uinta basin in eastern Utah together hold 2.8 trillion barrels of oil equivalent, making the area one of the world's largest untapped reservoirs of unconventional fuel.[41] "Western shale contains the most concentrated hydrocarbon deposits on earth," a team of energy analysts pointed out in the *Oil & Gas Journal*. "Recovery of even a small fraction of this resource would represent a significant energy source to supplement oil supply for many decades."[42]

Most oil shale is found in relatively shallow formations, lying some 1,000 to 2,000 feet beneath the surface. In essence, oil shale represents an early stage in the geologic formation of oil: the residue of ancient swamps and lake bottoms that was buried under sand and rock millions of years ago but never pushed far enough underground (and kept there long enough) to be transformed into crude petroleum. Instead, the hydrocarbons in oil shale take the form of kerogen, a solid organic substance that must be heated to between 530 and 930 degrees Fahrenheit in order to be transformed into a liquid.[43*] Extracting the shale from the ground and heating the kerogen to such temperatures require considerable energy inputs—which, in turn, produce significant carbon emissions. The process also consumes vast quantities of water, a precious resource in mostly arid Utah and Colorado. All of the companies seeking to produce liquid fuel from the shale deposits speak of their determination to minimize such impacts, but many experts believe that any exploitation of oil shale will inevitably pose significant environmental risks.[44]

Because of these environmental concerns, both federal and state government agencies have been relatively cautious in dealing with the shale issue. Most of the high-quality oil shale deposits in the United States are located on federal land, so no production can take place unless the government opens up its territory to private development. During the George W. Bush administration, Congress did vote for a measure allowing some federal lands in Colorado and Utah to be leased for oil shale research and demonstration projects; the bill also stated that these projects could be transformed into production operations if

---

*Oil shale—that is, relatively shallow layers of solid kerogen-bearing rock—is not to be confused with what is known as *shale oil*: mature, liquid petroleum trapped in deeper shale formations. In their attempts to extract shale oil, many energy companies are turning to the hydrofracking process, discussed in detail below.

the trials proved effective.[45] Additionally, President Bush retroactively inserted an amendment into all approved leases that would have allowed their owners to pay very low royalty rates when production began, and would have exempted them from strict environmental oversight. This move was widely condemned by environmental organizations, and was almost immediately reversed by the Obama administration: when Ken Salazar became secretary of the interior after Obama's inauguration, one of his first acts was to cancel the leasing plan.[46] Salazar later indicated that some of the demonstration projects would be allowed to proceed, but that more research would have to be done on the environmental impacts of oil shale extraction before full-scale production could be permitted.[47]

At present, the company that appears closest to developing a commercially viable process for exploiting oil shale is Royal Dutch Shell. The firm's method involves inserting electrical heaters into the underground shale formation; the heat slowly converts the kerogen into a liquid hydrocarbon, which can be brought to the surface by conventional pumps. To prevent any of the liquid from leaking into underground aquifers and threatening drinking supplies, Shell also inserts a "freeze wall"—an impermeable barrier of frozen earth—around the entire drill site. The company has conducted trial runs of the process on privately owned Colorado acreage, and now plans to lease several blocks of government land in the Piceance basin for full-scale testing. If all goes well, Shell hopes to begin commercial production of crude derived from oil shale by the middle of this decade.[48]

Several of Shell's competitors, meanwhile, are investigating other potential methods for extracting liquids from oil shale. ExxonMobil is focusing on the "Electrofrac" process, which involves using powerful water jets to fracture the underground stone before applying electricity to heat the kerogen.[49] Chevron, in partnership with the Los Alamos National Laboratory, is exploring the possibility of employing explosives to shatter the rock and then applying chemical solvents to break it down into oil. An even more exotic technology is being tested by Schlumberger, the world's leading oil-field services company: instead of trying to break down the underground shale with chemistry or electricity, Schlumberger plans to use radio-frequency microwave emitters.[50] All of these methods are still in the experimental stage, and none of them are guaranteed to yield significant quantities of liquid fuel affordably and with minimal environmental risk. The fact that so much money and effort are being expended on their development, though, speaks volumes about the oil companies' intense desire to exploit this untapped resource.

SHALE GAS

Underground shale formations have been attracting attention not only for their potential oil riches, as in the Piceance basin, but also for the vast reserves of natural gas trapped within them. Until recently those gas supplies have been considered inaccessible, because sedimentary shale basins are too dense to allow the recovery of natural gas through standard drilling methods. As with oil shale, however, major firms are now turning to extraordinary means—and investing billions of dollars—in their efforts to extract energy from this unconventional resource.

"We've always known the potential of shale; we just didn't have the technology to get to it at a low enough cost," says Amy Myers Jaffe of the Energy Forum at the Baker Institute of Rice University. "Now new techniques have driven down the price tag—and set the stage for shale gas to be the game-changing resource of the decade."[51] Consistent with this assessment, the U.S. Department of Energy now predicts that shale gas will account for more than one-fourth of all natural gas production in the United States by 2035—up from zero just a few years ago—and an even higher percentage in Canada and China.[52]

The most important of the new technologies that have been developed to extract gas from the dense shale formations are horizontal drilling and hydraulic fracturing, or "hydrofracking." In a typical application, energy firms use conventional drills to dig a vertical well down to the level of the shale, usually a mile or so underground; the drills are then steered sideways into the rock, often extending thousands of feet horizontally. Once numerous channels have been drilled and encased in concrete, small explosive charges are set off to puncture the concrete and shatter the rock. Finally, millions of gallons of water laced with sand, lubricants, and other chemical additives are forced into these fissures, widening the openings and allowing the gas to escape toward the central well and then be collected on the surface.[53]

The first tests of hydraulic fracturing as a way to extract natural gas from shale were carried out in the late 1990s by Mitchell Energy and Development Corporation, a small independent company based in the Houston area. Mitchell's success in unleashing natural gas from the Barnett shale formation, which lies at a depth of about 8,000 feet under and around the city of Fort Worth, Texas, soon attracted imitators.[54] Other companies began applying the hydrofracking technique at promising sites elsewhere in the country, including the Fayetteville shale formation in central Arkansas, the Haynesville formation in northern Louisiana and east Texas, and the giant Marcellus formation in West Virginia, Pennsylvania, and New York State.[55] Together, these reserves—or "plays," as they are called in the industry—extend over millions of square miles and are thought to house as much as 600 trillion cubic feet of untapped gas, representing roughly one-third of the total natural gas reserves in the United States.[56]

When shale gas formations began to be exploited in the early years of the twenty-first century, many independent enterprises saw this as their opportunity to establish a presence in "upstream" (extraction) operations without stepping on the toes of the giant energy companies. Some of the first wells in the Marcellus formation, for instance, were drilled by such smaller firms as Atlas Energy Resources, Cabot Oil & Gas, Epsilon Energy, Range Resources Corporation, and Ultra Oil & Gas.[57] Before long, however, larger companies such as Devon Energy, XTO Energy, and the Chesapeake Energy Corporation moved in, buying up some of the smaller businesses and acquiring significant drilling tracts of their own. (Mitchell, the hydrofracking pioneer, was sold to Devon in 2001 for $3.1 billion.) But interest in shale gas is so great that these relatively large companies, in turn, have now become takeover targets for even bigger corporations. Chesapeake has sold some of its shale interests to BP, Statoil, and Total,[58] while XTO Energy has been absorbed by ExxonMobil.[59] "This is really a significant event, a paradigm shift for our sector," said John H. Pinkerton, the chief executive of shale gas developer Range Resources, regarding Exxon's acquisition of XTO. Soon, he predicted, much of the acreage in the leading shale-gas areas will be controlled by the giant IOCs.[60]

As other sources of energy dry up and the new technologies become more widely available, the race for shale gas leases will only accelerate. According to energy market analysts Wood Mackenzie of Edinburgh, private companies spent $21 billion on acquiring such leases in the first six months of 2010 alone—as much as they expended in 2008 and 2009 combined.[61] Eager to further expand their resource base, the giant firms have also begun seeking out shale gas deposits in other parts of the world, especially Europe and China.[62] ConocoPhillips, for example, has teamed up with Lane Energy to develop a million-acre leasehold in Poland's northern Baltic basin, near the port of Gdańsk. Exxon has also acquired drilling rights in Poland, while a number of companies, including Devon and Total, are exploring prospective shale formations in southeast France.[63]

There is no doubt that shale gas has enormous potential as an energy source; indeed, many observers are now speaking of a "shale gas revolution." Before that full potential can be realized, however, the industry will have to overcome a number of environmental and regulatory challenges. With the giant energy firms now going beyond the established fields in Texas and Pennsylvania and acquiring production leases across the United States, government officials are beginning to pay much greater attention to the possible consequences of large-scale shale gas production. The *Deepwater Horizon* disaster has also added to the scrutiny of shale gas drilling, since some of the technological risks involved are the same in both kinds of operations. Many observers worry, for instance, that improper cementing of the wellbore—a key factor in the *Deepwater Horizon* explosion—could result in toxic liquids leaking from a shale gas well and contaminating local aquifers. The danger is all the more significant because some of the most promising shale gas plays are located in the northeastern United States, near the water supplies of major metropolitan areas.[64]

Even if wellbore cementing is performed correctly and no leaks occur, dealing with the wastewater produced by the hydraulic fracturing process is no simple matter. To shatter the shale beds and release the natural gas, hydrofracking uses as much as five million gallons of water per well. This water is mixed with various chemicals, many of them toxic; once the fracturing is complete, the remaining water and chemicals must be pumped back out of the well so the gas retrieval process can begin. In Texas, this "flowback" liquid is often stored in permanent underground caverns; however, such caverns are rare in the Northeast. Instead, drilling companies treat the flowback to remove the toxicants and return it to the environment—which means that any failure in the treatment process can poison rivers that supply drinking water to nearby communities. What's more, before being treated the flowback is usually stored in unlined holding ponds at the drilling site, and so if any liquid escapes from these ponds it, too, can endanger drinking supplies in the area.[65]

The energy companies, for their part, insist that the use of hydraulic fracturing in producing shale gas poses no danger to the environment. "It's a very reliable, safe, American source of energy," John Richels, president of Devon Energy, said in December 2009.[66] "We've done it 10,000 times in the company's history without incident," added Aubrey McClendon, chief executive officer of Chesapeake Energy, in an interview the following month.[67] But a number of recent events cast doubt on such confident assertions. In January 2009, gas from an improperly sealed well in Dimock, Pennsylvania, seeped into a surrounding aquifer, contaminating the water supplies of several neighboring households. Cabot Oil & Gas, the company that drilled the well, initially denied responsibility for the contamination, but later agreed to pay $4.1 million in order to settle claims with nineteen local residents.[68] A year and a half later, in June 2010, a well being drilled by EOG Resources in west-central Pennsylvania suffered a blowout, spewing 35,000 gallons of wastewater, mud, and poisonous chemicals seventy-five feet into the air. The company quickly built a dike around the site to contain the toxic stew, but some of the chemicals are believed to have made their way into underground aquifers.[69] And yet another blowout occurred in April 2011, this time in northeastern Pennsylvania. On this occasion, a well owned by Chesapeake Energy spilled thousands of gallons of chemical-laced water into nearby fields and streams before company engineers were able to bring it under control.[70]

Beyond such local incidents, a hazard of another order entirely was revealed in early 2011, when the New York Times conducted an extensive investigation of water contamination in Pennsylvania, a major site of shale gas production. According to corporate and government data collected by the Times, most of the 1.3 billion gallons of wastewater produced by shale gas wells in Pennsylvania between 2008 and 2010 was sent to public treatment plants not equipped to remove many of the toxic materials in the drilling waste. These materials included carcinogenic fracking fluids such as benzene, as well as radioactive particles of radium and uranium from naturally occurring underground deposits that were brought to the surface by the flowback. Some of the wells contributing to the toxic brew were found to be producing wastewater with 100 or even 1,000 times the level of radioactivity considered safe to drink; yet much of this drilling waste eventually found its way into rivers like the Monongahela and the Susquehanna, which provide drinking water for millions of people in Baltimore, Harrisburg, and Pittsburgh.[71] Industry officials insisted that the dumping of contaminated wastewater into public sewage systems was not a serious concern. "These low levels of radioactivity pose no threat to the public," said James E. Grey, chief operating officer of Triana Energy.[72] Many environmentalists and health officials, however, warn that if the radioactive materials accumulate in drinking water—or enter the food chain through fishing and farming—they are likely to produce an increase in cancer rates.[73]

As a result of the New York Times investigation and various gas well mishaps, some localities—including the states of Maryland and New

York and the city of Pittsburgh—have placed a moratorium on hydro-fracking pending further study. (New York's Department of Environmental Conservation, however, recently unveiled a proposal that would allow fracking across much of the state, excluding only the Catskill Mountains watershed area for New York City.) The federal government, too, is looking into instituting more stringent controls on the dumping of wastewater from shale gas wells. "The industry has failed to meet minimally acceptable performance levels for protecting human health and the environment," proclaimed Senator Benjamin L. Cardin of Maryland at a hearing held by the Senate Committee on the Environment and Public Works. "The promise of natural gas will be a promise unfulfilled if the human health and environmental impacts are not properly safeguarded."[74]

To a certain extent, the political debate over shale gas has followed predictable party lines. The concerns voiced by Cardin and other government officials, many of them Democrats, have been met with a barrage of reassurances from the mostly Republican allies of the large energy firms, who insist that hydraulic fracturing can be performed with minimal risk to the public. Recently, however, the shale gas industry has received support from an unexpected quarter: the administration of President Barack Obama. Proclaiming that increased domestic gas output can help the environment by diminishing reliance on dirtier fuels such as coal—and simultaneously enhance U.S. energy security by reducing the country's dependence on imported fuels—Obama has lauded the rapid rise of shale gas. "In 2010 . . . total U.S. natural gas production reached its highest level in more than 30 years," the White House noted in its 2011 *Blueprint for a Secure Energy Future*. "Much of this increase has the been the result of growing natural gas and oil production from shale formations as a result of recent technological advances. These resources, when developed with appropriate safeguards to protect public health, will play a critical role in domestic energy production in the coming decades."[75] To help overcome public anxieties about the dangers that shale gas production poses to drinking water and the environment, the Obama administration has appointed a panel of experts to study the industry and devise new federal guidelines for the hydrofracking process.[76]

Most energy experts believe that U.S. shale gas production will continue on a steep upward trajectory, especially if the industry adopts new safeguards intended to minimize the risk of environmental damage. There are, however, some drilling specialists who argue otherwise, saying the potential for growth is not as great as the conventional wisdom suggests. Although many of the wells drilled in the Barnett and Fayetteville formations have proved prolific, they point out, others—drilled just a mile or so away—have come up dry, suggesting a pattern of uneven and unpredictable results. Compared to typical oil and gas fields, moreover, shale gas fields tend to decline at a much faster rate after their initial development.[77] "This kind of data is making it harder and harder to deny that the shale gas revolution is being oversold," said Art Berman, a Houston-based geologist who worked for two decades at Amoco and is now one of the most vocal skeptics of shale gas economics.[78]

Though most hydrofracking applications so far have focused on shale gas fields, hydraulic fracturing is also increasingly being used in dense, low-permeability shale formations to access reservoirs of crude petroleum, which likewise cannot be reached with traditional drilling methods. For instance, between 3.0 and 4.3 billion barrels of technically recoverable oil are thought to be trapped within the Bakken shale formation, which stretches across 200,000 square miles of Montana and North Dakota; another large deposit is believed to be embedded in the Eagle Ford formation, located in South Texas.[79] Unlike the oil shale deposits in Colorado and Utah, where kerogen must be heated to produce a usable liquid, the petroleum in the Bakken and Eagle Ford formations is in mature, liquid form and so does not need to be treated in this fashion. But while some energy analysts see a bright future for shale oil production in the Bakken and Eagle Ford formations, others worry about the environmental risks of hydrofracking and express doubt that the process will be as effective with oil as it is with natural gas.[80]

Such concerns have not stopped the major energy firms from pouring more and more money into the development of shale gas and shale oil, so some significant increase in hydrofracking output—at least for the short term—currently appears to be inevitable. Precisely how big this increase will prove, and for how long it will persist, remains to be seen.

OTHER UNCONVENTIONAL FUELS

As the various efforts to develop "unconventional" fuels demonstrate, the planet harbors a variety of hydrocarbon materials that can—with substantial and costly effort—be converted into usable liquids and gas. At present, the major energy firms are focusing their attention primarily on Canadian tar sands, Venezuelan heavy oil, Rocky Mountain oil shale, and North American shale gas. But those four unconventionals are not the only possibilities, and in recent years other hydrocarbons— including coal-bed methane gas, coal-to-liquids, and methane hydrate— have also begun to attract corporate interest. While none of them are likely to provoke the same multibillion-dollar frenzy of development in the near future, all will play a role in the race to exploit the world's leftover energy reserves.

Coal-bed methane, as the name suggests, is methane gas (a pure form of natural gas) extracted from underground coal deposits. The process that produces coal from organic matter over the course of many millennia also generates large quantities of methane, which becomes trapped in the internal fissures of the coal bed. For coal miners, methane is a constant danger: if enough of it leaks out of the coal seam during excavation and is not properly ventilated, any contact with heat or flame can result in an explosion. Given this risk, most coal companies have historically sought to get rid of the methane in coal seams, installing giant fans to expel it from their underground caverns. But now the methane is seen as a valuable resource in its own right, and more and more energy firms are adopting plans to exploit the gas lodged in coal beds.[81]

According to the USGS, the contiguous United States (excluding

Alaska and Hawaii) holds approximately 700 trillion cubic feet of coal-bed methane, of which at least 100 trillion cubic feet is economically recoverable with existing technology—the equivalent of 19 billion barrels of oil.[82] Very large deposits of coal-bed methane are also found in Australia, Canada, China, Germany, and Indonesia. To extract this resource, energy firms drill wells into promising coal seams and allow the methane gas to rise to the surface, where it is collected and processed. The escaping methane is usually intermixed with large volumes of water, which also collects in the coal seam fractures; as part of the process, therefore, the wastewater has to be separated from the gas and disposed of. As with shale gas production, improper management of the wastewater can pose a risk to local water supplies.[83]

In the United States, production of coal-bed methane has averaged about 1.9 trillion cubic feet per year, or about 9.5 percent of total U.S. natural gas output. Because shale gas production is expected to rise so rapidly in the years ahead, coal-bed methane's share of the total gas output is projected to decline slightly over time, falling to 7 percent in 2035.[84] Nevertheless, several major energy firms, including Chesapeake, Devon, and ExxonMobil, are investing considerable effort in developing coal-bed methane assets in the United States. Even more ambitious plans are in progress overseas: Exxon has acquired some two million acres of land in Germany and began drilling for coal-bed methane there in 2010,[85] while ConocoPhillips has joined with Australia's Origin Energy to expand coal-bed methane production in Queensland.[86] And several Western firms, including Chevron and Texaco, are teaming up with Chinese companies to develop the vast reserves of coal-bed methane in that country.[87]

In addition to this exploitation of coal seams for their methane content, the big energy firms are now also seeking to develop another use for coal itself: as a raw material for the manufacture of liquid fuels such as diesel and gasoline. Coal is composed of the same hydrogen and carbon building blocks as petroleum and natural gas, albeit in different molecular combinations, and scientists have long been exploring ways to transmute it into usable liquids or gases. During World War II, Germany—which possesses large reserves of coal but very little oil—used one such method, known as the Fischer-Tropsch process, to convert coal into synthetic diesel and aviation fuel; later, during the apartheid era, South Africa's SASOL (from Suid Afrikaanse Steenkool en Olie, or South African Coal and Oil) turned to the same process to supply much of the country's diesel. Now, several of the major oil companies are exploring ways to convert coal to liquids (CTL) on a very large scale. Some, like Shell, are using variants of the Fischer-Tropsch process; others, including Chevron and Exxon, are researching new ways to achieve the conversion.

Introducing CTL technologies on a large scale could accomplish several objectives at once. It would increase the worldwide supply of liquid hydrocarbons at a time when conventional oil fields are facing systemic decline; it would help the United States and other countries to reduce their reliance on oil imports; and it would provide another use for coal, a relatively abundant fossil fuel. "For all the potential of heavy oil and oil shale," says Chevron, "coal to liquids could be even bigger, especially in the United States, sometimes called the 'Saudi Arabia of coal.'"[88] But the CTL approach is not without its own environmental risks. Any increase in the consumption of coal—whether it's converted to liquids or burned in conventional power plants—is likely to increase greenhouse gas emissions, hastening the onset of dangerous climate change. Energy officials talk of minimizing this risk by removing carbon from the fuel mix and burying or sequestering it, but that approach is technologically unproven and is likely to prove extremely costly.

Even further down the road of technological innovation is the idea of exploiting the earth's reserves of methane hydrate—a dense substance composed of methane molecules trapped within a crystalline lattice of frozen water. Such formations occur only in places where temperatures are low and pressures are great; if a hydrate is either warmed or depressurized, it separates into water and natural gas. But the right conditions do exist beneath the Arctic permafrost and at the bottom of oceans, so the world's overall supplies of methane hydrate are believed to be quite extensive. What's more, because one cubic meter of hydrate releases 164 cubic meters of natural gas, these supplies theoretically add up to a colossal fuel resource—potentially containing twice as much energy as all the oil, coal, and conventional gas deposits on the planet combined.[89]

Such enormous hydrocarbon riches make methane hydrate a very attractive prospect for the world's energy needs, but no economically viable method for mining the hydrates and safely extracting the methane trapped within the crystals has yet been developed.[90] (Because methane is a potent greenhouse gas, possessing twenty-one times the heat-trapping capacity of carbon dioxide, the crystals must be mined in some fashion that prevents any gas from escaping into the atmosphere.) At this point, the scientific and technological challenges are so complex that most research on the commercial possibilities of methane hydrate is being conducted by governments, not private companies. Between 2000 and 2010, the U.S. Department of Energy devoted some $119 million to investigating the technological requirements for extracting natural gas from the hydrate formations while minimizing the environmental risks.[91] The United States has also agreed to exchange information with India, Japan, and South Korea, which have launched extensive methane hydrate research projects of their own.[92]

Of the several countries seeking to exploit methane crystals, by far the most ambitious has been Japan—a resource-scarce nation eager to increase its domestic energy supplies. With copious funds provided by the government, the Japan Oil, Gas, and Metals National Corporation (JOGMEC) is putting together plans to extract methane gas from crystal beds in the Nankai Trough, located off the Pacific coast of south-central Japan. "Some estimates indicate that the reserves of methane hydrate correspond to a 100-year supply of natural gas for Japan, making it an important potential source of energy," JOGMEC indicates on its official Web site.[93] The scheme has alarmed environmentalists, who worry that drilling for undersea hydrate deposits might accidentally release methane gas into the atmosphere and therefore accelerate climate change through the greenhouse effect. Despite these concerns,

JOGMEC hopes to begin commercial production of methane gas from hydrates in 2018.[94]

Most of the world's conventional, easy-to-extract reserves of oil and natural gas have now been exhausted. The major energy companies are doing everything they can to prolong the life of existing fields and to develop new deposits in previously inaccessible areas, such as the Arctic and the deep waters of the Gulf of Mexico; increasingly, however, they will be forced to rely on unconventional hydrocarbon sources to sustain the flow of oil and gas. Many such sources do exist, some in great abundance—but as we have seen, exploiting them is usually more expensive and environmentally risky than using conventional fuels. Still, until noncarbon alternatives such as wind and solar energy are developed on a very large scale, the incentive for producing unconventional hydrocarbons will remain strong. Paul Allison, a manager of Chevron's research in this field, sums up the corporate outlook succinctly: "Humankind is going to need all the unconventionals, so we need to create technologies for them all."[95]

5 ▸ MINING'S NEW FRONTIERS

The tropical rain forest of eastern Gabon, a former French colony in West Africa, is one of the world's last few unspoiled preserves for jungle wildlife. Large populations of elephants, chimpanzees, forest buffalo, and lowland gorillas make their home among the greenery, while pristine rivers form spectacular rapids and waterfalls. Similar areas in adjoining countries have been ransacked by loggers and poachers, but Gabon's rain forests have largely escaped invasion: the country has been an oil supplier for many decades, and its ruling elites were generally content to live off the proceeds of energy production. Oil output, though, has been declining since the late 1990s, and Gabon's government—desperate to find new sources of revenue—has opened the interior to mineral exploitation, selling massive tracts of land to some of the biggest mining firms in the world. Now, roads are being slashed through the jungle and preliminary work has begun on establishing open-pit mines in areas currently occupied by wild animals and scattered local tribes.[1]

The asset of greatest interest to international miners in Gabon is the Belinga iron ore field, located in the remote northeast some 300 miles from Libreville, the country's capital. Iron ore is the primary ingredient of steel, and Belinga is thought to hold some 500 million tons of high-

WEST AFRICA

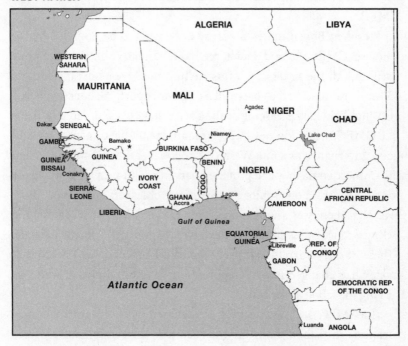

grade ore—making it one of the world's largest untapped deposits of iron. With many long-established iron mines in other countries showing signs of irreversible decline, the major mining firms are eager to exploit Belinga's rich deposits. Once operations are fully up and running, Belinga could yield as much as 30 million tons of iron ore per year, propelling Gabon into the top ranks of major producers.[2]

In March 2005, anxious to see work begin, the Gabonese government awarded an initial exploratory contract to the Companhia Vale do Rio Doce of Brazil (now Vale S.A.), the world's leading producer of iron. But when Vale submitted its preliminary study the following year, it received a rude shock: Gabon's president and absolute ruler, Omar Bongo Ondimba, announced that the company would not be allowed to perform the actual mining. Instead, the exclusive right to develop the Belinga field would be given to the China National

Machinery and Equipment Import and Export Corporation, known as CMEC.[3]

President Bongo touted an array of benefits to be provided by the Chinese: CMEC, he said, had agreed to invest $3.5 billion in the mine itself and all the necessary infrastructure improvements, including a 330-mile railroad to the coast and a deepwater port.[4] Gabonese officials also highlighted the ease of dealing with state-backed Chinese firms like CMEC, which do not impose requirements for transparency and good governance as some Western developers are wont to do. "When the Chinese come they can provide financing, without a lot of strings or moralizing," said one senior figure.[5] Many observers speculated, however, that there was another, unspoken reason why CMEC gained the Belinga concession: sizable bribes given to top government officials. "There was never irrefutable proof that this happened, but I heard that money had changed hands," reported one Western diplomat who was serving in Gabon at the time.[6]

The CMEC deal was roundly condemned by environmental organizations in Gabon, both for the secretive, unseemly nature of the arrangement and for the threat it poses to some of Gabon's natural wonders. To provide power for the mines, CMEC intends to build two hydroelectric dams on the Ivindo River, one of the principal streams flowing through the rain forest. This river is the source of the Kongou Falls, widely considered to be among the most beautiful in sub-Saharan Africa. "Local pygmy and Bantu ethnic groups have revered the Kongou Falls for centuries, and it is easy to understand why," notes an account in the *New York Times*. "The falls begin as a steep set of rapids that fracture in half a dozen directions, funneling churning chutes down sheer cliffs into frothy pools. Further down, two branches of the Ivindo River gush down twin falls known as the Sun and the Moon."[7] The falls and surrounding area are located within Ivindo National Park, and so should, by law, be protected from any form of development. With President Bongo's permission, however, CMEC began working in the park in 2007, building roads and otherwise damaging the environment.[8] "Whatever happens, whatever anyone says, [the Belinga project] will go ahead," Bongo declared.[9]

At present, the exact future of the endeavor is unclear. Bongo died in 2009, and his son, who won the ensuing presidential elections, has promised to review the CMEC contract and consider alternative options for the mine's development. Reportedly, he is entertaining a competing proposal from Vale, which still wants to be involved with the project.[10] Most observers expect that CMEC will retain control of Belinga but that Vale will be brought in as a junior partner—helping to provide technical assistance as well as political cover for the Gabonese government.[11] Whatever the specifics, though, all signs point to the eventual development of the massive iron ore deposits.[12] Environmentalists can only hope that the review process will grant enhanced protection to Ivindo National Park and other sensitive ecological areas.

Although distinctive in many ways, the situation in Gabon is representative of what is occurring in many parts of the world as the major mining companies look to extend their reach. Currently, most of the world's mineral ores are still being extracted from mines that were established in the decades following World War II and, up to now, producers have been able to cope with depletion by digging deeper into existing deposits and by employing sophisticated techniques to extract valuable minerals from lower-quality ores.[13] But boosting output at current locations is proving increasingly difficult, while global demand is growing by the day. Finding fresh sources of supply, therefore, is becoming essential.

This race for new mineral reserves extends to virtually all of the basic industrial metals, including copper, iron, tin, titanium, and bauxite (the source of aluminum). A large part of the increased demand for these materials is coming from industrializing countries such as China and India, where a growing middle class is rapidly acquiring larger homes, new automobiles, kitchen appliances, and other amenities. China, in particular, is enormously hungry for minerals, and has already become the world's leading consumer of aluminum, copper, steel, tin, and tungsten. At the same time, the populations of prosperous Western countries are buying more and more computers, televisions, air conditioners, and other devices whose manufacture requires significant quantities of metals; many of these items are also made in China, further increasing that country's need for mineral supplies.

Just like the oil and gas companies, however, major mining firms seeking added reserves are finding that most of the world's easily accessed deposits have already been fully exploited. And while many other, harder-to-reach deposits of industrial metals are known to exist, setting up mining operations in such "frontier" areas will prove difficult and hazardous. Some of these deposits, like many of the world's remaining hydrocarbon reservoirs, are located in environmentally challenging areas of the Arctic; others are found in countries that are at war or ruled by corrupt and authoritarian regimes. Almost invariably, these mineral frontiers currently lack the infrastructure necessary to support large-scale mining operations and transport massive volumes of ore to distant ports and smelters.

Still, despite such challenges, senior executives of major mining firms see no choice but to gamble vast sums on exploration and expansion. Without new deposits to exploit, a mining company would almost certainly lose market share to more aggressive competitors and eventually risk going out of business altogether. As the struggle for untapped reserves becomes more intense, only the largest companies are likely to survive, and even they risk losing their investments to unscrupulous rulers or rival firms. The main victims of the contest, though, are likely to be indigenous peoples and pristine natural landscapes—trampled underfoot, as at Belinga, in the battles of the mining giants.

GUINEA'S IRRESISTIBLE MINERAL WEALTH

Guinea, like Gabon, exemplifies both the opportunities and the problems that arise as major mining companies rush to the mineral frontiers. A former French colony on the western bulge of Atlantic Africa, Guinea is known to possess very large reserves of iron ore, bauxite, and other valuable minerals. Several Western firms established bauxite operations in Guinea in the past decades, and today the country accounts for about one-tenth of the world's total bauxite supply. Like many other African nations, however, Guinea has been a persistent victim of the "resource curse": its mineral riches have produced little broader development, leading instead to government corruption, widespread poverty, and internal strife. In this unstable environment, Guinea's promising iron ore deposits have been deeply embroiled in political difficulties—and the battle that several major firms are waging over them has made the situation more complicated still.

The biggest mineral prize among Guinea's iron reserves is the Simandou field, which lies in the country's remote southeastern corner, far to the east of the capital city of Conakry. Some experts consider Simandou to be the largest undeveloped iron ore deposit in the world,[14] and it is thought to be capable of producing 350 million metric tons of iron ore per year—more than all but a handful of the world's most productive mines.[15] Installing the infrastructure to extract that ore and transport it to loading facilities on the Atlantic Ocean coast will be a costly and complex task, but the potential gains are large enough to make Simandou an irresistible target for the mining firms.

In 2006, Guinea's longtime dictator Lansana Conté granted a concession to develop the Simandou mine to Rio Tinto, a giant multinational mining enterprise with headquarters in London and Melbourne. After confirming Simandou's vast potential, Rio Tinto spent an estimated $680 million clearing the land, building roads and power lines, and otherwise preparing for mining operations.[16] But just as Vale discovered in Gabon, Rio Tinto found in Guinea that no contract awarded by a corrupt, unscrupulous regime can ever be fully relied upon. In mid-2008, acting on the flimsy pretext that the company was not moving fast enough to begin production, Conté seized half of Rio Tinto's concession and awarded it to the Israeli company BSG Resources Limited. BSG, in turn, sold a 51 percent stake in the half concession to Vale, which this time turned out to be a beneficiary rather than a victim of government skullduggery.[17]

Rio Tinto vigorously protested the seizure, but Guinean officials told the company that if it persisted in trying to regain its lost half of

Simandou, it would be expelled from the iron ore field entirely. Confronted with such threats, Rio Tinto eventually admitted defeat: in April 2011, it agreed to drop its claim to the tracts it lost in 2008 and to pay the Guinean government $700 million to reconfirm its legal title to the remaining part of the concession. In addition, Rio Tinto announced that it would develop its share of Simandou jointly with the Aluminum Corporation of China, known as Chinalco. By entering into the partnership, Rio Tinto gained $1.35 billion in additional financing—and also, it is believed, put itself back in good graces with the Guinean government, which has established close ties with Beijing.[18]

As in Gabon, Chinese companies seeking to secure mineral deposits in Guinea have benefited from their willingness to overlook issues of good governance and human rights. After Conté died in December 2008 and a military junta seized control of the country, many Western powers shunned the new regime, but the Chinese showed no compunction about working with the military rulers. Indeed, in October 2009—just two weeks after the junta's soldiers attacked an opposition rally in Conakry, killing at least 156 people—the China International Fund announced that it would spend $7 billion on modernizing Guinea's infrastructure in return for a significant share in all future mining ventures. Although the Hong Kong–based CIF is nominally a private firm, it is believed to have close ties to the Chinese government, and so the $7 billion offer was widely regarded as China's implicit endorsement of the junta's hold on power.[19]

How all of these international machinations will play out remains to be seen. After many problems and false starts, Guinea finally conducted a reasonably fair national election in November 2010, and a former opposition leader, Alpha Condé, became the country's president. Condé has promised to revise any mining contracts that do not return adequate revenues to the Guinean people, and to make sure that any future contracts are granted in a more transparent manner. He is also seeking to secure a greater role for Guinea's own firms in any major mining operations.[20] But Condé's grasp on power appears tenuous: in July 2011, a group of disgruntled army officers invaded his Conakry home and tried to kill him.[21] Although Condé survived the attack, it is impossible to predict how much longer he will remain in control of the country, and whether he will be able to implement his ambitious plans for reform.

URANIUM EXTRACTION IN NIGER

The resource curse that plagues Gabon and Guinea has also made itself felt in Niger, a former French colony in west central Africa. Niger is lacking in most natural resources, but it does possess deposits of one mineral that is of great interest to outside powers: uranium, the principal fuel of nuclear power plants and atomic weapons. Ever since the early Cold War period, when Niger was still under French rule, uranium extraction has been a significant industry in the country, but it has mostly enriched only a few well-connected government officials and the companies that own the mines. Few of Niger's sixteen million people have ever seen any benefits from the mining, and two-thirds of them still live on less than $1 per day, making Niger one of the poorest nations on earth.[22] As a result, tensions between the mining firms and the Nigerien population have long been high, and the disputes have turned deadly on several occasions.

The first uranium deposits found in Niger were discovered by the French government in 1958, in the Tim Mersoï basin in the northern region of Agadez. Originally, ore from this region was used to manufacture French nuclear weapons; later, it was used to supply France's ambitious nuclear power program.[23] (France generates more than three-quarters of its electricity from nuclear power, a far higher proportion than any other country in the world.)[24] After Niger won its independence from France in 1960, uranium extraction continued to remain largely under French control. Although other mining companies are now allowed to operate in the country, the dominant producer is the French nuclear enterprise Areva, which is 90 percent owned by the government of France.[25]

At present, Areva obtains the bulk of its ore from two mines in the Agadez region, at Arlit and Akouta. Together, these facilities produce approximately 4,000 metric tons of uranium per year, or about one-tenth of the total world output. But that amount is apparently not enough for Areva, which wants to ensure a steady supply of uranium ore and expand its nuclear power business. Accordingly, the company is working to open a third operation in the Agadez region, at a deposit known as Imouraren—an undertaking that Areva describes as "the largest uranium mine in Africa and the second largest in the world." In keeping with this massive scale, the company's agreement with the Nigerien government promises that Areva will invest $1.5 billion in the new project. When production begins in 2013, Imouraren is expected to yield 5,000 tons of uranium per year, more than doubling Niger's current production.[26]

Areva's executives insist that its mining activities are promoting development in Niger and helping to alleviate hunger and poverty. But the company's dominant role in the Nigerien economy—and its close association with corrupt government leaders—has alienated it from significant sectors of the population. Opposition has been particularly fierce among the nomadic Tuareg peoples, who inhabit large areas of the arid northwest, where Areva's major mines are located. Under the banner of the Nigerien Movement for Justice (known as MNJ for its initials in French), Tuareg rebels have repeatedly mounted attacks against the central government, driven in large part by dissatisfaction with the government's economic and mining policies. According to the Tuaregs, the uranium mining brings little economic benefit to the surrounding community while poisoning their pastures and water supplies with uranium dust.[27] "This wealth needs to be used to help the people, not the politicians," said Aghali Alambo, president of the MNJ. "Otherwise it's just plunder."[28]

To press their cause, the MNJ has conducted several attacks on Areva's mining operations in northern Niger. In April 2007, for example, MNJ forces attacked Areva's Imouraren exploration camp, killing one worker and wounding four.[29] Another incident occurred the following year, when four Areva employees were kidnapped by MNJ militants while jogging in the town center of Arlit.[30] (They were later released unharmed.) And although the Nigerien government finally signed a peace agreement with the MNJ in 2009, promising the Tuaregs more high-paying mining jobs and other economic benefits as well as immunity from prosecution,[31] other groups continue to target mining workers in the country. In September 2010, for instance, a militant Islamic organization with loose ties to al-Qaeda kidnapped seven foreigners from the mine at Arlit,[32] four of whom still remained in captivity more than one year later.[33]

Despite the popular protests and the continuing risk of violence, Areva remains committed to the production of uranium in Niger. But its current dominance in that field might soon be threatened by the same type of challenge that has confronted Western iron mining companies in Gabon and Guinea: the arrival of aggressive Chinese firms, ready to do whatever it takes in their own pursuit of new mineral supplies. China's ambitious nuclear plans—it already has eleven nuclear reactors in operation and intends to build sixteen more over the next few years—mean that it will require significant quantities of uranium, most of which will have to come from abroad.[34] The state-owned China Nuclear International Uranium Corporation (known as Sino-U) has already begun production at its own mine in the Agadez region and by 2015 expects to be exporting as much as 2,500 tons of uranium per year.[35]

Many Nigerien politicians have welcomed the arrival of the Chinese firms, seeing it as a way to break France's near-monopoly and secure higher prices for the country's uranium assets. The Tuaregs and other marginalized groups, though, have regarded the Chinese mining companies with the same distrust and hostility they've shown Areva. In July 2007, after Sino-U allegedly provided money to the Nigerien government to fund counterinsurgency operations, the MNJ kidnapped a Sino-U executive and held him captive for four days.[36] Chinese officials, of course, insist that they do not intend to interfere with Niger's internal affairs and only wish to assist in the country's development. Still, with nearly all the benefits from new mining operations once again accruing to

Nigerien authorities and foreign mining firms, resentment from Niger's broader population is not likely to disappear anytime soon.

AFGHANISTAN'S DANGEROUS ALLURE

Like many countries in Africa, Afghanistan has long been known to harbor significant reserves of valuable minerals but has been regarded by most mining companies as too hazardous to operate in. Invaded and occupied by Soviet forces in 1979, plunged into civil war after the Soviet withdrawal a decade later, and since 2001 the site of a continuing struggle between U.S.-led forces and Taliban insurgents, Afghanistan has now suffered from more than thirty years of almost continuous bloodshed. Although the U.S. and NATO armed presence is currently providing a degree of stability in Kabul and other parts of the country, violence remains the norm in many outlying areas—and most observers fear even greater disorder when American and European troops start to withdraw. Nevertheless, mining firms desperate for new resources are now taking a closer look at Afghanistan's potential, and some are considering making substantial investments there.[37]

The first systematic exploration of Afghanistan's mineral wealth took place in 1980s, when the country was under Soviet control. The occupiers were too busy defending themselves from U.S.-armed Islamic insurgents to start developing any of the deposits they identified, but many of the survey maps drawn up at that time were hidden away and preserved by Afghan scientists after the Soviet departure. Some three decades later, the U.S. Geological Survey used those maps as the starting point for its own detailed investigation of potential mining sites in Afghanistan. Over the course of several years, the USGS efforts added up to what one reporter called "the most comprehensive geologic survey of Afghanistan ever conducted"—including advanced aerial imaging that offered a three-dimensional profile of mineral deposits below the earth's surface.[38]

The results of the study were nothing short of astonishing. At a site called Aynak in Logar Province, about twenty miles from Kabul, the

American geologists found what might be the world's largest untapped deposit of copper, containing at least 12 million metric tons of high-grade ore—with another 17 million metric tons dispersed in nearby areas. A little farther away, at Hajigak, the survey crew came across what was described as "the largest unexploited iron ore deposit in Asia." Elsewhere in Afghanistan, the USGS noted promising deposits of baux-ite, gold, lead, tungsten, and zinc, along with specialty materials such as rare earth elements and niobium.[39] All told, the unexploited minerals in Afghanistan were estimated to be worth well more than $1 trillion.[40]

The calculation of Afghanistan's tremendous mineral wealth sparked an intense debate about the potential impact of intensive mining on Afghan society. President Hamid Karzai's spokesman Waheed Omar called the USGS data on mineral resources "the best news we have had over many years in Afghanistan."[41] American military officials also spoke of the rediscovered mineral ore fields in glowing terms, suggesting that mining would bring new jobs and income to the war-torn country. "There is a stunning potential here," said General David H. Petraeus, then commander of the U.S. Central Command. "There are a lot of ifs, of course, but I think potentially it is hugely significant."[42] Other observers, however, were less optimistic, suggesting that the development of Afghan reserves would most likely enrich well-connected elites and warlords while providing little or no benefit to most Afghan citizens. "Countries with a history of conflict have perverse effects from mineral wealth—more war, more corruption, less democracy, and more inequality," noted Terry Lynn Karl, a political science professor at Stanford University and an expert on the resource curse.[43]

The prospect of large-scale mineral extraction in Afghanistan also raises the difficult question of security in the mining regions. Although Aynak is very close to Kabul, and Hajigak is less than ninety miles away from the capital, both of these areas are periodically attacked by insur-gents, and the roads leading to them are not always safe. Large contin-gents of Afghan police and army forces would be needed to protect the sprawling mining facilities, and few of these outfits are considered entirely capable or reliable. Indeed, by comparison with Afghanistan's security problems, the periodic attacks and kidnappings experienced by Areva and Sino-U in Niger appear quite small-scale.

Despite these risks, however, the Afghan government's 2007 auction for rights to develop the Aynak copper mine attracted a number of significant suitors. After a complicated bidding process, the eventual winning offer of $2.8 billion came from the state-owned China Metallurgical Group Corporation, known as MCC—beating out such competitors as U.S.-based mining giant Phelps Dodge (now part of Freeport-McMoRan) as well as groups from Russia, Canada, and the United Kingdom. As with the Chinese bids for the Belinga iron ore field in Gabon, the MCC offer for Aynak included promises of major infrastructure development in the country: the corporation agreed to build a railroad to connect Aynak with both Uzbekistan and Pakistan, as well as a power plant that could help supply electricity to Kabul.[44] And, as in Gabon, some observers suspect that the official pledges of massive investment were supplemented by less formal payments, including a $30 million bribe given to Mohammad Ibrahim Adel, the Afghan minister of mines at the time.[45] (Adel denied the allegations but was subsequently fired by President Karzai.)

Despite high expectations, work at the Aynak mine has proceeded slowly so far. Visitors to the site have described it as being little more than a cluster of prefabricated dormitories surrounded by a massive wall made of sandbags.[46] Construction of the railroad has not yet begun, and other major infrastructure projects are said to be a year to eighteen months behind schedule. Chinese officials blame poor security for the delays, even though the Kabul government has deployed a dedicated force of 1,500 police officers to the area.[47] Afghan authorities, for their part, still insist that Aynak will be producing and exporting refined copper by 2014, the delays notwithstanding.[48]

In the United States, meanwhile, the award of Aynak development rights to a state-owned Chinese firm has provoked considerable discussion about U.S. involvement in Afghanistan. Some analysts maintain that by giving well-paid jobs to Afghans and generating tax revenues for the tottering central government, China is contributing to the ultimate American goal of stabilizing the country. Others, however, have complained that China is gaining an unfair advantage by exploiting Afghanistan's mineral resources while doing virtually nothing to improve the security situation. "We do the heavy lifting, and they pick the fruit," said S. Frederick Starr, the chairman of the Central Asia-Caucasus Institute in Washington, D.C.[49] It has not escaped notice, for example, that the 1,500 Afghan police officers assigned to protect MCC's Aynak operations have all presumably received their training and weapons from NATO and the United States.

The controversy about China's unfair advantage is particularly relevant because MCC has also expressed interest in the Hajigak iron deposit, the next big mineral field that Afghanistan is likely to open to competitive bidding. The territory around Hajigak is considered even more dangerous than the Aynak area, so it is unclear whether any companies are currently ready to begin operations at the site.[50] However, given that Hajigak is thought to hold approximately 2 billion tons of high-grade ore, it is hard to imagine that major mining companies will ignore this field forever; indeed, an auction scheduled for November 2011 attracted interest from many giant firms. No matter what happens in Afghanistan over the coming years, some corporation will almost certainly find a way to develop Hajigak and other such deposits.

As in Gabon and Guinea, what will happen next to the mining projects in Afghanistan is almost impossible to predict. It is conceivable that mining will flourish and eventually support Afghanistan's recovery, just as American officials hope. However, the mineral riches can just as easily contribute to the country's balkanization, with various mines falling under the sway of different militant groups or the Taliban's religious leaders. In that scenario, the advantage would most likely fall to producers from China and the former Soviet Union, which are more prepared to pay off local warlords in return for security. The mineral ores would still be extracted, but not with the speed—or the benign consequences— that General Petraeus and others envisioned just a few years ago.

MONGOLIA'S MINERAL OPENING

As countries like Guinea, Niger, and Afghanistan grapple with the influx of foreign mining companies, they would do well to study the experience of Mongolia—a newly democratic nation that is still struggling to establish effective controls over the mining industry. For most of the twentieth century, the country was a Soviet-style "people's republic," and aside from some production of coal and other materials deemed valuable by the USSR, there was no systematic effort to develop its mineral resources. A democratic awakening in the early 1990s, however, ushered in multiparty elections, market reforms, and the possibility of significant foreign investment. Soon, mineral prospectors were crisscrossing the country in search of promising deposits, and their discoveries have been breathtaking: by some accounts, the combined worth of Mongolia's untapped reserves exceeds $1.3 trillion.[51] For a sparsely populated, largely agricultural country that even now has a GDP of just $2,000 per capita, this is a stupendous bonanza, and mining has quickly emerged as a major driver of the economy. But dealing with the giant multinational corporations eager to exploit the reserves—as well as with geopolitical pressures from neighboring China and Russia—has proven to be no easy task.[52]

For the moment, the legacy of ties to the USSR still dominates Mongolia's mining operations. Most of the country's copper, for instance, currently comes from a mine that belongs to the Erdenet Mining Corporation, which was established in 1978 as a Mongolian-Soviet joint venture and is now owned by the Mongolian and Russian governments in a 51–49 split.[53] Starting in 2013, however, EMC's operations will yield pride of place to a vast new facility under construction at Oyu Tolgoi (Turquoise Hill), located about 350 miles from the Mongolian capital Ulan Bator. First discovered by an American firm in 1996, Oyu Tolgoi is now owned primarily by Ivanhoe Mines of Canada, which describes it as the largest undeveloped copper-gold resource in the world. Believed to hold as much as 38 million metric tons of copper and 1,500 tons of gold, the mine is on track to become Mongolia's leading source of revenue and one of its top employers.[54]

MONGOLIA

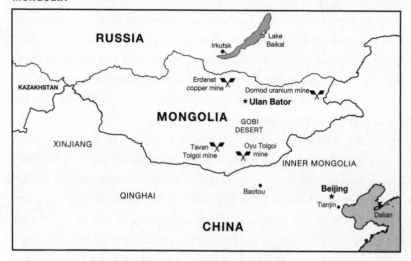

Bringing Oyu Tolgoi into production has required Ivanhoe and its partners—notably Rio Tinto, which has acquired a 48.5 percent stake in the Canadian firm—to overcome a number of significant logistical difficulties at the remote, undeveloped desert site. To construct the thirty-one-story headframe for the main mineshaft, for instance, Ivanhoe erected the largest ready-mix concrete plant in Mongolia, capable of producing enough concrete to fill two Olympic-size swimming pools every day.[55] The company also built a sixty-mile paved highway to the Mongolia-China border (where other roads will carry copper to Chinese processing plants) and a regional airport capable of accommodating Boeing 737–sized aircraft.[56] All told, the cost of building the necessary facilities has added up to $4.5 billion.[57]

Far more daunting than these practical problems, however, have been the political dimensions of the project. When Ivanhoe acquired the Oyu Tolgoi mining licenses in 2002, Mongolia had not yet finalized its mineral laws, and its population was deeply divided over the extent to which private companies should be allowed to own and manage large mining properties. Debate over various proposed regulations went on for years, preventing Ivanhoe from obtaining final government approval for its work. The mining controversy also dominated Mongolia's 2008 parliamentary elections, during which riots broke out and five people were killed in clashes with government troops.[58] Eventually, Ivanhoe did secure the necessary approvals—but it was first required to yield a 34 percent stake in Oyu Tolgoi to the Mongolian state, and the government is now pressing the company to give up an even bigger share.[59]

Partly because of the tensions surrounding Ivanhoe's Oyu Tolgoi operation, the Mongolian government has tried to take a different approach to some of the country's other large-scale mineral deposits. Prominent among these is the Tavan Tolgoi coking-coal project, located in the South Gobi Desert. Coking coal, used in steelmaking, is a higher-grade ore than the type of coal normally used to generate electrical power, and the Tavan Tolgoi prospect is considered the world's largest untapped deposit of this type, with reserves of some 7.5 billion metric tons.[60] Originally, the government had planned to develop Tavan Tolgoi as a joint venture with an international mining firm, along the same lines as its partnership with Ivanhoe at Oyu Tolgoi, but in February 2010 Prime Minister Sükhbaataryn Batbold announced that Mongolia would retain full ownership of the coking-coal deposit. Rather than sell development rights, the Mongolian government would bring in foreign firms on a contractor basis, hiring them to perform specified mining services for a predetermined fee.[61]

Even this kind of arrangement, however, has not necessarily allowed the Mongolian government to fully control the fate of Tavan Tolgoi, whose overall value has been estimated at $15 billion. Bidding for the massive service contract attracted such major firms as Peabody Energy of the United States and Mitsui of Japan, but neither one of them prevailed. Instead, after intense lobbying by the Chinese government, the primary contract was given to China's state-owned mining giant Shenhua International—an outcome that might have been driven more by Mongolia's need to appease its powerful neighbor than by purely commercial calculations. The Japanese government, convinced that Japanese firms were unfairly excluded from participation in the project, has filed an official diplomatic protest.[62]

A similar tug-of-war has erupted over Mongolia's largest uranium deposit. The site, at Dornod in eastern Mongolia, was originally developed in the late 1980s by Soviet geologists, but Russian extraction efforts there ceased in 1995. The rights to the mine were subsequently sold to Khan Resources of Toronto, which believes that large quantities of untapped uranium still remain in the deposit.[63] Mongolian officials, though, are said to be under enormous pressure from Moscow to give the mine to a Russian firm. In 2009, the Mongolian Nuclear Energy Agency revoked Khan's licenses to Dornod, allowing Russia's state-owned Atomredmetzoloto to make a bid to acquire it. Khan's rights to Dornod have been reaffirmed by a number of court proceedings in Ulan Bator, however, so its ultimate fate remains unclear.[64]

The twists and turns in the ownership battles over Oyu Tolgoi, Tavan Tolgoi, and Dornod demonstrate the difficulty of Mongolia's situation. A young democracy with relatively little experience in overseeing multibillion-dollar mining projects, Mongolia is just beginning to establish the necessary legal and regulatory structures to govern the mining industry, and the process has been a slow and difficult one. At the same time, while most of its citizens seek to preserve their nation's autonomy, Mongolia cannot afford to offend its powerful neighbors. Both China and Russia play a vital role in Mongolia's trade and transportation, and both seek access to Mongolia's mineral wealth. Many key mining decisions, therefore, will be governed by geopolitical rather than economic considerations. Some Mongolians will, in the end, benefit from employment in the mines and the country as a whole will gain much-needed tax revenues; the principal beneficiaries of Mongolia's mineral boom, though, are likely to be foreign companies, whether private or state owned.

THE LURE OF THE NORTH

In addition to expanding their operations in such places as Guinea and Afghanistan that had once been avoided for political reasons, the giant mining companies are also increasingly venturing into the harsh geography of the Arctic region. Some mineral extraction, of course, has long been conducted in northern latitudes, from gold mining in Alaska to nickel production in Siberia; the new projects now being considered, however, are often on a far grander scale. With their prospects declining elsewhere, many of the mining firms—like their counterparts in the energy industry—regard the Arctic as one of their best remaining bets for developing untapped reserves of natural resources. But just as with Arctic drilling for oil and gas, any increase in Arctic mining is bound to pose a significant risk to the fragile northern environment and to the indigenous peoples who live there.

Alaska provides a particularly vivid example of both the potential appeal and the potential dangers of Arctic mining. The mineral industry has been a significant part of Alaskan economy ever since the Klondike Gold Rush of 1897, and today Alaska ranks sixth among all U.S. states in its output of nonfuel minerals, yielding some $3.5 billion of gold, zinc, lead, silver, and other materials per year.[65] But all of the state's existing mines would be overshadowed if a controversial new excavation currently under consideration is allowed to proceed: the Pebble Project at Iliamna Lake, some 200 miles southwest of Anchorage. If given the go-ahead, the Pebble Project could prove to be the biggest gold mine and the second biggest copper mine in North America, as well as a major source of molybdenum, an element used as an alloying agent in high-strength steel. Pebble's gold reserves alone are estimated at 67 million ounces, making them worth more than $100 billion at current market prices—an extraordinary enticement for the investors involved.[66]

Since 2001, the mining rights to the Pebble prospect have been held by Northern Dynasty Minerals, a Vancouver-based enterprise, which itself is owned in part by Rio Tinto and Mitsubishi of Japan. As the magnitude of the project gradually became clear, Northern Dynasty has sought out other partners, and eventually forged a fifty-fifty joint venture with Anglo American, one of the world's leading mining companies.[67] Operating as the Pebble Partnership, these companies plan to develop the field in two sections: an open-pit operation intended to dig out some 4.1 billion metric tons of combined ore, and a giant underground mine that would produce another 3.4 billion metric tons.[68] From this raw output—much of it consisting of porphyry, a hard, reddish rock flecked with feldspar and quartz—the partners hope to extract an estimated 55 billion pounds of copper, 3.3 billion pounds of molybdenum, 140 million ounces of silver, and those attention-grabbing 67 million ounces of gold.[69]

Producing all of this ore would require an industrial-scale mining operation quite unlike anything yet seen in Alaska. The open-pit section of the mine is expected to be two miles long, a mile wide, and 1,700 feet deep—a mammoth gash that would be visible from outer space. The porphyry taken from this giant hole would be treated with arsenic, mercury, and other toxic chemicals to leach out the gold and copper, leaving mounds of unused rock and a thick slurry of poisonous mine waste, or tailings. To prevent the tailings from contaminating surrounding rivers and streams, Pebble Partnership plans to construct artificial lakes covering 14 square miles, more than ten times the size of New York's Central Park. The processed minerals themselves are to be trucked along a new highway that would have to be built through a wilderness area surrounding Lake Clark National Park, eventually reaching to a new port at Cook Inlet on Bristol Bay, some ninety-five miles distant.[70]

The construction of these massive facilities could bring much-needed income to the surrounding area, but the plans have also provoked significant opposition from many environmentalists and local residents.[71] The protesters note that Bristol Bay and the streams that feed into it constitute the world's most prolific salmon fishery: every year, hundreds of millions of salmon return to the bay and swim up its rivers to spawn and die. For thousands of years, Native American communities have relied on the annual salmon runs to provide a significant part of their annual food supply; more recently, a $100-million-per-year commercial fishing industry has developed here, employing some 12,500 people.[72] If the toxic chemicals used in the mining process were to leak into the intricately connected waterways, the salmon would perish in vast quantities and thousands of local residents would suffer accordingly.[73]

Mining officials connected with the project, unsurprisingly, insist that Pebble can be developed in an environmentally friendly way. "I certainly don't want my legacy to be that we destroyed a fishery," said John T. Shively, the chief executive of the Pebble Partnership. "But if we can do it correctly, I'd love to see it done, because I think the benefits are huge."[74] Pro-development politicians such as Sarah Palin are also supporting the mine; when she was governor of Alaska, Palin backed several measures designed to advance the work.[75] But some mining experts insist that it is almost impossible to prevent environmental damage from a project this vast, especially given how many rivers and streams will run through the mine site and associated infrastructure. "You cannot point to a porphyry copper [mine] in the proximity of water resources that hasn't caused problems," says Jim Kuipers, a consulting mining engineer for the Center for Science in Public Participation. "There are things that can be done to mitigate it, but in many cases the mitigations aren't adequate."[76] What's more, the Pebble mine site is located just a few dozen miles from an active volcano and even closer to a major earthquake fault, placing at risk any earthen walls constructed to contain poisonous tailings.[77]

The opposition to the project among Native Alaskans has not been universal: some, despairing of their people's unrelenting poverty, believe that the Pebble work should go ahead. "Yeah, we need to save the fish, but we also need to save our people," insisted Trefon Angasan of the Alaska Peninsula Corporation, an association of Native villagers. "We need to look at the opportunity to develop the mine without impacting the environment."[78] But many others in the surrounding Native communities fear that mining activity will mean the end of their way of life. "I live here," said Raymond Wassillie, chief of the village of Newhalen. "I breathe the air, I fish the waters, I hunt the lands. That's the way the traditional life of my culture has been, and I like it. And if it goes away, I'm dead."[79]

The Pebble Partnership plans to request a permit from the State of Alaska in 2012 to begin work on the mine. Whether it will receive this approval and manage to clear numerous other legal and regulatory hurdles still remains to be seen. One new barrier was raised in October 2011, when residents of Alaska's Lake and Peninsula Borough, where the mine would be located, voted to impose a strict ban on any project that endangered salmon fishing in the area. (Lawyers for the Pebble Project say they will contest the legality of the measure in state courts.) At this point, advocates and opponents of the project are descending on Juneau and Washington, D.C., to press their respective views. But it is hard to imagine that $100 billion worth of gold—not to mention an equal treasure in copper and other minerals—will be allowed to remain in the ground forever.

OTHER ARCTIC VENTURES

Similar temptations are drawing miners to other parts of the Arctic—and wherever they go, mining firms are running into the same sort of problems that they face in Alaska. Canada, for instance, provides a particularly clear illustration of the miners' dilemma. Intensive mineral extraction has long been conducted in Canada's southern reaches, but many existing deposits there are facing imminent depletion, so mining executives must look ever northward in their search for new sources of supply. Yet the farther north they go, the more severe the weather and the more costly it is to construct the necessary infrastructure. To further complicate matters, Canada has ceded control over its northern territories to the Native population, which is deeply divided over the value of mineral extraction. While some tribal groups view such activities as a boon to development, others see them as a dire threat.

Existing mines in Canada's Far North already demonstrate the extreme difficulty of operating in such an environment. One such enterprise—the Voisey's Bay nickel mine in northern Labrador, owned by a Vale subsidiary—decided early on that the remote and often bitterly cold site was too harsh to house anybody there permanently. Instead, the mine runs a "fly-in/fly-out" operation, with workers arriving for a two-week rotation and then being transported out again. While onsite, they live in a self-contained complex that contains cafeterias, medical facilities, shops, and recreational areas, much like on a large offshore oil rig.[80] But even these amenities have not been enough to make the situation easily bearable: in August 2009, workers at Voisey's Bay went on strike for higher pay and better working conditions. The dispute lasted for eighteen months and was resolved only when Vale offered a substantial increase in wages and benefits.[81]

Nevertheless, planning is currently under way for a potential iron mine at Mary River on Baffin Island, in the Native-controlled territory of Nunavut, where conditions are likely to be far more demanding than at Voisey's Bay. Attracting workers to the project will be a particular challenge because Mary River, located some 370 miles north of the Arctic Circle, receives no sunlight at all from mid-November until late January. The engineering difficulties are also extraordinary: before production can begin, the project's developer, Baffinland Iron Mines Corporation, will have to build a ninety-mile railroad from the mining site to a new port on the coast, running a rail bed over permafrost and unstable soils. The company also plans to build a costly new fleet of icebreaking ore carriers to transport the iron to markets abroad.[82] What's more, the Inuit inhabitants of Baffin Island have been agitating against the project, worried that Baffinland's construction and icebreaking activities will threaten the survival of walruses and other marine mammals considered vital to their culture.[83] Yet despite these obstacles, and the $4 billion price tag for the necessary infrastructure, the lure of the Mary Bay deposit—believed to hold 365 million metric tons of high-grade iron ore—is apparently too powerful to resist.

A similar northward drive, with all its attendant problems, is also under way in Russia and the Scandinavian countries—all of which have long operated mines in the upper reaches of their respective territories, but are now placing increasing emphasis there as production elsewhere has slipped into decline. Sweden, for example, has stepped up its production of iron ore in the Kiruna district, the country's northernmost region,[84] while a Norwegian company is trumpeting its discovery of a $3 billion copper deposit in the country's Finnmark territory, even farther to the north.[85] Russia, too, is actively developing new mines nearby, particularly in the Kola Peninsula, which lies adjacent to Finnmark and juts out into the Barents Sea.[86] In all three countries, the mining shift

northward has provoked anger and complaints from the area's indigenous Sami people, who say that reindeer hunting—essential to both
their economic and cultural existence—has been disrupted by the intensified mineral extraction work.[87]

Finally, just like the giant energy firms, major mining companies are
also now expanding to the previously untouched expanses of Greenland. The Canadian enterprise Quadra FNX Mining plans to establish a
large open-pit mine at Malmbjerg, on Greenland's east coast, with the
goal of eventually producing 7,500 to 10,400 metric tons of molybdenum there per year.[88] Another firm, Greenland Minerals and Energy, of
Australia, has acquired the right to develop a combined mine for uranium, zinc, and rare earths at Kvanefjeld, near the country's southwestern tip.[89] All these endeavors, like those in Canada, will require extensive
investment in new infrastructure and will pose significant risk to the
fragile northern environment. And in Greenland, as in other Arctic
locales, the miners are meeting strong resistance from indigenous peoples, who fear for the survival of their traditional ways of life.[90]

Up to this point, the world's declining supply of basic metals such as
iron and copper has been noticed primarily by mining company executives, who foresee diminishing production and rapidly increasing demand
in the years to come. The fierce contest for new ore reserves on mining
frontiers like Guinea, Afghanistan, and the Arctic is still largely focused
on the future, as private and state-owned mineral companies jockey to
establish a leadership position for the leaner decades ahead.

There is another class of minerals, however, that also concerns the
world's giant corporations: unusual elements, including lanthanum, lithium, palladium, and tantalum, whose relatively tiny annual production
belies their crucial importance to modern high-tech industry. And when
it comes to these exotic materials, the worldwide shortage of supplies is
already upon us.

6 ► RARE EARTHS AND OTHER CRITICAL MINERALS

On September 22, 2010, the international news media reported a startling and unprecedented development: Chinese customs officials were blocking all shipments of rare earth elements bound from China to Japan. The rare earths are a crucial ingredient in many high-tech products, from mobile phones to hybrid cars, so the Chinese move produced widespread consternation in Japan—especially given that several leading Japanese manufacturers were completely dependent on Chinese imports for all their rare earth needs. Government officials in Beijing issued no formal statement on the matter, but most foreign observers assumed that the suspension of these deliveries was related to another international drama then under way: Japan's arrest and detention of a Chinese fishing captain, who had been accused of ramming his trawler into Japanese coast guard vessels in the East China Sea.[1]

The Chinese captain, Zhan Qixiong, had been arrested about two weeks earlier, shortly after his boat allegedly collided with the Japanese ships near a cluster of uninhabited islands claimed by both China and Japan. The tiny island chain, called Senkaku by the Japanese and Diaoyu by the Chinese, is located between Taiwan and Japan's Okinawa prefecture, and has been a source of Sino-Japanese friction for many years. When informed of Zhan's arrest, officials in Beijing demanded his immediate release, indignantly noting that he was apprehended in waters that China regards as its own. "If the Japanese side clings obstinately to its course," warned Foreign Ministry spokesman Ma Zhaoxu, "China will take strong countermeasures and Japan will bear all the consequences."[2] A few days later, all Japanese imports of China's rare earths were cut off. To what degree this influenced Japan's official thinking cannot be ascertained, but Zhan was freed several days later—handing China what was widely regarded as a major geopolitical victory.[3]

The struggle between China and Japan over contested waters in the East China Sea is itself, as we have seen, a product of the race to secure scarce natural resources. The Diaoyu/Senkaku Islands are of little economic value in themselves, but whoever controls them can also claim large swaths of surrounding maritime territory, including areas believed to hold significant underwater deposits of natural gas. China's rare earths embargo, though, brought to the forefront a different aspect of global resource scarcity: the coming battle over access to vital minerals. Exotic elements such as rhodium and niobium, lanthanum and samarium may not be as familiar as oil and gas, but their absence would wreak havoc with much of modern industry, and governments around the world are taking urgent measures to ensure that their countries will not be left without these indispensable materials.

In Japan, the realization that China had a near monopoly on such vital supplies produced much anguished commentary and calls for immediate action. In response, government officials quickly announced a $1.2 billion plan to expand the nation's rare earth stockpiles, with roughly half of that amount devoted to overseas mining projects.[4] "Securing stable long-term supplies of mining resources including rare earths is one of Japan's important diplomatic goals," said Foreign Minister Seiji Maehara. "We will work as a team to provide strong support for our private companies."[5] Shortly thereafter, Japan's prime minister held meetings with the leaders of Mongolia and Vietnam to discuss possible Japanese involvement in rare earth mines being developed in those countries.[6]

The Chinese ban on rare earth exports to Japan also provoked concern and consternation in the United States, which is a significant consumer of rare earths for military and commercial applications.[7] A week after China stopped its Japan-bound shipments, the U.S. House of Representatives passed legislation calling on the Department of Energy to commence an intensive research effort aimed at ensuring "the long-term, secure, and sustainable supply of rare earth materials sufficient to satisfy the national security, economic well-being, and industrial needs of the United States."[8] David Sandalow, the DoE's assistant secretary of energy for policy and international affairs, told the Senate Committee on Energy and Natural Resources that the Obama administration was watching the issue closely and would give high priority to establishing such a supply.[9]

Japan's release of Zhan did not immediately result in China resuming its rare earth deliveries to the country. As weeks passed with Japanese rare earth orders still going unfulfilled, the atmosphere grew increasingly tense. Secretary of State Hillary Clinton met several times with her Japanese counterpart, Seiji Maehara, to discuss the matter, and demanded assurances from Beijing that China would honor its commercial obligations.[10] In late November 2010, two and a half months after the crisis began, some rare earths finally began flowing from China to Japan, but it was clear that the shipments would not be completely restored to precrisis levels. Indeed, China soon officially tightened its rare earth export quotas by some 35 percent, ensuring that the world would face a significant shortage of the vital materials.[11]

The Chinese actions provoked a barrage of questions in the mass media, the U.S. Congress, and other public arenas: What are rare earths? Why are they so important? Why does China play such a pivotal role in their production, and what can be done to diminish its dominance in this arena? These are crucial issues, and they will only become more important as the world's reliance on rare earths continues to increase.

The rare earth elements (REE) include seventeen different metallic substances with distinctive characteristics. Most of them are located in a continuous stretch of the periodic table of the elements, beginning with lanthanum (at number 57 in the periodic table) and extending to lutetium (number 71); in addition, the group also includes yttrium and scandium, two lower-numbered elements with similar chemical properties. The rare earths are distinguished by their ability to form unusually strong and lightweight magnetic alloys with other metals, and by their unique optical properties, including fluorescence and emission of coherent light.[12] Most of the rare earths have significant industrial applications, as detailed in Table 6.1.

Many of today's portable electronic devices—including cell phones, laptops, and iPods—contain rare earths, and these materials have also long been used for a wide variety of other purposes. Liquid crystal displays in computer monitors and televisions, for example, use europium as the red phosphor, while fiber-optic telecommunications cables rely on laser repeaters infused with erbium. Several rare earths are essential constituents of catalysts used in petroleum refining and of the catalytic converters used to reduce automotive exhaust emissions. And virtually all polished glass products, from ordinary mirrors and eyeglasses to precision camera lenses, are finished with solutions of cerium.[13]

More recently, rare earths have received a boost from the growing popularity of energy-efficient "green" technologies. According to the U.S. Department of Energy, clean energy applications currently account for about 20 percent of the consumption of REE, and this proportion is expected to grow over the coming decades.[14] For example, rare earths play an especially vital role in advanced electromagnets and lightweight batteries—both of which are widely used in green energy products. Ordinary magnets, made from iron, cobalt, and nickel, eventually lose their magnetization when exposed to high temperatures, but alloys made with rare earths remain magnetic even when exposed to great heat, making them highly desirable for use in wind turbines and motor engines. Meanwhile, batteries that incorporate rare earths are lighter than those made from lead or cadmium-nickel alloys, and retain their charge for a longer period—an ideal set of characteristics for hybrid and all-electric vehicles.[15] The Toyota Prius, the world's most popular hybrid car, is particularly dependent on rare earths: according to one

TABLE 6.1: THE RARE EARTHS AND THEIR USES

RARE EARTHS	ATOMIC NUMBER	INDUSTRIAL USE
Scandium	21	Aluminum alloys, semiconductors, stadium lights
Yttrium	39	Lasers, fiber optics, energy-efficient lightbulbs
Lanthanum	57	Hybrid electric motors and electric car batteries
Cerium	58	Lens polishers
Praseodymium	59	Searchlights, aircraft parts, portable electronics
Neodymium	60	High-strength magnets, hybrid electric motors, portable electronics
Promethium	61	Portable X-ray units
Samarium	62	Glass manufacture, high-strength magnets

estimate, each Prius electric motor requires two pounds of neodymium and each Prius battery uses twenty-two to thirty-three pounds of lanthanum.[16]

The distinctive properties of rare earths make them especially valuable for military applications. According to a 2010 briefing prepared for Congress by the Government Accountability Office (GAO), "the use of rare earth materials is widespread in defense systems. These include, among others, precision-guided munitions, lasers, communications systems, radar systems, avionics, night vision equipment, and satellites." Specific systems cited by the GAO included the Aegis SPY-1 radar, which contains samarium-cobalt magnet components; the M1A2 Abrams tank, which uses similar technology; and the DDG-51 destroyer, which relies on a hybrid drive system employing neodymium magnets.[17] Samarium-

Europium	63	Energy-efficient lightbulbs, fiber optics
Gadolinium	64	Neutron radiography
Terbium	65	High-strength magnets, hybrid electric motors, portable electronics
Dysprosium	66	High-strength magnets, hybrid electric motors, portable electronics
Holmium	67	Glass tint
Erbium	68	Metal alloys
Thulium	69	Lasers
Ytterbium	70	Stainless steel
Lutetium	71	None currently

Sources: U.S. General Accounting Office, *Rare Earth Materials in the Defense Supply Chain*, April 1, 2010; Keith Bradsher, "China Tightens Grip on Rare Minerals," *New York Times*, September 1, 2009.

cobalt magnet motors are also used to steer many precision-guided bombs and missiles and to power the tail fins of high-performance fighter aircraft such as the F-22 Raptor.[18]

The fact that rare earths are vital to so many high-technology applications is one reason why the Chinese restrictions on their shipment provoked such a global panic. Even more troubling to the general public was the sudden realization that China has completely monopolized the mining, processing, and refining of these materials. David Sandalow of the DoE estimates that China now accounts for some 95 percent of total worldwide rare earths production, and other experts place the figure as high as 97 percent.[19] This is not because the world's REE reserves are located exclusively in China: several other countries, including Australia, Canada, and the United States, possess significant deposits as well,

TABLE 6.2: RARE EARTHS: MINE PRODUCTION AND RESERVES
(in metric tons)

	ESTIMATED RESERVES	MINE PRODUCTION, 2010
Australia	1,600,000	0
Brazil	48,000	550
China	55,000,000	130,000
Former Soviet Union	19,000,000	not available
India	3,100,000	2,700
Malaysia	30,000	350
United States	13,000,000	0
Other countries	22,000,000	not available
World total (rounded)	114,000,000	134,000

Source: U.S. Geological Survey, "Rare Earths," *Minerals Commodity Summaries*, January 2011.

and the United States used to have its own domestic REE supply chain.[20] But natural concentrations of rare earths are uncommon, and so normally they must be extracted from composite ores containing many other minerals—including, in many cases, radioactive materials—through a costly and hazardous process.[21] The procedure usually involves using acids of various kinds to leach rare earths from the surrounding stone, producing toxic wastes that can poison farms and water supplies unless they are carefully disposed of. By overlooking the environmental risks and lowering its production costs, China was able to undercut the other REE suppliers, eventually leading nearly all of its competitors to suspend their operations (see Table 6.2).[22]

Having firmly established itself as the world's dominant REE producer, China has been eager to use this position to its advantage. Even before the September 2010 ban on rare earth deliveries to Japan, Chinese authorities were gradually imposing more state control on the rare earths industry and reducing the country's REE export quotas. The limit for annual exports of all rare earth elements was lowered from 53,000 tons in 2008 to 35,000 tons in 2009, and shipments of certain metals were restricted even further.[23] Additional quota cutbacks were announced in 2010 and 2011, and deliveries are now running at significantly lower levels than in past years.[24] The official reason given for the tightened controls was that the Chinese government seeks to eliminate unregulated "pirate" operations and reduce environmental degradation in the country; many observers believe, however, that the export limits are also intended to encourage foreign firms to move their REE-dependent high-tech manufacturing operations into China. Many rare earth mines are located in relatively poor areas of the country such as the Inner Mongolia Autonomous Region, and officials there have made no secret of their desire to attract more foreign enterprises to the area.[25]

Whatever the underlying motivation, the Chinese efforts to restrict rare earth exports have caused significant anxiety in Western government and industry circles. In March 2010, half a year before China's embargo on Japan-bound REE shipments, Representative Mike Coffman of Colorado—a Republican whose district includes several major mining firms—described the situation as a "looming crisis," and introduced a bill calling for the federal government to provide support for new rare earths facilities in the United States.[26] Coffman's initial proposal failed to pass, but he reintroduced it in April 2011, emphasizing again that China's monopoly on rare earths poses "a serious threat to both the economic and national security of the United States."[27] Several other prominent members of Congress have also taken up the issue,[28] and China's actions against Japan—demonstrating that Chinese leaders are clearly willing to use the rare earths as a bargaining chip—have given new urgency to the concerns.

THE HUNT FOR NEW RARE EARTH DEPOSITS

Chinese authorities now insist that they will provide an uninterrupted supply of rare earth elements to key customers abroad, albeit at substantially lower levels than in the past. But with most analysts predicting an ever-greater demand for these materials, the incentive to establish new rare earth mines has never been greater. According to one estimate, global REE demand will jump from 124,000 tons in 2010 to 185,000 tons in 2015, an increase of nearly 50 percent.[29] With consumption increasing so swiftly and Chinese output unlikely to grow, many observers expect to see a high-stakes race among potential REE suppliers around the world. Some of them will try to reopen old mines that had previously been shut down by Chinese competition; others will work to develop new deposits elsewhere.[30]

In the United States, the greatest hope for renewed rare earths production rests on plans to rehabilitate an abandoned REE mine at Mountain Pass, California, just across the border from southern Nevada and about sixty miles from Las Vegas. The Mountain Pass mine first began producing rare earths in 1965, and for the following two decades it was the world's leading rare earths supplier. During most of that time the United States was largely self-sufficient in rare earths, with China playing a relatively minor role in the global trade. By the late 1980s, however, the costs of extraction at Mountain Pass had risen substantially, while China had opened new low-cost mines in Jiangxi and Inner Mongolia. In addition, stricter environmental regulations enacted during the 1990s made it difficult to operate Mountain Pass without costly upgrades, and the mine's owners shut it down in 2002. Now, however, a group of private investors working through Denver-based Molycorp Minerals have acquired the mine and are trying to resume production, claiming that the use of advanced technologies will allow them to improve the rate of REE extraction at the site.[31]

Restoring Mountain Pass to full operating capacity will not be easy. Recent visitors to the mine report that all of its original processing facilities have fallen into decay and will have to be replaced. Environmental concerns, too, remain a major worry: the mine's 2002 closure was prompted in part by an incident in which a leaking pipeline spilled radioactive wastewater into the Mojave Desert. Bringing the facilities into compliance with federal and state regulations will cost Molycorp an estimated $187 million, while repairing the existing infrastructure and introducing new technology will require $300 million or more beyond that. Still, the company has succeeded in raising the necessary cash and is confident that the mine will soon resume full-scale operations.[32]

Ambitious investors are also gearing up to establish new REE mines in other countries. Australia, in particular, has been attracting significant attention from the industry, with two major projects currently under way. One venture, being undertaken by Arafura Resources, involves extracting rare earths from the Nolans Bore deposit in the Northern Territory and shipping them by rail to a processing facility in South Australia, about 250 miles from Adelaide; Arafura expects to have the mine up and running in 2013.[33] At the same time, the Lynas Corporation has begun developing the Mount Weld rare earth deposit in Western Australia, considered one of the world's largest. By 2013, Lynas plans to be producing about 9,000 tons of rare earths per year.[34]

Ironically, both of these Australian rare earth ventures have been the target of Chinese buy-in efforts. The East China Mineral Exploration and Development Bureau (ECE) made a bid to acquire a 22 percent stake in Arafura, enough to make it the firm's single largest shareholder, while the China Nonferrous Metal Mining Group (CNMC) offered $210 million for a majority stake in Lynas. These proposals caused considerable anxiety in Australia, especially as they came on the heels of several Chinese attempts to acquire control of other Australian mining companies—attempts that many politicians and other public figures denounced as a threat to Australia's security and independence. After much deliberation, ECE's bid for minority ownership of Arafura was eventually given government approval, but CNMC's offer for a majority stake in Lynas was not allowed to proceed.[35]

Like the planned restoration of the Mountain Pass mine, Australian rare earths projects are provoking serious concerns about potential radioactivity leaks, and Lynas's operations are causing particular worry. Possibly to avoid Australia's strict environmental regulations, Lynas intends to ship ore extracted at Mount Weld across the sea to Malaysia, where it is building a new rare earths refinery. But engineers employed at that site have raised an alarm about improper construction techniques, saying that the facility is not properly shielded and might allow toxic materials to escape. The Malaysian government has ordered Lynas to draft a detailed plan for the long-term disposal of radioactive wastes at the site before it will issue an operating permit for the refinery, which had been expected to open in September 2011.[36]

When (and if) Lynas's Malaysian plant does begin production, most of its output will flow to Japan, which has been scouring the world in the search for new sources of rare earths. This effort began even before China's September 2010 interruption of REE deliveries, but gained considerable momentum after that point. "Some countries have started taking steps to seek various options," said Foreign Minister Seiji Maehara on October 1, 2010. "I think it is quite a healthy development for each country to start resource diplomacy after developing a sense of crisis because of the latest incident."[37] In Japan's case, the resource diplomacy has centered on assertive regional negotiations by the country's prime minister, Naoto Kan, and a heavy infusion of government cash channeled through the state-run Japan Oil, Gas, and Metals National Corporation (JOGMEC).

Among the first steps taken by Tokyo to enhance Japan's access to rare earths was an overture to Mongolia, which is thought to possess significant untapped REE reserves. In October 2010, Kan met with Mongolian prime minister Sükhbaataryn Batbold to propose a joint REE venture, declaring that "development of mine resources in mineral-rich Mongolia will benefit both countries."[38] After the meeting, Kan indicated that a Japanese research team would soon depart for Mongolia to begin searching for promising rare earth deposits, with financing to be provided by JOGMEC.[39]

A few weeks later, Prime Minister Kan made his way to Hanoi to discuss rare earth projects with senior Vietnamese officials. Here, too, he extolled the virtues of a joint approach, and after meeting with his Vietnamese counterpart Kan announced that the two countries had established a "strategic partnership" to mine rare earths in Vietnam.[40] This intergovernmental endeavor will presumably dovetail with related corporate efforts, as Vietnam's state-run Coal and Mineral Industries Group has made plans to work with the Toyota Tsusho Corporation—the trading arm of the Toyota Motor Corporation—to develop the Dong Pao rare earths deposit located northwest of Hanoi. As one of the world's leading consumers of rare earth elements, Toyota has a natural interest in securing multiple sources of supply, and the Dong Pao operation is expected to begin exporting rare earths to Japan in 2013.[41]

Toshiba, another major rare earths consumer, is taking steps of its own to procure foreign sources of rare earths: it has established a joint venture with Kazakhstan's state-owned nuclear holding company Kazatomprom to mine and process rare earths and other specialty metals in that country.[42] And other Japanese companies are venturing even farther afield in their REE search. The large trading house Sojitz, for instance, is joining with JOGMEC and Lynas to develop a new rare earths project in the landlocked African country of Malawi.[43]

Indeed, miners searching for rare earths supplies are starting to resemble oil and gas prospectors in their willingness to seek out new deposits in remote locations. As noted in the previous chapter, an Australian firm hopes to obtain rare earths from a uranium-zinc mine it plans to develop at Kvanefjeld, near the southwestern tip of Greenland.[44] Some visionary entrepreneurs are also thinking of extracting rare earths from manganese nodules—potato-sized rocks that litter the deep-ocean floor and contain rare earth elements along with copper, cobalt, and other minerals.[45] The rocks are difficult to collect using existing technology, but some analysts expect that with REE prices climbing the industry will eventually develop the necessary harvesting techniques.

How many of these assorted ventures will pan out in the years ahead remains to be seen. Establishing the infrastructure to mine and refine rare earths can be very costly, and the process involves significant environmental risk. Nevertheless, with China restricting its REE output—and with the global demand for rare earths expected to soar thanks to increasing emphasis on "green" technology—all signs point to a frenzied effort to develop new sources of supply, wherever they might be found.

THE ALARM OVER OTHER "CRITICAL MINERALS"

Rare earths are not the only specialized ingredients that play a vital part in high-tech industries, and the international alarm over REE supplies has prompted broader concerns about the availability of other exotic natural resources. Accordingly, various governmental agencies around the world have been urgently reviewing their countries' vulnerability to disruptions in the supply of what have been termed "critical minerals"— materials that are essential to modern technology but are not abundantly available, either because their deposits are genuinely scarce or because they are concentrated in just a few problematic locations. The "critical minerals" category includes such elements as indium, gallium, lithium, niobium, palladium, tantalum, and vanadium: substances largely unfamiliar to the general public, but no less indispensable for all that.

Many of these minerals are used as additives in making specialized steel and aluminum for applications that require great heat resistance and durability. Niobium, for example, is used to make high-performance alloys for oil and gas pipelines; manganese and vanadium are used in the manufacture of corrosion-resistant, high-strength steels; and lightweight titanium alloys are highly prized by the aerospace industry. Other critical minerals are needed for building clean energy systems: gallium and indium, for instance, are used in making photovoltaic solar cells, while lithium is a component of advanced motor-vehicle batteries. Any given application might require only a relatively small quantity of these materials, but it is often impossible to achieve the desired results without them.[46] (See Table 6.3.)

As with the rare earths, the global demand for these critical minerals is likely to soon exceed their supply on international markets. "Mineral availability—or more precisely, unavailability—has emerged as a potential constraint on the development and deployment of emerging energy technologies," Roderick G. Eggert of the Colorado School of Mines told a Senate subcommittee in September 2010, urging senators to focus more government attention on the issue. Part of the problem, Eggert explained, is that our reliance on these materials has increased in tandem with the growing complexity and sophistication of modern technologies. Computer maker Intel, he noted, used only eleven mineral-derived elements in the 1980s, but may use up to sixty such elements in the near future. At the same time, whether because of the "basic geologic

TABLE 6.3: CHARACTERISTICS AND APPLICATIONS OF SELECTED CRITICAL MINERALS

Mineral	Atomic Number	Characteristics	Industrial Use
Gallium	31	A soft, silvery metal that melts at relatively low temperatures	Electronic devices, primarily high-speed semiconductors and light-emitting diodes; also used in photovoltaic cells.
Indium	49	A soft, silvery gray, malleable metal	Used in indium-tin-oxide (ITO) coatings for flat-panel displays; also used in infrared detectors, high-speed transistors, and photovoltaic cells.
Lithium	3	A soft, silvery white metallic element; the lightest of all solid elements	Wind turbines; lithium-ion batteries in hybrid-electric vehicles.
Manganese	25	A silvery metallic element	Essential to steelmaking; also used for making stainless steel, aluminum alloys.
Niobium (also called columbium)	41	A soft, gray, ductile material; usually found in association with tantalum	Used in specialty steels and superconducting alloys.
Platinum	78	A silvery white, lustrous, ductile, and malleable metal	Automotive catalytic converters; hydrogen fuel cells.
Tantalum	73	A hard, blue-gray, lustrous metal that is highly corrosion resistant; usually found in association with niobium	Automotive electronics, pagers, personal computers, and portable telephones.
Titanium	22	A strong, lustrous, corrosion-resistant metal with a silver color; usually found in rutile and ilmenite ores	Air and space vehicles, lightweight armor.
Vanadium	23	A soft, silvery gray, ductile metal	An alloy for high-strength steel.

Sources: U.S. Department of Energy, *Critical Materials Strategy*, December 2010; U.S. Geological Survey, *Mineral Commodity Summaries*, January 2011.

scarcity" of certain elements or because of export restrictions that some countries may place on raw materials, future availability of these minerals is by no means guaranteed.[47]

There is currently no formal definition of which minerals qualify as "critical," but a 2008 study conducted by the National Research Council (NRC) concluded that the term should apply to any material "that is both essential in use (difficult to substitute away from) and subject to some degree of supply risk." One example of difficult-to-substitute minerals is provided by the platinum group of metals, which are a crucial component in automotive catalytic converters and have no known alternative for that purpose. "Supply risks," meanwhile, exist whenever a given mineral is extracted or processed by only a few companies, since an interruption at any one of these producers is likely to affect availability worldwide. When a particular mineral is both irreplaceable *and* vulnerable to supply disruptions, it is said to have a high degree of "criticality," or high economic risk.[48]

The NRC study identified five minerals and mineral groups as being particularly critical for commercial and military users in the United States: indium, manganese, niobium, platinum-group metals (PGMs), and the rare earths. Another six elements—copper, gallium, lithium, tantalum, titanium, and vanadium—were deemed less critical, but nonetheless worthy of significant attention. Additional research is needed, the NRC said, to identify promising sources of all these materials and the best ways of extracting, refining, and processing them.[49]

The U.S. Department of Defense has been paying increased attention to the problem of critical minerals and taking steps to ensure that the military does not suffer from a lack of any of them. Of course, concern about supplies of vital natural resources is not an entirely new phenomenon: during the Cold War era, the DoD accumulated huge quantities of industrial materials including cobalt, tin, and zinc through the Defense National Stockpile Center, which runs a series of vast mineral storehouses scattered across the country. At the end of the Cold War, though, most of these materials were sold off, and many of the storehouses were shut down. As recently as 1995, the defense stockpile held 90 different types of commodities in 85 separate locations; today, it holds a mere 20 commodities in just 10 facilities. Now, the DoD is again planning to expand its mineral reserves—this time with a focus on critical materials such as specialty steels, lithium, and rare earth elements.[50]

Major agencies in other countries have also taken up the issue of rare and specialized minerals. In 2009, the European Commission (the European Union's administrative arm) established a working group charged with defining "critical raw materials" and making recommendations for European policy. Like their counterparts in the United States, the members of this group decided to assess the "criticality" of key materials by plotting them on a matrix with two separate axes: the relative economic importance of a given mineral and the danger that its supply might be interrupted. Using this approach, the EU group identified fourteen minerals as especially critical, including many of the same materials that were similarly classified by the NRC. Both lists included rare earths, PGMs, gallium, indium, niobium, and tantalum; in addition, the EU group also sounded warnings about antimony, beryllium, cobalt, fluorspar, germanium, graphite, magnesium, and tungsten. (Like other critical minerals, the additional materials on the EU list are used as alloys in high-strength metals or have specialized industrial functions.) A shortage of any of these materials, the group warned, could cause serious damage to European economies.[51]

Japanese officials, too, are keenly aware of the need to secure reliable supplies of critical materials. The state-owned JOGMEC is charged with ensuring "a stable source of natural resources for Japan," a duty it fulfills in part by helping to procure "risk money" that Japanese mining firms need for starting up new operations. In 2008, the government boosted JOGMEC's $42 million budget for metals exploration by 50 percent, pushing it to increase spending on specialty minerals and uranium.[52] Aside from supporting efforts by Japanese firms to obtain rare earths from varied foreign sources, JOGMEC has partnered with Nippon Steel and other companies to acquire part ownership of a niobium mine in Brazil.[53] In addition, it has established a strategic alliance with Brazilian mining giant Vale to search for manganese, nickel, zinc, PGMs, and other specialty minerals in Africa.[54]

As the demand for specialty minerals continues to grow in the years ahead, such efforts to secure reliable supplies of these materials will become increasingly important. All of the exotic elements described above will no doubt be sought after with great intensity, but several are likely to attract particular attention. Chief among these are lithium, the platinum group metals, and tantalum.

LITHIUM

Lithium is a soft, silvery metal that has long been employed in various commercial products, including heat-resistant glass and ceramics. Its powerful tranquilizing effects have also made it useful in mood-altering drugs. More recently, however, lithium has gained its greatest importance in another area altogether: the manufacture of rechargeable batteries. Because lithium is lighter than most other materials used to make batteries and holds a charge for longer, lithium-based rechargeables have become the standard in most cell phones and laptop computers, as well as a growing array of cameras and portable tools. Even more significant, many automobile manufacturers—whether they are working on hybrid-electric vehicles (HEVs), plug-in hybrid vehicles (PHEVs), or pure electric vehicles (EVs)—plan to employ lithium-ion batteries as a power source. The Chevrolet Volt, a plug-in hybrid introduced with much fanfare in 2011, is among the various cars that run on a lithium-ion battery, as are many of the PHEVs and EVs now being developed by other auto companies.[55]

Many experts believe that global efforts to increase the popularity of hybrid and all-electric vehicles—and thereby slow the buildup of greenhouse gases in the atmosphere—will depend in large part on how innovatively manufacturers can use lithium to produce advanced, lightweight batteries. Nissan's all-electric Leaf car, for instance, was made possible by a rectangular laminated lithium-ion battery that has twice the capacity and twice the power of a conventional cylindrical battery of the same weight, yet takes up only half as much room.[56] And the U.S. Geological Survey reports that a promising new approach, the lithium metal-air battery, may eventually be able to deliver ten times as much energy density as the best lithium-ion technology of today.[57]

Much of the original research on lithium batteries for hybrids, plug-ins, and all-electric vehicles was conducted by Japanese companies, especially Nissan, Mitsubishi, and Toyota. Recently, however, China announced its intention to become a world leader in the manufacture of hybrids and electric cars, making it another major player in the lithium market. A Chinese car company called BYD is already using lithium-ion batteries in the country's first plug-in hybrid, the F3DM, and its first all-electric car, the e6.[58] (Evidently impressed by BYD's leadership in PHEV and EV technology, American investor Warren Buffett acquired a 10 percent stake in BYD in 2008.)[59] As part of its Five-Year Plan for 2012–17, China's government will spend some $15 billion to promote further development of electric vehicles by Chinese companies, with much of that investment targeted at advanced lithium battery research.[60]

American automobile companies have also been looking to hybrid and all-electric cars as crucial to their long-term prosperity, and President Obama has been especially fervent in his support for advanced battery development. In the administration's 2009 economic stimulus package, some $940 million was allocated to lithium battery producers and their suppliers.[61] "When folks lift up their hoods on the cars of the future, I want them to see engines and batteries that are stamped: Made in America," Obama told employees at A123 Systems, one of the battery makers that benefited from this government funding.[62]

All of these initiatives, of course, mean that worldwide consumption of lithium is bound to increase. In the short term, some additional supply can come from current producers of the metal, most of which are concentrated in Australia, Chile, China, and the United States. But existing lithium deposits are not considered adequate to meet the surge in demand that's expected to come from all of the battery projects now under way around the world. Finding and developing new reserves of this critical mineral, therefore, will soon prove essential.[63]

Of all the potential sources of lithium, none appear to hold greater promise than the remote southern highlands of Bolivia. Near the Bolivia-Chile border lies the Salar de Uyuni, the world's largest salt flat and a treasure trove of lithium-infused brine. Covering some 4,000 square miles—twice the size of Delaware—the Salar is a vast uninterrupted desert of blindingly white salt. "As far as the eye can see, [there is] nothing," wrote one visiting journalist. "Not a shrub or tree, not a hill or

BOLIVIA: SALAR DE UYUNI

valley, just an endless expanse of white."[64] According to the USGS, this thick crust of salt, about a dozen feet deep, sits above a sea of brine that contains as much as 5.4 million tons of lithium—an amount roughly equivalent to all the other lithium deposits in the world combined. If the brine were extracted and the salty water allowed to evaporate, leaving its dissolved minerals behind, the Salar de Uyuni could satisfy the world's lithium requirements for many decades to come.[65]

But many obstacles stand in the way of exploiting the Salar's lithium riches. The giant salt lake sits in the Andes Mountains at nearly 12,000 feet of elevation, far from any railways, airports, or paved roads. Bolivia also lacks an outlet to the Pacific Ocean, and is wary of exporting any raw materials through neighboring Chile or Peru. In addition to such infrastructure difficulties, an even more significant complication lies in the fiercely nationalistic attitude of Evo Morales, Bolivia's outspoken president. Elected in 2005 with the enthusiastic support of his country's marginalized indigenous communities, Morales—himself descended from Aymara Indians—has pledged to impose state control over all of Bolivia's natural resources. Their exploitation, he says, must redound to the benefit of the nation, not the multinational corporations. Morales's pledge applies not only to Bolivian oil and natural gas, but also to the lithium-rich brine beneath the Salar de Uyuni.[66] "The government of Bolivia will never give away control of this natural resource," he declared in June 2009.[67]

Morales insists that his government is willing to cooperate with foreign companies to develop the country's lithium deposits, but he is demanding a very high price: any prospective partners are expected not just to share profits from the extraction and processing of lithium, but also to help establish an electric battery and automobile manufacturing industry in Bolivia. "From this brine, there will be lithium cars coming out of Bolivia," Morales told Lawrence Wright of the *New Yorker*. "This is the dream. Without dreams, what's anything worth? Dreams become reality."[68] Most outside analysts believe, however, that such lofty aspirations are impracticable in one of Latin America's poorest and least developed countries. "Bolivia's ideological face does not square with business and commercial realities," argued Carlos Alberto López, a former Bolivian minister of energy who went on to become a consultant with Cambridge Energy Research Associates. "I doubt lithium's potential [in Bolivia] will be realized in the short or medium term."[69]

If Bolivia ends up not supplying the lithium needed by the automotive industry, where else might it come from? One potential source is the Salar de Olaroz, a salt flat in northwestern Argentina just across the Bolivian border.[70] The Salar de Olaroz is much smaller than the Salar de Uyuni, but its brine is thought to contain fewer impurities, and the Argentinean government has not objected to its exploitation. In January 2010, Toyota Tsusho—the same trading firm that is involved in rare earth procurement for Toyota Motors—announced a multimillion-dollar joint venture with Orocobre, an Australian exploration company, to develop the Argentine site, and they hope to begin production in 2012.[71]

Another possible future source for lithium is Afghanistan, a veritable cornucopia of untapped minerals. Most mining attention so far has been focused on Afghanistan's massive copper and iron ore deposits, but American geologists working with the U.S. Department of Defense also say that dry salt lakes in western Afghanistan are likely to harbor lithium deposits on a par with those found in Bolivia. According to an internal DoD memo seen by a reporter for the *New York Times*, some Pentagon analysts believe that Afghanistan could become the "Saudi Arabia of lithium."[72] But starting up lithium operations in Afghanistan would involve tremendous challenges, including a lack of infrastructure, pervasive corruption, and recurring violence. Whether any major mining firms will make an attempt to overcome these difficulties remains to be seen.

PLATINUM-GROUP METALS

Like lithium and the rare earths, the platinum-group metals (PGMs) are expected to play an increasingly significant role in advanced electronic and transportation systems. Aside from platinum itself, the PGMs include five other rare minerals with similar physical and chemical properties: palladium, iridium, rhodium, ruthenium, and osmium. Each of these elements has its own distinct characteristics, but all of the various PGMs are known for their exceptionally high melting points, superb electrical conductivity, outstanding catalytic capabilities, and excellent resistance to corrosion. These properties make them ideal for use in catalytic converters—the devices used to remove harmful emissions from automobile exhaust—as well as in jet engines and portable electric devices. It is estimated that one-quarter of all manufactured goods sold today either contain PGMs directly or were manufactured on equipment that uses PGMs, and for some key industrial applications no substitutes are known to exist.[73]

Outside the technology circles, of course, platinum is best known for its use in jewelry, where it is often alloyed with gold. Worldwide, however, only about 20 percent of platinum output goes into jewelry, high-end watches, and similar luxury products, while industrial applications take up a much greater share. According to the U.S. Geological Survey, 44 percent of all platinum used worldwide in 2008 went into automotive catalytic converters; such converters also accounted for 47 percent of palladium consumption and 81 percent of all rhodium use.[74] In addition, PGMs are widely employed in computer hard drives, liquid crystal displays, and miniaturized electronic circuits.

The use of PGMs in automotive catalytic converters is essential: no other materials have proven as effective in converting carbon monoxide, nitrogen oxide, and other noxious emissions into water vapor and less-toxic gases. As governments push automakers to produce cleaner, more fuel-efficient vehicles with engines that operate at higher temperatures, the need for PGMs will only grow. In addition, platinum is a critical component of hydrogen fuel cells, which some experts believe will power future generations of electric cars.[75] (Fuel cells produce electricity by combining hydrogen and oxygen, with platinum as a catalyst; the technology is particularly attractive because no greenhouse gases are emitted in the process.)

But while PGMs might seem like miracle minerals, there is a catch: every one of these elements is exceptionally rare. The total world output of platinum and palladium in 2010 was just 836,000 pounds, a truly meager amount when compared to the millions of tons of iron, copper, bauxite, and other basic minerals mined every year.[76] Like gold, the PGMs are found in very small quantities in just a handful of locations, and their prices accordingly hover in the same stratospheric range. In the first half of 2008, for example, palladium reached a high of $585 per troy ounce; platinum peaked at $2,275 per troy ounce; and rhodium, the most expensive mineral in the group, soared to above $10,000 per troy ounce. (For comparison, the all-time high price for a troy ounce of gold is around $1,800.) The global financial crisis that began in the fall of 2008 knocked down the cost of most PGMs from their record highs to a certain extent, but the prices began rising again the following year and have been increasing ever since.[77]

The global supply chain for PGMs is especially tenuous because most of the world's production of these elements currently comes from just two countries: Russia and South Africa. The United States does have two PGM mines of its own, both located in south-central Montana, but the metals extracted there in 2010 added up to less than 26,000 pounds of palladium, 8,000 pounds of platinum, and a few dozen pounds of rhodium for the entire year. Canada's platinum and palladium mining, carried out by several firms in the Sudbury region of Ontario, is on a similar scale. Overall, therefore, the combined North American operations make up less than 10 percent of the world's total PGM output—leaving Russia and South Africa in a dominant position in the market.[78]

Those two leading PGM producers, however, are having to grapple with significant problems of their own. Norilsk Nickel—the top Russian supplier and the source of almost half the world's palladium—traces its history back to the Soviet era, when the enterprise was established to exploit giant mineral reserves in the Norilsk area of northern Siberia. Located well above the Arctic Circle and far from other populated areas, the Norilsk mines were originally developed in the 1930s using slave labor from the Gulag political prison settlements.[79] Today, Norilsk Nickel is a private company and mining is conducted by well-paid workers, but the operations are facing severe criticism for their abysmal environmental record. "The snow is black, the air tastes of sulfur and the life expectancy for factory workers is 10 years below the Russian average," reports the Blacksmith Group, an environmental organization that has ranked the city of Norilsk as one of the ten most polluted places in the world.[80]

Meanwhile, South Africa—which in 2010 accounted for 75 percent of the world's platinum output, 37 percent of the world's palladium, and a significant proportion of the other PGMs—has been confronted with recurring work stoppages and labor unrest at several of its major mines. Workers at Anglo Platinum, the country's largest PGM producer, have repeatedly staged strikes to protest unsafe mining conditions, despite the company's assurances that it scrupulously follows occupational standards.[81] Similar troubles have been plaguing Impala Platinum, South Africa's second biggest PGM producer, for most of the past decade. In June 2004, Impala fired 1,700 rock drill operators who had participated in an illegal strike over harsh working conditions at the Rustenburg mine, northwest of Johannesburg; although the operators were later reinstated, all 17,000 workers at the mine went on strike three months later to again insist on better conditions and demand higher wages.[82] Periodic strikes at Anglo's and Impala's various South African mines are continuing to this day.

Anglo Platinum has also become embroiled in a controversy regarding its aggressive expansion plans in Limpopo Province, in far northern South Africa. Eager to increase its platinum output, the company is developing several new open-pit mines in Limpopo, which have involved the relocation of thousands of indigenous people from their ancestral lands. Although Anglo has built new towns for the displaced villagers, some have resisted the relocation and have had to be driven off by armed police firing rubber bullets.[83]

Given the insecure state of the current PGM supply, developing new sources of platinum and related metals is of immense importance. The world's largest untapped platinum reserves, however, are thought to be located in Zimbabwe—a country that many Western governments have placed under economic sanctions to protest President Robert Mugabe's brutal suppression of pro-democracy movements. With most Western mining firms avoiding any involvement in Zimbabwe, its platinum reserves have largely become the domain of the two familiar South African PGM mining giants, Impala and Anglo Platinum. Both companies are making major investments in their cross-border plans: Anglo Platinum expects to spend $400 million on developing the Unki platinum mine, while Impala has undertaken a $500 million expansion of its existing Ngezi mine in central Zimbabwe.[84] Even these projects, though, have been hampered by political complications, as Mugabe insists that all foreign mining firms must sell a 51 percent stake in their local operations to black Zimbabweans under the government's "indigenization" policy. The program is officially intended to promote domestic economic development, but it is widely seen as merely a device to enrich Mugabe's political allies, and its implementation is bound to cause further difficulties in bringing Zimbabwe's platinum to the market.[85]

TANTALUM

Tantalum is a hard, blue-gray metal with excellent electrical conductivity and superb resistance to corrosion; it is often recovered together with niobium from a shared mineral stock known as columbite-tantalite, or "coltan." It has long been employed for industrial purposes such as making specialty steels, including those used in jet engines and nuclear reactors.[86] More recently, it has become a crucial ingredient in the production of miniature capacitors for cell phones and other compact electronic devices. The amount of tantalum used in these products is often very small, but demand for the element is rising, especially in the electronics industry, and few substitutes with the same key chemical properties are known to exist. To further complicate matters, some of the world's richest deposits of coltan are located in war-torn areas of the Democratic Republic of the Congo, making their extraction dangerous and problematic.[87]

Given its importance to vital industries and the paucity of viable mining sites, tantalum has long been flagged for special attention by the U.S. government. "Because the United States has no niobium or tantalum ore reserves," the USGS noted in 2010, "domestic supply has been a concern during every national military emergency since World War I."[88] Throughout the Cold War, the Defense National Stockpile Center held significant inventories of the metal in its warehouses. Much of that supply was later sold off, but with Congress now eager to bolster America's reserves of critical minerals, all such sales from the defense stockpile have been halted.[89]

In 2010, the entire worldwide production of tantalum amounted to just 670 metric tons, or a little less than 1.5 million pounds of the material—making it only three or four times more common than platinum or palladium. As with all critical materials that have growing high-tech applications, mining companies are eagerly scouring the globe in search of new sources of supply. At the moment, however, most of the world's tantalum comes from just a handful of countries, with Brazil, Mozambique, Australia, and Rwanda officially accounting for about 70 percent of the total production and supply.[90]

The Democratic Republic of the Congo, with its substantial coltan deposits, does not formally figure on that list of the largest producers. Nonetheless, experts estimate that as much as one-fifth of the world's tantalum supply comes from small-scale, clandestine mining operations in the eastern Congo that connect to world markets through circuitous routes, often going through Rwanda. (Indeed, it is generally believed that Rwanda is not actually a significant producer in its own right, and functions only as an export platform for tantalum covertly extracted elsewhere.) Because much of the money from the clandestine Congolese mines flows to rebel militias or rogue elements of the DRC army, tantalum and other metals obtained from such sources have acquired the unusual sobriquet of "conflict minerals," and international

EASTERN CONGO

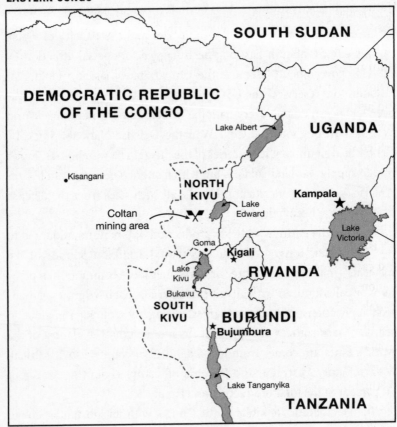

groups have been trying—though with only limited success—to suppress the trade in them through sanctions and legislation.

The history of the illicit coltan mines is rooted in the long-standing strife among ethnic groups in the region, including Hutus and Tutsis. Many of the inhabitants of Congo's eastern provinces of North Kivu and South Kivu are ethnic Tutsis, with ties to the Tutsis of neighboring Rwanda and Burundi. In 1994, however, when a Tutsi-led government took control of Rwanda after Hutu *génocidaires* had killed over half a million Tutsis in that country, many of Rwanda's Hutus—fearing reprisals—fled across the border into the Kivu provinces. There, the Hutus established ethnic enclaves of their own and set up armed militias to protect themselves from pursuing Rwandan forces. Congo's native Tutsis, in turn, created their own militias to defend against the Hutu intruders, as did various other ethnic groups in the area. The various factions have fought for control of eastern Congo ever since, and neither peace agreements signed among the groups nor the deployment of a large United Nations peacekeeping contingent has succeeded in ending the violence.[91]

To finance their ongoing operations, many of the warring groups have seized control of mineral-rich areas in North and South Kivu and are forcing local civilians to dig for tantalum, tin, tungsten, gold, and other minerals. There is no machinery or electricity, so all of the mining is done by hand; the extracted ores are then placed into large sacks and carried by human porters over many miles of jungle trails to collection sites scattered around the region. Militia commanders collect illegal "taxes" at every stage of the process, extorting fees from the miners, the merchants who sell them provisions, and the local traders in Goma and Bukavu (the principal cities of North and South Kivu, respectively), who arrange for the shipment of the ores onward to their destinations. Eventually, the minerals are shipped to major DRC trading centers, then to Burundi, Rwanda, and Uganda—and from there to smelters in East Asia.[92]

A reporter from the *New York Times* who visited one such mining operation in North Kivu described "columns of men, bent double under 110-pound sacks of tin ore," emerging from a pit that had been "carved hundreds of feet into the mountain with Iron Age tools powered by human sweat, muscle, and bone." Just to gain access to the mining town—the only source of employment for impoverished families in the area—prospective workers had to walk "30 miles down a winding, muddy footpath through dense, equatorial forest." Soldiers from a renegade brigade of the national army collected tolls at several stops along the way, both coming and going. It was, the reporter wrote, "a Darwinian place where those with weapons and money leech off a desperate horde."[93]

Because mines of this sort finance many rebel groups and feed the unremitting violence against civilians in the region, the United Nations has tried to suppress the illegal trade in coltan, tungsten, and tin ores. Under Security Council Resolution 1807, which was passed in 2008, all states, businesses, and individuals are prohibited from providing arms or material support to rebel organizations in the eastern Congo—which has been interpreted to include any black-market dealings in coltan and other conflict minerals. The measure also obliges the countries abutting the eastern Congo—Burundi, Rwanda, and Uganda—to block the illicit transport of weapons and conflict minerals across their national borders. According to a later UN investigation, however, the resolution has done little to improve the situation, and trafficking in conflict minerals continues unabated.[94]

The U.S. government has also taken notice of the link between illegal mining, armed militias, and the continuing bloodshed in the eastern Congo. "I am particularly concerned about the exploitation of natural resources" that helps sustain the violence, Secretary of State Hillary Clinton declared during a 2009 visit to the country.[95] To address the problem, the United States is financing UN efforts to improve official Congolese government oversight of the mining industry. In addition, a 2010 law (the Wall Street Reform and Consumer Protection Act, also known as Dodd-Frank) requires U.S. manufacturers to review their supply chain and report whether any of their products incorporate conflict minerals from the DRC—aiming thereby to deter such usage.[96]

Despite such efforts, experts agree that curbing the illicit trade in tantalum and other conflict minerals will prove extremely difficult. The DRC government remains too weak and riddled with corruption to effectively police the export of ores from North and South Kivu, while the neighboring states seem either unwilling or unable to prevent their territories from being used as way stations for the transport of these materials to global markets.[97] It is likely, therefore, that for the foreseeable future a certain percentage of the laptops, cell phones, and other electronic devices carried by well-off consumers around the world will contain tantalum that originates in the war zones of eastern Congo.

Aside from rare earths, lithium, tantalum, and the platinum-group metals, a variety of other uncommon minerals received high "critical-ity" scores from the National Research Council, indicating that these materials play key roles in high-tech applications but are vulnerable to supply problems of one sort or another. The NRC report expressed particular anxiety about gallium, a soft, silvery metal that is used in integrated circuits, light-emitting diodes (LEDs), and lasers; indium, a very soft metal used as a coating for flat-panel displays and solar cells; and vanadium, an extremely tough metal employed in making super-strength alloys for various aerospace applications. Notably, virtually no supplies of these elements are currently produced in the United States itself: the country is dependent on imports for 99 percent of its gallium use and for a full 100 percent of its indium and vanadium.[98]

Given that the global minerals trade is a well-established part of modern commerce, the fact that the United States is importing all of these minerals "is not in itself a reason for concern," the NRC noted in its 2008 report. On the other hand, the study continued, "import dependence can expose a range of U.S. industries to political, economic, and other risks that vary according to the particular situation."[99] For instance, 37 percent of America's gallium supply and 44 percent of its indium comes from China, which has already proven itself willing to cut off key mineral shipments for political reasons. Moreover, since China is seeking to become a leading manufacturer of many electronic products that rely on gallium and indium, it is likely to eventually restrict the export of these materials, just as it has imposed quotas on foreign purchases of rare earths.[100]

All this adds up to an important precautionary note. In recent years, many analysts and politicians have spoken optimistically about a "green" high-tech future in which our current reliance on heavily polluting fuels will give way to new, environmentally friendly alternatives. That scenario may indeed come to pass, but getting there will not be a simple task—and the critical minerals are one potential major problem. As we have seen, many advanced green technologies depend on relatively scarce, hard-to-acquire specialty elements whose future availability cannot be ensured. As time goes on, struggles over the control of these materials could prove no less intense and significant than the past battles over petroleum, copper, and other basic commodities of the Industrial Age.

7 ► GLOBAL "LAND GRABS"
AND THE STRUGGLE FOR FOOD

King Abdullah of Saudi Arabia is no stranger to impressive gifts from around the globe—falcons from the government of Pakistan, a sixteenth-century engraving from Pope Benedict XVI, and other such offerings as befit a monarch.[1] At a formal ceremony in Riyadh on January 26, 2009, however, Abdullah received a gift at once more humble and more significant than most: a batch of Ethiopian-grown rice, harvested there on land acquired by Saudi investors under a special royal decree. Following the global food crisis of 2008, during which some of Saudi Arabia's major international grain suppliers had temporarily halted all exports to satisfy consumers at home, Abdullah had established a multibillion-dollar fund to facilitate Saudi farming operations in foreign countries—intending thereby to ensure that food deliveries to the kingdom would never be interrupted again. Now, seated in a large audience chamber, the Saudi ruler was offered the first products of this undertaking. "King Abdullah praised the positive outcome of the project and urged its directors to double their efforts to achieve the desired goals," said a report on the event released by the Saudi Ministry of Foreign Affairs.[2]

Until the 2008 shortages, Saudi Arabia had been content to acquire most of its food supply through purchases on the international market;

the country has very little arable land of its own, so growing rice or other foodstuffs domestically is not a viable option. Seeing the market system break down, though, Abdullah concluded that the kingdom could no longer rely on foreign merchants for its food security. If Saudi Arabia's own soil was inadequate, then Saudi companies needed to acquire cropland abroad and grow food for export to the homeland. The Saudi government, for its part, would subsidize them as required via the newly established King Abdullah Initiative for Saudi Agricultural Investment Abroad.[3]

Obtaining farmland in Ethiopia has been made easier by the involvement of Mohammed Hussein Al Amoudi, an Ethiopian-born businessman who is one of Saudi Arabia's richest and most influential figures.[4] It was Al Amoudi's Ethiopian farming enterprise, Saudi Star Agricultural Development, that grew the first batch of rice under the royal food initiative, and it was he who presented the samples to King Abdullah at the January 2009 ceremony in Riyadh.[5] Saudi Star now operates a 25,000-acre pilot project, devoted largely to rice, in Ethiopia's Alwero region, and eventually plans to grow a wide array of crops for Saudi consumption on the 750,000 acres it has acquired from the Ethiopian government. All told, Al Amoudi expects to spend between $3 billion and $5 billion on these endeavors.[6]

Other Saudi corporations have also joined King Abdullah's drive for Saudi food security, initiating their own pilot projects. Hail Agricultural Development Company (Hadco), a prominent Saudi firm with close ties to the government, has acquired 22,800 acres in northern Sudan, and is making an initial investment of $45 million to start growing wheat, corn, and soybeans there for export to the kingdom. A state-owned enterprise, the Saudi Industrial Development Fund, is expected to provide 60 percent of Hadco's costs for launching this endeavor.[7] Another major Saudi firm, Savola Foods Company, is likewise planning to grow food crops in Sudan for export to foreign markets.[8]

The proliferation of Saudi agricultural projects in desperately poor African nations such as Sudan and Ethiopia has produced some striking scenes. Nancy Macdonald of *Maclean's*, who visited the Saudi Star pilot operation in Alwero, described guards with AK-47s protecting humidity-controlled greenhouses that are watered by computerized irrigation systems—high-tech plantations set in the middle of a country where farming is still conducted with sickles and ox-drawn plows and where millions suffer from chronic malnutrition. "Every day, a workforce of 1,000 locals pick, pack and load hundreds of tons of fresh produce onto waiting trucks," Macdonald wrote. "After reaching the capital, Addis Ababa, the produce is flown to a handful of Middle Eastern cities, entirely bypassing Ethiopia, one of the hungriest places on the planet."[9]

And Saudi Arabia is far from alone in seeking to acquire agricultural territory abroad to produce food for the homeland. Around the world, countries flush with cash but poor in arable land are now rushing to secure vast amounts of acreage in land-rich but underdeveloped nations. In theory, of course, such trades could benefit both sides, but in practice they usually raise extraordinarily troubling ethical and political questions. What's more, the rapidly growing international market in cropland has also begun to attract private investors, who see fertile farm plots as a lucrative new asset class with very high potential returns. For these banks, hedge funds, and other investors, land shortages are just another way to make a profit, and the risks of hunger and starvation in the developing world are even further removed from the calculation.

Underlying all of these land-buying sprees—or "land grabs," as critics often call them—is the conviction that arable land is becoming a premium commodity, just like oil, gas, copper, platinum, and other materials described in the previous chapters. The key characteristic of all of these resources is a persistent mismatch between supply and demand, with existing reserves increasingly depleted and production levels failing to keep up with global consumption. In the past, cropland had usually not been viewed in this fashion, since new farms could always be brought into cultivation on the peripheries of existing settlements. Today, however, there are few agricultural frontiers left to explore, while existing farmland is being whittled away by desertification, urbanization, and other powerful forces. With population growth ensuring an ever-increasing need for additional foodstuffs, the race for land is now under way.[10]

Precisely how severe the food situation will become in the years ahead is a matter of considerable debate.[11] Some experts believe that technology can help avert disaster: if we make a sufficient investment in new agricultural techniques, they say, and develop bioengineered crops designed to withstand the high temperatures and persistent drought expected from climate change, then it should be possible to feed the entire human population, which is expected to surpass 9 billion in 2050.[12] Others, however, are far less sanguine. "Arable land is disappearing," notes Lester Brown of the Earth Policy Institute. "Topsoil is eroding faster than new soil forms on perhaps a third of the world's cropland." Unless governments take urgent steps to conserve soil and water, reduce carbon emissions, and constrain population growth, he warns, soaring food prices will throw the world into chaos.[13]

As Brown sees it, the looming food shortages are a matter for universal concern; international cooperation, in his view, is the only way to prevent a potential collapse of civilization itself. But the large-scale buyers of land have drawn a very different conclusion from the situation. Private investors—many of whom regularly cite Brown's research in their own presentations[14]—see it merely as an extraordinary money-making opportunity, a chance to reap enormous gains from the expected surge in land values as supplies dwindle and demand continues to rise. "Farmland is the new gold," Euromoney magazine proclaimed in 2008; "there are not many markets left in which it would be safe to invest, but agriculture should be a safe bet."[15] For King Abdullah and other government leaders, meanwhile, the prospect of food shortages has inspired a rush to protect their own countries above all. By acquiring land in the developing world, these rulers seek to guarantee that no matter what happens, their domestic populations will be fed—even if this means that people in the supplying countries are not.

A PERSIAN GULF IMPERATIVE

The drive to secure cropland abroad has been especially pronounced among the nations of the Persian Gulf, which see such acquisitions as the only sure way to guarantee adequate food supplies for the years ahead. The combined population of Bahrain, Kuwait, Qatar, Saudi Arabia, and the United Arab Emirates (UAE) is expected to jump from 27 million in 2000 to 62 million in 2050,[16] an extraordinary increase that is unlikely to be accompanied by any increase in domestic agricultural output. At the same time, international food markets are becoming less reliable; as global warming disrupts agricultural production, exporting countries are liable to impose restrictions on food shipments just as they did in 2008. This is the impetus behind the King Abdullah Initiative and the comparable measures being adopted by the four other countries on the southern side of the Persian Gulf.

All of these plans work in a similar way: through grants or low-cost loans, government agencies subsidize efforts by private or state-owned companies to grow crops abroad and export them back to the home country. For such schemes to work, the companies need to find land that is both reasonably fertile and available for purchase or long-term leasing—a condition that usually narrows the search to Africa and other developing areas where the government is keen to attract foreign investment and willing to overlook existing claims to the land by indigenous peoples. Other attractive targets include the former Soviet Union, where immense swaths of once-productive cropland now sit fallow because of changing economic priorities, and South American countries that seek to encourage development in sparsely populated regions such as Patagonia and the Amazon.

Ethiopia, which sits relatively close to the Arabian Peninsula, has been a particularly enthusiastic partner for the Persian Gulf states. "We have vast land resources and a lot of water resources," said Aberra Deressa, Ethiopia's state minister for agriculture and rural development, at a 2009 conference hosted by Saudi Star. "If investors with potential come, we will give them land."[17] Many local protesters point out that the lands in question are already used by indigenous pastoralists—traditional cattle herders who often travel across vast distances to find fresh pasture for their livestock.[18] Ethiopian officials and foreign investors, however, insist that no one is being displaced by the foreign programs. "There is lots of land in Ethiopia, especially in the lowland areas," declared Haile Assegide, the CEO of Saudi Star. "Where we have leased, there is no settler."[19]

While Saudi Star has focused its attention on Ethiopia and firms such as Hadco have been acquiring tens of thousands of acres in Sudan, other Saudi companies are making substantial investments in parts of Asia, Europe, and South America. The state-backed group Agroinvest, for instance, reportedly intends to spend some $500 million over the next few years to establish agricultural operations in Brazil, which it has praised as a promising location for grain and poultry farming.[20] And since the King Abdullah Initiative is said to have more than $5 billion at its disposal, even more such large-scale Saudi acquisitions can be expected in the near future.

Other Persian Gulf states are similarly hurrying to secure foreign farmland that can be used to grow crops for consumption at home.[21] The small, mostly arid nation of Qatar, for example, relies on imports for as much as 90 percent of its food supplies, so it found the 2008 disruptions of international food markets extremely alarming. In response, the Qatar Investment Authority—the nation's multibillion-dollar sovereign wealth fund—established an agricultural investment arm, Hassad Food, to oversee the acquisition of farmland abroad. So far, Hassad Food has already purchased a sugar plant in Brazil capable of providing all of Qatar's sugar requirements, and a Brazilian farm that will supply 60 percent of the country's poultry and eggs. It has also concluded a $500 million deal with Sudan, acquiring 245,000 acres to grow rice and wheat for Qatari consumption. And the shopping spree is set to continue, with Qatar officials investigating assorted farming opportunities in Argentina, Australia, Brazil, Ghana, Sudan, and Turkey, among other countries.[22]

Government-backed agricultural firms in the UAE, meanwhile, now control some 700,000 acres of farmland in Sudan, which they are using to grow a variety of produce for export to the Emirates.[23] UAE-based Jenaan Investment has also secured some 100,000 acres in Egypt, with a goal of sending home 350,000 tons of wheat per year as well as corn and other crops.[24] And at least one enterprising UAE company, the state-backed Minerals Energy Commodities Holding (MEC), is even combining the pursuit of farmland with the global race for other natural resources, treating them all as part of the same operation. In Indonesia, MEC is leasing 245,000 acres near a coal mine that the firm is developing; the land will be used for cultivating rice and other crops, while a railroad that the company began building to service the mine will now be used to carry agricultural produce as well.[25]

CHINA, INDIA, AND SOUTH KOREA, TOO

Although Saudi Arabia and other Persian Gulf nations are the most avid seekers of foreign cropland, they are by no means the only countries trying to enhance national food security in this manner. Among the most conspicuous in this regard have been China, India, and South Korea. These three countries, unlike the arid nations of the Persian Gulf, have substantial cropland reserves of their own and so can obtain a significant share of their food requirements from domestic farms; nevertheless, as their populations grow, they will have to import an ever-increasing share of their food supplies. And like King Abdullah, their leaders have decided that simply buying food from international sellers is no longer a reliable option: to be secure, they must control the agricultural land itself.[26]

South Korea is in a particularly difficult bind. Although still self-sufficient in rice, it has become heavily reliant on imports for many other food products, and there is little undeveloped land remaining in the densely populated country. Accordingly, its leaders have become convinced that acquiring foreign cropland is essential.[27] "The government will give companies as much support as possible," the Ministry for Food, Agriculture, Forestry, and Fisheries proclaimed in March 2011.[28] Without identifying the companies it was aiding, the ministry indicated that some sixty South Korean firms were conducting farming operations in sixteen foreign countries by the end of 2010, harvesting approximately 87,000 metric tons of grain.[29]

A prominent South Korean company was, in fact, the first large firm to spark international concern over the "land grab" phenomenon. In 2008, the Daewoo Logistics Corporation (part of the giant Daewoo conglomerate) obtained a government lease to some 3.2 million acres of farmland in Madagascar,[30] hoping to grow some 50 percent of all corn consumed in South Korea on the large African island.[31] If the plan had been realized, Daewoo would have taken control of about half of Madagascar's arable land, displacing many small farmers and their families. But popular resentment over the deal helped spark a rebellion against Madagascar's president Marc Ravalomanana, forcing him to surrender his post in March 2009.[32] Ravalomanana's successor, Andry Rajoelina, canceled the Daewoo deal shortly after taking office. "Madagascar's land is neither for sale nor for rent," he declared emphatically.[33]

The Daewoo setback has not stopped other South Korean firms from looking to secure promising farmland abroad. In June 2008, the Sudanese ambassador to Seoul, Mohamed Salah Eldin Abbas, said that Korean companies had been granted the right to develop fully 1.7 million acres of farmland in his country.[34] Meanwhile, Hyundai Heavy Industries Company, the world's largest shipbuilder and a major component of the giant Hyundai conglomerate, has acquired tens of thousands of acres of farmland in Siberia and is planning to add more acreage in the near future.[35] Another branch of the same conglomerate, the Hyundai Corporation, is planning to buy large parcels of farmland in Brazil.[36] With strong government support, South Korean firms aim to control a combined one million acres of foreign farmland by 2018, enabling them to supply 10 percent of the country's annual imports of corn, wheat, and soybeans.[37]

For South Korea to seek overseas farmland to produce food for domestic consumption is not altogether surprising, given the country's relatively large population and limited growing area. The fact that China and India are also engaging in such activity might at first glance seem harder to explain, since they possess vast agricultural sectors and huge numbers of farmers. But the same factors that figure elsewhere—rapid population growth and the loss of domestic farmland to urbanization, soil erosion, and other forces—have now become a significant concern for the Chinese and Indian governments.

The situation in India could become especially perilous. The country's population is expected to grow by some 300 million people between 2010 and 2050, so its need for additional food will become gargantuan. At the same time, the so-called Green Revolution in crop productivity, based on high-yield grains and extensive fertilizer use, appears to be reaching its limits. Squeezed between these two forces, "India may find it extremely difficult to depend on farm land within her boundaries for our future food security needs," says Rana Kapoor, founder of Yes Bank in Mumbai. To avoid a food shortage, he argues, "it is thus imperative for policy makers of the country to seriously explore the option of transnational farmland opportunities."[38]

India's corporate leaders, both public and private, are heeding the call. The government-owned Minerals and Metals Trading Corporation of India (MMTC), for instance, is buying land across sweeping stretches of Africa to grow legumes and vegetable oil. Existing foreign food suppliers are unreliable, explains H. S. Mann, MMTC's acting chairman, "so we want to diversify in countries such as Tanzania, Ethiopia, Kenya, Malawi, and Mozambique."[39] At the same time, the privately held Karuturi Global of Bangalore—one of the world's leading suppliers of roses and other cut flowers—is also focusing on Ethiopia, where it has acquired 770,000 acres to produce rice, palm oil, and sugarcane. About one-third of this land is in Ethiopia's remote Gambela region, where Karuturi plans to spend an estimated $350 million to construct its own energy and irrigation systems.[40]

China is charting a similar course. Although China's population is not growing as fast as India's, it suffers from a severe shortage of suitable farmland: about two-thirds of its territory is arid grassland or desert, and a significant amount of arable land is being lost every year to urbanization, industrial expansion, and creeping desertification. Climate change, of course, will only worsen the situation, depriving many farming areas of adequate rainfall while inundating others through rising sea levels. So the Chinese government, too, is calling on Chinese firms to start seeking farmland abroad.[41] "The time is ripe for the country's agricultural companies to embark on a 'go outward strategy,'" Han Changfu, the minister of agriculture, declared in December 2010.[42]

China's efforts may have started slightly later than those of its competitors, but they are being carried out on an enormous scale and with blistering speed. In April 2011, just a few months after Han's "go outward" speech, China's state-run Chongqing Grain Group Company announced that it would join with other enterprises from Chongqing Municipality—now China's most populous city—to set up a $2.5 billion soybean operation in the Brazilian state of Bahia. Chongqing Grain's partners in Bahia will provide it with some 500,000 acres of land, and the company will build a processing facility capable of producing two million tons of soybean oil per year.[43] A month later, another group of Chinese companies announced an even more ambitious scheme to grow soy in Brazil: a $7 billion plan to acquire and develop farmland in the vicinity of Uruaçu, in Goiás state.[44]

Chinese companies have also sought large tracts of land in Africa, though details of these deals are sometimes hard to come by, since both the Chinese firms involved and their partner governments often seek to conceal the magnitude of the transactions. In Mozambique, for example, Chinese companies are believed to have been promised vast parcels of farmland in exchange for millions of dollars in development assistance, but specifics of the agreement have not been made public.[45] Chinese firms have also been welcomed by Robert Mugabe's regime in Zimbabwe, which is shunned by most Western governments but enjoys good relations with Beijing. Grateful for this support, the Mugabe government has given the state-owned China International Water and Electric Corporation the right to farm 250,000 acres of corn in the southern part of the country.[46] Other Chinese firms are said to be active in Benin, Cameroon, Mali, Uganda, and the Democratic Republic of the Congo.[47]

And the list of China's target countries extends far beyond Africa and Brazil. In March 2011, Beidahuang Land Cultivation Group—which functions as the corporate vehicle of China's Heilongjiang provincial government and is largely responsible for feeding that northeastern province's 38 million inhabitants—announced plans to secure 500,000 acres of farmland abroad to add to the 1.5 million acres that it manages in Heilongjiang itself.[48] With a flexible approach, Beidahuang will employ whatever strategy works best in a given country: leasing the land in some places, buying it outright in others, and setting up farming partnerships elsewhere. "In Venezuela and Zimbabwe, the Group mainly provides machinery and laborers, and takes about 20 percent of the harvest in return," explained Beidahuang chairman Sui Fengfu. "In Australia, it is mainly through the acquisition of farmland. In Brazil and Argentina, the business model involves renting land."[49] Russia and the Philippines are also on Beidahuang's list, while other Chinese companies are obtaining substantial tracts in Southeast Asia, Central Asia, and various countries of the former Soviet Union.[50]

GLOBAL AGINVESTING

For the governments of China, India, South Korea, and the Persian Gulf countries, farmland abroad is valuable primarily as a means of nourishing their own growing populations—a way to bypass unreliable grain dealers and thus promote national food security. But for many private investors around the world, foreign farmland has a different attraction: money. More and more wealthy individuals and corporate investment funds now regard arable land as a very lucrative asset, with the forthcoming land shortages providing an unprecedented opportunity for profit.

The increasing popularity of this outlook was on full display recently at the "Global AgInvesting 2011" conference, held at the luxurious Waldorf Astoria hotel in New York City. Organized by the agribusiness consulting firm Soyatech to highlight "the opportunities and challenges of investing in agriculture," the event promised to bring together "end-investors, ag-managers, academics, policy experts, and agribusiness industry executives" to discuss "the opportunities and challenges of investing in agriculture."[51] The prospect proved attractive enough to pull in representatives from hundreds of prominent firms and institutions, including Bank of America, Black River Asset Management, Credit Suisse, Deutsche Bank, GE Asset Management, IBM Retirement Funds, J. Paul Getty Trust, Merrill Lynch Wealth Management, and a host of colleges and universities.[52] At one point, a participant reported, the Waldorf's ballroom was so packed with hundreds of bankers, fund managers, speculators, and corporate farming executives that conference administrators had to warn the crowd not to block the fire exits.[53]

The 2011 Waldorf Astoria extravaganza was the third annual meeting of its sort in New York City, but investors from other parts of the world are hardly being left behind. Soyatech is also offering regional AgInvesting conferences in Switzerland, Singapore, and Abu Dhabi,[54] while *Africa Investor* magazine sponsors an "Agribusiness Investment Summit" in South Africa.[55] Animating all of these events is the conviction that prime cropland will become increasingly scarce and valuable in the coming years, providing an unparalleled source of income to those in the know. "Bankers and fund managers are scrambling to build up rural expertise in response to rocketing investor demand to buy entire farms as an inflation hedge," noted a Reuters report on the 2010 AgInvesting Europe conference. "Investment funds worldwide have put an estimated $15 billion to $20 billion in agriculture globally, and interest is also growing from ultra-rich investors and pension funds, which see farmland as tangible, strategic assets."[56]

Many advocates of farmland buying contend that agricultural property is not only a valuable addition to a portfolio of more conventional assets, but is superior in many respects to other resource investments. Paul Kanitra, a consultant on agricultural securities, argues that forthcoming shortages of tillable land could be as significant as the expected contraction of global petroleum output: "The term 'peak soil' would soon become as common as 'peak oil.'" Indeed, he says, hydrocarbons could someday be replaced by renewable sources of energy, whereas the need for food will never disappear, so farmland "will prove to be of greater long-term strategic value than oil and gas."[57] Investment analyst Doug Hawkins, of London-based Hardman and Company, agrees: "By 2050, it is possible to argue that food-producing land might have a superior value to all other asset classes."[58]

To satisfy the explosion of investor interest in cropland, various banks and investment firms have been setting up special accounts devoted to acquiring agricultural properties around the world. Dow Chemical, for example, has established a $6 billion subsidiary, Black River Asset Management, to undertake large-scale investments in farmland overseas. Black River now controls 125,000 acres of productive land in South America and is planning to make equally large land acquisitions in Asia.[59] Another large asset management firm, the BlackRock group of New York, has introduced its own farmland investment fund, which raised more than $450 million within a year.[60]

A particularly aggressive company in this field is Emergent Asset Management of England, which has as much as $750 million at its disposal, and whose founder and CEO, Susan Payne, is regularly featured as a speaker at AgInvesting conferences. Payne's views on global food availability combine the nineteenth-century precepts of Thomas Malthus—who predicted that overpopulation would inevitably lead to mass starvation—with twenty-first-century statistics showing declining water levels in China and India, increasing desertification from global warming, and, of course, global population levels rising by some 80 million people per year. All of these factors, Payne explains, could lead to significant food shortages by 2020, giving anyone who controls large areas of farmland the chance to accrue colossal profits.[61]

The arguments offered by Payne, Hawkins, Kanitra, and other promoters of farmland investing have clearly proven persuasive for many hedge funds, pension funds, and wealthy individuals across the globe. In a recent study of foreign cropland purchases, the World Bank noted that such acquisitions averaged approximately 10 million acres per year until 2008, but soared to an estimated 110 million acres in 2009—an area the size of Sweden.[62] And if the Global AgInvesting conferences, which attract larger crowds with every annual gathering, are any indication, the cropland-purchase numbers for the coming years are sure to be higher still.

"THE NEW SCRAMBLE FOR AFRICA"

In addition to highlighting the overall rise of farmland purchases abroad, the World Bank also examined the geographical breakdown of all these operations—both those driven solely by investment motives and those carried out by governments concerned about food security. As of 2010, the World Bank revealed, fully half of cropland acquisition projects involved locations in sub-Saharan Africa. What's more, because the African acquisitions tended to be larger than those elsewhere, when measured by land area they accounted for an even higher proportion of the total: roughly two out of every three acres involved in major land-buying operations around the world.[63] To a very considerable extent, then, any discussion of the race for land is a discussion of Africa.[64]

Africa beckons as a prime farmland-buying locale for several reasons. Whereas most other farming regions, including those in North America, Europe, and Asia, are already intensely cultivated, Africa possesses large untilled areas that can be acquired at comparatively low prices. Most African governments are anxious to attract foreign investment and are therefore very accommodating to potential buyers. Moreover, while global warming is likely to reduce the amount of rainfall in some African states, it is expected to bring increased precipitation to others, boosting the productivity of their croplands. By choosing wisely, therefore, savvy investors can gain control over vast parcels of valuable farmland at bargain-basement prices.[65]

Susan Payne's Emergent fund is among several companies that are placing particular emphasis on Africa when planning their cropland acquisitions. "Africa is the final frontier," Payne declared at the 2009 Global AgInvesting conference in New York City. "It's the one continent that remains relatively unexploited."[66] Describing Africa's attractions in a *New York Times* interview, Payne similarly noted that its "land values are very, very inexpensive, compared to other agriculture-based economies." Moreover, she said, "there's accessible labor. And there's good logistics—wide open roads, good truck transport, sea transport."[67] Citing Africa's extraordinarily low costs and excellent growing conditions, Emergent promises to achieve an unusually high rate of return on investment—exceeding 25 percent per year.[68]

For African farmers themselves, of course, the cheerful language of asset managers conceals a grimmer reality. Payne's mention of "accessible labor," for instance, is a thin euphemism for massive joblessness and underemployment, while the continent's "wide open roads" say less about Africa's investment in infrastructure than about its pervasive poverty. Many local activists would also contest Payne's description of Africa as "unexploited,"[69] noting the lands acquired by outsiders are often already used by pastoralists and other indigenous peoples employing traditional agricultural techniques. Such objections, though, carry little weight with investors from the outside.[70]

According to a July 2009 report in *Der Spiegel*, Emergent now controls more than 370,000 acres of prime African farmland, with its largest holdings located in South Africa, Zambia, and Mozambique.[71] The company is also reported to have acquired land in Angola, Botswana, Swaziland, and the Democratic Republic of the Congo.[72] Approximately 30 percent of this land is owned outright by Emergent, and the rest is secured by contracts that will last for generations. "We only operate in countries where we can have clear land title," says Payne. "If we can't get this, or we don't have a 99-year lease from the government then we won't operate in that country." Brushing off accusations that her company is engaging in hostile "land grabs," Payne insists that "we are seeing amenable terms because local groups, including governments, want us there."[73]

Middle Eastern and South Asian land buyers also find Africa particularly attractive, for both geographical and historical reasons. Sudan and Ethiopia are just across the Red Sea from the Arabian Peninsula, and East African ports on the Indian Ocean provide easy access to the South Asian subcontinent. Arab and Indian merchants have been plying these waters for thousands of years, so there is a long history of business ties—and, often, family connections—stretching across the region. For Arab investors, there is the added appeal that Islam has made significant inroads in Africa, creating cultural and religious links as well. This is especially evident in northern Sudan, an Arab Muslim nation that is receiving significant attention from the Saudi government.

As state-owned companies and private investors from across the globe rush to lock up African farmland, some observers, invoking the continent's colonial past, describe the situation as "the new scramble for Africa."[74] Unlike nineteenth-century European colonization, this new wave of land acquisition is mostly being carried out with the support of African national governments themselves, who see in it a chance to replace subsistence agriculture with high-payoff cash crops. Local residents of the territories in question, however, often believe that their traditional land rights are being trampled upon, and react with anger and resistance.

It would be impossible to fully describe every facet of this ongoing struggle, both because it is so extensive and because many of the land transactions are conducted in secrecy. A few examples, however, can help to suggest its magnitude.

Democratic Republic of the Congo: Eager to attract foreign agricultural investment, Congolese authorities have awarded vast swaths of land to foreign investors, often running roughshod over the rights of poor farmers and indigenous groups who have long inhabited the areas involved. In 2009, the government promised an astonishing 7 million acres to a Chinese firm, ZTE Corporation, for a palm-oil plantation (though only a fraction of that total is likely to be developed); two years later, it gave some 1.2 million acres to a Malaysian firm, Atama Plantation, for the same purpose.[75] Congo's minister of agriculture, meanwhile, has ceded control over 200,000 acres of prime farmland to a South African company that plans to use them for growing corn, rice, and soybeans.[76] Local farmers have protested these transactions, but to no avail.

Kenya: In a bid to promote economic development, the government of Kenya is encouraging foreign investment in the Tana River delta, one of the country's most pristine areas and a major wild bird habitat. Although long occupied by subsistence farmers, the delta region is now being cleared to make room for plantations of sugarcane and jatropha, a shrub whose nuts are used to produce biofuels. A Canadian company, Bedford Biofuels, has been given 25,000 acres to grow jatropha, while a British firm, G4 Industries, has received 70,000 acres toward the same goal.[77] In exchange for Qatar's offer to finance a new deepwater port on the Indian Ocean, the Kenyan government has also awarded 100,000 acres to various companies from Qatar for growing fruits and vegetables.[78] But no matter how enthusiastically promoted by officials in Nairobi, these moves are provoking increasing hostility from inhabitants of the delta. "We know there are people who have sold our land when it isn't theirs to sell," said one of the delta residents. "They are criminals, and we will fight them, with guns and sticks."[79]

Liberia: Long embroiled in internal strife, Liberia is now opening its land for agricultural development, particularly palm-oil production. Sime Darby, the world's biggest publicly listed planter and one of Malaysia's leading corporations, has acquired a sixty-three-year lease to 545,000 acres for this purpose and plans to spend some $3.1 billion developing the land.[80] The venture is strongly supported by the Liberian government but has provoked vocal opposition from local residents, who maintain that some of the land in question has long been occupied by their tribal ancestors. "We are concerned and greatly disappointed over the continuous lack of protection and respect for our distinct ways of life, traditions, and customs," said a statement written by residents of Grand Cape Mount County, the site of one of Sime Darby's plantations.[81]

Mali: In a multimillion-dollar scheme to produce rice for his own country, Libyan dictator Muammar el-Qaddafi acquired 250,000 acres of land in the inland Niger River delta of Mali and constructed a vast canal system for irrigation.[82] The undertaking, known as the Malibya Project, required displacing hundreds of local farmers and depriving many others of an essential water supply, but the Malian government— long dependent on Libya for economic assistance—has allowed the work to proceed.[83] "We are responsible for developing Mali," explained one government bureaucrat. "If the civil society does not agree with the way we are doing it, they can go jump in a lake."[84] Mali's slavish subservience to Qaddafi has left the country in difficult straits, however: with the rebellion in Libya and Qaddafi's death, Libya has been unable to meet its financial obligations, putting the Malibya project at risk.

Senegal: Hoping to attract significant foreign investment, Senegalese government officials are negotiating a lease that would provide Saudi corporations with up to 1 million acres of prime farmland, much of it in the fertile Senegal River valley.[85] One of the major parties in these talks is Foras International Investment Company, a Saudi-based business partly owned by the Bin Laden Group—the giant construction firm established by Osama bin Laden's father. Foras is seeking to secure 370,000 to 500,000 acres of Senegalese land to grow rice, much of it intended for export to Saudi Arabia.[86] As elsewhere, government officials insist that the parcels in question are unoccupied (and thus available for development by outsiders), but many observers disagree. "The land is not empty," said Lamine Ndiaye, the head of economic justice at Oxfam Senegal; it is "occupied by the community, it's just that they're not recognized as owners of that land."[87]

Many similar farmland-acquisition projects are under way in other African countries as well: an inventory conducted by the International Food Policy Research Institute in 2009 included Angola, Cameroon, Egypt, Gabon, Malawi, Mozambique, Nigeria, Tanzania, Uganda, and Zimbabwe among the nations being targeted by foreign investors.[88] Even that tally is incomplete, since many of the deals carried out by Emergent Assets and other private investment funds have not been publicly reported. And despite all the millions of acres already awarded to foreign governments and corporations, the new scramble for Africa is by no means over yet: as the advisory firm Dalberg Global Development told investors at the 2010 Agribusiness Investment Summit, they are confident that there is "specifically a huge amount of arable land in Africa" still available and untapped.[89]

BACK TO THE USSR

While the African countryside has so far attracted the greatest attention from private investors and specialized government agencies, the rush to secure arable land is also making a significant impact on other areas of the world. Among these, perhaps the most intriguing recent development is the massive surge of agribusiness funds flowing into Russia and other states of the former Soviet Union (FSU), as well as into various former Soviet allies in eastern Europe. A number of major investment firms, such as New York–based Morgan Stanley, have now bought or leased immense parcels of cropland in Russia and Ukraine, while agriculture officials from Qatar and other Middle Eastern countries have also sought land in the region.[90] Although these transactions have not received as much publicity as similar endeavors in Africa or South America, they represent an important and growing aspect of the global "land grab" phenomenon. In 2009, according to the detailed World Bank study, eastern Europe and the FSU accounted for the third largest share of all cropland sales by area, behind only Africa and East/South Asia.[91]

Unlike in Africa, where farmland awarded to foreign buyers is usually touted as uncultivated, "virgin" territory, much of the land now being traded in the FSU had once been intensely used. During the Soviet era, it had belonged to large farms—either state run or collectively owned— that carried out agricultural operations in accordance with centralized planning. When the USSR broke up and communist economic policies were abandoned, these industrial-scale farms frequently were divided into small plots, typically of under ten acres apiece, and distributed to the former farm workers. Yet making a decent living on those plots often proved extremely difficult in the harsh economic climate of the post-Soviet era, when loans were hard to come by and few could afford to invest in modern agricultural equipment. As time went on, more and more farmers—tired of the endless drudgery and meager profits—abandoned their fields and moved away to the cities, leaving the land lying fallow. It is this history of collapse and rural decay that has now provided an opening for foreign investors, who can reaggregate the small plots into large corporate farms and employ high-tech farming techniques to ensure substantial crop yields.[92]

Aside from the cheapness of the neglected countryside—several acres of prime Russian farmland can be acquired for a few hundred dollars, a small fraction of what they would cost in Europe or the United States[93]— foreign buyers have also been attracted to the FSU by the extraordinary fertility of the soil. Russia and Ukraine both possess colossal expanses of chernozem, or black earth: a soil rich in humus, the dark organic matter produced by the decomposition of plants. Land of this type has a high capacity to retain moisture, making it ideal for growing wheat and other grains. Indeed, as Eleonore Demy of Agence France-Presse puts it, the "appeal of black earth" has now overshadowed even the lure of "black gold"—Russia's massive reserves of petroleum—that had previously drawn foreign investors to the Russian market.[94]

One company that has placed particularly large bets on Russian cropland is Black Earth Farming, headquartered in Jersey of the British Channel Islands. Founded by Michel Orloff, a former director of the Carlyle Group's Moscow office, BEF began buying up rural Russian properties in 2006; half a decade later, it controlled approximately 740,000 acres, an area bigger than Rhode Island. "In Moscow, they said I was crazy for going into agriculture," Orloff said at one of the company's farms outside Podlesny. "Now, they all envy us."[95] Using modern agricultural techniques, BEF has nearly doubled the yield of the fields under its ownership,[96] and it is considering additional land acquisitions.[97]

A dozen or so other entrepreneurial companies have also been active in the region, including Alpcot Agro of Sweden (which now controls about 420,000 acres of Russian cropland) and Trigon Agri of Denmark (approximately 250,000 acres).[98] According to one report, total foreign investment in Russian agriculture jumped from $156 million in

2005 to $862 million in 2008, an increase of more than 450 percent in just three years.[99] Many analysts believe that such investment will only continue to grow, given the rising international demand for grain and the ready availability of prodigious quantities of fallow land. A recent report in the *Moscow Times* noted that as much as 60 percent of Russian black earth—some 120 million acres—is currently idle, and the total amount of Russian land reserves suitable for cultivation is greater still.[100]

Other eastern European countries of the old Soviet bloc are also now attracting major investors. Landkom International, for example, now controls 182,000 acres of black-earth farmland in Ukraine, while AgroGeneration has already acquired 110,000 acres in the country and plans to double its holdings there.[101] The financial services giant Morgan Stanley, a company better known for managing stock offerings and corporate mergers, has also bought itself 100,000 Ukrainian acres.[102] And across the Ukrainian border, the former Soviet ally Romania is drawing its own share of praise from real estate analysts for its fertile soil, good climate, and unusually low land prices.[103] As a result, according to one estimate, nearly 2.5 million acres of Romanian farmland— approximately 12 percent of the country's entire arable territory—is now in foreign hands.[104]

Although the greatest interest in FSU farmland so far has come from private European and American corporations, some of the major Middle Eastern governments are also keenly aware of the region's potential. In 2009, for example, the president of Ukraine arranged an official visit by a delegation from the UAE, offering to lease them as much as 250,000 acres.[105] The following year, the head of Qatar's food security efforts announced that his agency was planning to put upwards of $100 million into Ukrainian agriculture.[106] Qatar has also been looking into potential investments in the former Soviet republic of Moldova, while UAE authorities have been investigating agricultural opportunities in Romania and Bulgaria.[107]

Local opposition to such deals in the former Soviet republics has been much more muted than in Africa, but it is hardly nonexistent. Russia and Ukraine have strong agrarian roots, and many people there resent the intrusion of foreign companies—especially Western corporations—into what they see as a core part of the national identity. Perhaps hoping to forestall more vocal protests, Russian and Ukrainian governments have recently introduced legislation barring foreigners from buying land outright; local farmers will still be allowed to lease their land to investors from abroad, but only under strict controls.[108] "The main task of land reform is to enable Ukrainian citizens to feel like masters of their own land," declared Mykola Prysyazhnyuk, Ukraine's minister of agriculture.[109]

"WIN-WIN" SOLUTION OR TRIGGER FOR CONFLICT?

State-backed and private investors who acquire farmland abroad invariably proclaim that their projects benefit not just the foreigners who ultimately consume the food grown on those farms, but also the population of the hosting region. "It's a win-win solution," says Wang Yunkun, deputy director of the Agriculture and Rural Affairs Committee of China's National People's Congress, regarding Chinese plans to set up farming operations outside the country. "Countries in South America, for example, have arable land and need our technology and investment, and they welcome our companies."[110] George Aboagye, director of Ghana's Investment Promotion Centre, uses similar phrasing when discussing potential Ghanaian investments by Qatar's Hassad Food. "We have a lot of water and land but we need to build dams to save wasted water. As Qatar is interested in food preservation and production, together we can create a win-win situation for both."[111]

Central to the "win-win" argument is the claim that foreign agricultural projects bring fresh capital and modern technology to the target countries, thereby generating new jobs and promoting overall rural development. "Without private pools of capital like we are providing, there will not be the jump-start to get Africa growing rapidly in agriculture," says Susan Payne of Emergent Asset Management. "There is a lot of enthusiasm for this and there should be."[112] Emergent's farming operations typically make use of advanced agricultural techniques and high-yield "miracle" seeds, making them more productive than indigenous farms in the area. If those techniques are imitated by the surrounding African farmers, the argument goes—and if sufficient capital is made available to them to buy the required seeds and machinery—then foreign ventures like Emergent's could have a ripple effect, boosting incomes throughout the region.

Many observers, however, are skeptical about such rosy scenarios. They note that large-scale land purchases represent a significant disruption of traditional farming and herding communities, and therefore risk causing social displacement and unrest. If the acquisitions are not handled very carefully, says Sindiso Ngwenya, chairperson of the Common Market for Eastern and Southern Africa, "you end up with an enclave economy, prosperous on cheap labor in the countryside but without integrating the locals."[113] Such privileged enclaves, placed in the middle of still-impoverished rural communities, are certain to engender resentment among residents who were promised the benefits of foreign investment but find themselves no better off than before.

The question of whether farmland purchases are indeed giving a "jump-start" to agricultural development in low-income countries, as Payne and other boosters maintain, was a key focus of the detailed examination of such investments that the World Bank carried out in 2010. The report's findings were not encouraging. Theoretically, the bank noted, foreign investments in farmland could well result in positive outcomes, "by generating jobs, providing social services, increasing knowledge, and improving the asset base of the local population."[114] But the study determined that investors in farmland often did not follow through on promises that they had made to local governments and communities. Under those circumstances, the study concluded, many of the projects "failed to live up to expectations and, instead of generating sustainable benefits . . . left local people worse off than they would have been without the investment."[115]

An even bigger problem with many instances of farmland acquisition, as we have seen, is that territories presented to foreign investors as "virgin" or "uninhabited" are rarely actually empty or unused. More frequently than not, they are occupied by pastoralists or other indigenous peoples, who may lack official title to the land but have been living there for centuries and using the fields for a wide variety of purposes. What's more, these peoples often adhere to traditional belief systems that view the land as sacred, and so perceive any attempt by foreigners to fence it off as a threat not only to their livelihoods but also to their very identity.

The discrepancy between official assurances and on-the-ground reality is particularly evident in areas such as the Gambela region of southwestern Ethiopia, a major focus of the Ethiopian government's efforts to attract foreign agricultural investment. All told, some 7.5 million acres in the region have been promised to foreigners—an area the size of Belgium. "Everywhere we want to increase the amount of land to be leased," explains agriculture minister Aberra Deressa. "We have abundant land available."[116] But the residents of Gambela say the land is not vacant, but properly belongs to them under customary land rights. "There is no empty land in Gambela without a history," says one critic of the government's land giveaways. "They can't sell that land, it's not theirs. That land is ancestral land."[117] Clashes between local farmers and government troops sent to force them off the land have already led to numerous casualties, and more such confrontations are likely. "You cannot speak freely about the land issue now," one Gambela resident told the BBC. "You can be arrested or even killed for this."[118]

Bloodshed also seems imminent in Kenya's Tana River delta, where the central government is awarding large parcels of land to foreign companies for jatropha plantations. "Tana Delta is in chaos," says Francis Kagema of the conservation group Nature Kenya, bluntly summing up the situation. The delta's original inhabitants "have lived here for hundreds of years, but suddenly someone writes up a piece of paper and they're [made into] squatters on their own land." Nobody in Nairobi has taken notice, Kagema says, because until now the delta residents have only conducted nonviolent protests. But when the foreign investors arrive to "pick up their shares with their bits of paperwork . . . it will be war. The day is coming."[119]

Similar stories are emerging in other parts of the world where large tracts of supposedly uninhabited land are being given away in willful disregard of the populations who do, in fact, inhabit those areas. News articles collected by GRAIN, a nongovernmental organization based in Barcelona, tell of clashes between rural villagers and government agents in a score of countries, including Liberia, Madagascar, Mali, Sudan, Tanzania, and the Philippines.[120] Indeed, violence is likely to be an increasingly conspicuous feature of the "land grab" phenomenon, as more and more people are expelled to make room for foreign agricultural operations in impoverished, hunger-stricken areas. Land ownership has always been a source of conflict in the countryside, especially where notions of customary land rights collide with formal decrees handed down by distant, often suspect government bureaucracies; when the official new owners are foreigners who appear completely oblivious to the historic claims and customs of the people they are displacing, the hostility will be far greater still.

For all the importance and forthcoming scarcity of oil, gas, and vital minerals, perhaps the fiercest resource struggle in the coming decades will involve food and the land it is grown on. Although billions of people in the more affluent, climate-blessed areas of the world are likely to have their nutritional requirements met in the years ahead, billions more are destined to find themselves in countries too short of water or arable land to satisfy their basic needs. For anyone in this latter category, buying up farmland in more agriculturally favorable areas of the world may seem like an appealing option; hence the King Abdullah Initiative for Saudi Agricultural Investment Abroad and similar efforts by countries ranging from China to the UAE. This apparent solution, however, is likely to prove ephemeral. As the global climate continues to deteriorate and food becomes less abundant, it is doubtful that people in Ethiopia and elsewhere will allow the bounty of their fields to keep being shipped to other countries when their own children are starving. Exactly when and where the eruption will come cannot be foreseen, but it is hard to imagine that these pent-up pressures will remain dormant for long.

8 ▸ SHAPING THE COURSE OF HISTORY

The global pursuit of vital natural resources has long shaped human history, providing the impetus for campaigns of exploration and conquest stretching back across the millennia. Ancient Rome continually added new colonies to satisfy the ever-increasing food and material requirements of central Italy, while the great European empires sent fleets of sailing ships to foreign territories in search of gold, silver, spices, furs, timber, and a host of other commodities for the homeland. For a few decades in the twentieth century, from the rise of fascism in the 1930s to the collapse of the Soviet Union in 1991, resource concerns became overshadowed by ideological strife as the main cause of international conflict. But now the importance of natural resources has reasserted itself, and as time goes on the race for what's left will play an increasingly dominant role in world affairs.

To see the signs of this intensifying struggle, one needs only to open a major daily newspaper. Virtually every day brings more articles about territorial disputes in resource-rich areas, more coverage of bidding wars over remote oil fields and mineral mines, and more debates about the environmental risk of offshore drilling and the proper regulatory response. The *Deepwater Horizon* disaster of April 20, 2010—a direct consequence of the race for what's left—dominated U.S. and international news for that entire summer, until the oil leak was finally capped in August. Just a month later, in September 2010, came prominent headlines about China's ban on the export of rare earth elements, a category of minerals that few people had heard of until then. Likewise, the hydraulic fracturing technique for extracting natural gas from shale deposits was once rarely discussed outside of industry circles, but in 2010 stories of toxic chemical leaks in rural Pennsylvania had begun to attract national attention, and by the spring of 2011 states across the USA (and countries around the world) were debating whether or not to permit the practice.

And this is only the beginning. As the race for what's left gains momentum, it will intrude with greater force into world affairs, threatening the survival of animal species, local communities, giant corporations, and entire nations. The global economy as it currently stands cannot grow and prosper without an increasing supply of numerous critical resources—but acquiring these materials will pose an ever-greater threat to the safety and stability of human society and the natural world. Only if we abandon the race altogether, focusing instead on developing renewable resources and maximizing efficiency, can we hope to avoid calamity on a global scale.

THE END OF "EASY" EVERYTHING

In February 2005, David O'Reilly, the chairman and CEO of Chevron, startled participants at an annual oil-industry conference in Houston by declaring that their business was at an epochal turning point. After more than a hundred years during which the global availability of petroleum had always kept pace with rising world demand, he said, "Oil is no longer in plentiful supply. The time when we could count on cheap oil and even cheaper natural gas is clearly ending."[1] In widely distributed advertisements, Chevron then put the matter in even starker terms: "The era of easy oil is over."

A closer look at O'Reilly's speech shows that he was less interested in defining a momentous historic transition than in lobbying for more favorable government policies and reduced environmental regulation. Nevertheless, his description of the global situation has been widely embraced as an explanation for prevailing energy trends. The *Wall Street Journal*, for example, recently summed up a story on the rise of unconventional petroleum in Saudi Arabia with the headline, "Facing Up to the End of 'Easy Oil.'" As the paper explained, "Saudi Arabia became the world's top oil producer by tapping its vast reserves of easy-to-drill, high-quality light oil. But as demand for energy grows and fields of 'easy oil' around the world start to dry up, the Saudis are turning to a much tougher source: the billions of barrels of heavy oil trapped beneath the surface."[2]

The impact of the changeover from "easy oil" to tougher alternatives is partly financial: extracting light crude in Saudi Arabia had once been accomplished for a few dollars per barrel, whereas making a barrel of usable liquid from the sulfurous heavy oil can cost as much as $60 or $70.[3] But the pursuit of new petroleum sources to replace the exhausted "easy" deposits also has other costs, such as a growing reliance on oil acquired from countries at war or from nations controlled by corrupt dictators. And as the *Deepwater Horizon* disaster in the Gulf of Mexico demonstrates, the rush to exploit hard-to-reach oil reserves at the outer limits of current technology also carries tremendous environmental risks. Any future drilling mishap on the frontiers of oil exploration— whether in the fragile Arctic or the offshore areas of Brazil—is likely to prove just as devastating.

The outlook for other types of hydrocarbons is similarly problematic, since "easy" sources of supply are running out for them as well. Although many analysts have hailed the tremendous potential of shale gas deposits, for example, few would claim that the hydraulic fracturing technology used to extract natural gas from these formations is simple or trouble-free. "Shale gas is also tough energy," Daniel Gross wrote in *Newsweek*, noting the risk that chemical solvents used in the "fracking" process could filter into underground aquifers, causing severe environmental damage.[4]

Coal, too, is becoming increasingly more difficult and dangerous to extract. In the American West, many formerly prolific coal deposits have been exhausted, forcing miners to dig more deeply into the earth—increasing the risk of cave-ins and seismic jolts known as "bounces," since less and less stone is left to carry the weight of the mountains above. "Typically, where you have problems with bounces is where cover depth exceeds 1,800 feet," observed Kim McCarter, a professor of mining engineering at the University of Utah.[5] In August 2007, six miners and three rescuers were killed following an underground tremor at one such ultra-deep mine, located in Huntington, Utah. "The days of easy, shallow coal are gone," said James Kohler, chief of the solid minerals branch of the federal Bureau of Land Management in Utah, in the aftermath of the tragedy. "By necessity, we're going deeper."[6]

And what is true of oil, gas, and coal is also true of many other natural resources necessary for modern industry, including iron, copper, cobalt, and nickel. "With Easy Nickel Fading Fast, Miners Go After the Tough Stuff," read one characteristic headline in the *Wall Street Journal*, describing the ongoing mining difficulties on the South Pacific island of New Caledonia.[7] At one time, New Caledonia's ore had been so rich—as much as 15 percent nickel—that miners could simply dig it out with pickaxes and haul it away on donkeys. Those reserves are long gone, however, and the mine's current owner, the Brazilian mining giant Vale, has been left trying to extract the valuable metal from ores that contain less than 2 percent nickel. This requires treating the rough ore with acid under intense heat and pressure—an inherently costly and risky process.[8] Massive acid spills have occurred on several occasions, delaying the opening of Vale's $4 billion nickel refinery. Adding to the company's problems, local indigenous groups have repeatedly stormed the site, demanding that Vale halt its operations and restore the original forested landscape.[9] When, and whether, the project will be completed is still uncertain.

Even food production, as we have seen, is experiencing a transition from "easy" to "tough" sources of supply. With most of the desirable cropland in Europe, Asia, and the Americas already in the possession of

well-established farmers and agribusiness, the companies and governments searching for more lands to till are turning to less developed, less
stable areas such as Sudan, Liberia, and the Philippines. These countries
may have investor-friendly central governments, but their populations
are hardly eager to surrender large swaths of their traditional territory
to outsiders, so such projects are always at risk of disturbances and
protests—such as those that already drove Daewoo out of Madagascar
and are currently roiling the Gambela region of Ethiopia.

As easy-to-access reserves of all these various natural resources disappear, the price of basic commodities will rise, producing extreme
hardship for the poor and requiring lifestyle changes—sometimes quite
significant ones—from those of greater means. The increased cost of
gasoline, for example, has already forced some Americans to curb their
discretionary driving, affecting suburban commerce and tourism-related
industries. The rising price of heating fuel is compelling home owners
to lower the temperature on their thermostats and to invest in energy-
saving insulation. Aging gas guzzlers are giving way to smaller, more
fuel-efficient vehicles; new homes, too, are smaller on average than those
built in the previous decades. New factories, schools, stores, and office
buildings are likewise being designed with energy efficiency in mind to
a much greater extent than before.

The end of easy oil is also closely linked to rising food prices. The
cost of corn, rice, wheat, and other key staples doubled or tripled in
2008, producing riots around the world and leading to the collapse of
Haiti's government; then, after a brief retreat, food prices rose again in
2010 and 2011, reaching record highs and sparking a fresh round of
protests. Analysts have given several reasons for this alarming trend,
including soaring global demand, the scarcity of cropland, and pro-
longed drought in many parts of the world (widely attributed to global
climate change).[10] But according to a World Bank analysis, the catastrophic 2008 spike, at least, was largely driven by rising energy costs.
The report notes that "the increase in oil prices raised the price of fuels
to power machinery and irrigation systems; it also raised the price of
fertilizer and other chemicals that are energy-intensive to produce."

With fuel, fertilizer, and chemicals accounting for as much as 34 percent of the cost of producing corn in the United States, a threefold increase in the price of petroleum—as occurred between 2005 and 2008—was bound to have a powerful impact on the price of food.[11]

Even if it is technically feasible to produce enough grains, vegetables, and meat to feed the planet's growing population, most analysts believe that food prices will remain stubbornly high in the decades to come—causing malnutrition and starvation for hundreds of millions of people unable to afford the rising costs, and profoundly affecting world affairs. Most middle-income people will be able to adjust to increases in the price of oil, coal, copper, iron, and so forth by making do with less, but steady and substantial increases in the price of food are certain to produce widespread suffering among the poor and trigger periodic explosions of rage. This is evident, for example, in the wave of antigovernment protests that swept through Arab countries in the spring of 2011: though they were propelled primarily by political concerns, resentment over rising food prices also fueled the tumult. "The government is humiliating us, they are raising the price of sugar," explained one protester at an early demonstration in Algiers. "We have to pay the rent, electricity, water, sugar, and oil. We are all poor."[12]

Skyrocketing commodity prices are among the most visible effects of the end of "easy" resources, and they will be felt by virtually everyone on the planet. But the transition away from an easy-resource world will not only affect individuals: it will also set the stage for ferocious competition between major corporations and for perilous wrangling among rival nation-states. These struggles, too, will shape the course of history.

WINNERS AND LOSERS

As global supplies of raw materials dwindle and developing the planet's remaining reserves becomes riskier and more expensive, only a handful of giant resource firms are likely to secure control of enough exploitable deposits to prosper and thrive. All others will shrink, go bankrupt, or become absorbed by the more powerful companies. For nation-states, the fight for resources has equally high stakes: those that retain access to adequate supplies of critical materials will flourish, while those unable to do so will experience hardship and decline. The competition among the various powers, therefore, will be ruthless, unrelenting, and severe. Every key player in the race for what's left will do whatever it can to advance its own position, while striving without mercy to eliminate or subdue all the others.

The corporate crisis that engulfed BP after the *Deepwater Horizon* disaster provides an early but telling indication of how this process is likely to unfold. At the time of the explosion, BP was listed by *Fortune* magazine as the fourth largest publicly held corporation in the entire world, with 2009 revenues of $367 billion.[13] Yet as soon as the extent of the damage caused by the oil spill became known, many on Wall Street began to speak of the company's imminent demise.[14] In fact, with BP liable not only for cleanup costs in the Gulf but also for punitive damages on every barrel of oil spilled as a result of its reputed negligence—charges that conceivably could run as high as $50 billion—an outright bankruptcy did not appear implausible.[15] And although BP has so far managed to preserve itself, it is significantly weakened, having had to sell off many of its oil and natural gas assets in order to raise cash to settle various claims and lawsuits.[16] Whether the company will come out of the entire episode as an independent major corporation still remains to be seen.

The cutthroat behavior of BP's principal competitors in the months after the explosion is particularly revealing. At first, the other major oil firms working in the Gulf of Mexico offered some support to BP's efforts to plug the leaking well, aware that if public opinion turned against deep-offshore drilling it would affect their operations as well. As soon as Congress started investigating the disaster, however, they rushed to present BP as a willful villain in the case, further weakening the battered company. "We would not have drilled the well the way they did," said Rex W. Tillerson, the chief executive of ExxonMobil, at a June 2010 hearing on the Gulf of Mexico spill. "It certainly appears that not all the standards that we would recommend or that we would employ were in place," declared John S. Watson, the chairman of Chevron. "It's not a well that we would have drilled in that mechanical setup," avowed Marvin E. Odum, the president of Shell.[17]

The executives' grandstanding hardly meant that their companies wanted nothing whatsoever to do with BP. On the contrary, keen to exploit BP's plight, at the height of the crisis several of its competitors apparently considered the possibility of acquiring BP outright—evidently believing that it could be bought at a bargain-basement price. According to various reports, ExxonMobil and Royal Dutch Shell both considered making an offer for the struggling company, with ExxonMobil going so far as to ask the Obama administration to provide preliminary approval for such an acquisition.[18] (The White House is said to have given its agreement.)[19] Though ExxonMobil and Shell eventually decided not to go ahead with takeover proceedings, neither firm has ruled out such a step for the future, so they remain ready to snap up BP if it runs into further economic or legal difficulties.[20]

In the meantime, even if no company has yet made a bid for BP as a whole, many have eagerly exploited its need to urgently raise vast amounts of cash. In what has been described as a feeding frenzy by savage vultures, many of BP's competitors have come away with some of its most prized oil and gas fields—often at prices far lower than those resources would have commanded if sold in a more orderly fashion.[21] Over the course of just a few months in 2010, the assets sold by BP included its oil fields in Colombia, an exploration concession in Egypt, hydrocarbon deposits in the United States and Canada, and a majority stake in Pan American Energy, the second largest energy company in Argentina.[22] The series of divestments netted BP nearly $18 billion for its immediate needs—helping it pay for the cleanup of the Gulf of Mexico, but depriving it of many billions in future profits.

The image of vultures gathering for a feast is equally applicable to recent developments in the mineral fields of sub-Saharan Africa, where a multitude of mining firms are fighting for control over the handful of large projects now getting under way. As we have seen, these firms show little compunction about acquiring valuable ore deposits with a dubious past: when corrupt Guinean officials took away half of the mammoth Simandou iron mine from Rio Tinto, for example, Vale did not hesitate to add that land to its own portfolio. Similar machinations have occurred in the Democratic Republic of the Congo, where government officials seized copper mines belonging to First Quantum Minerals of Canada and then sold them, through various circuitous and suspect means, to the Eurasian Natural Resources Corporation of Kazakhstan.[23] First Quantum is now suing ENRC in the British Virgin Islands, where some of these shadowy transactions took place, but few analysts believe the Canadian firm will ever regain control of its Congolese properties.[24]

In addition to fighting one another, private companies such as BP, Shell, Vale, and Rio Tinto are also increasingly coming into conflict with state-owned enterprises from China, Russia, and other major powers. In these sorts of collisions, the private firms must contend not only with well-financed competitors but also with agencies of the state—as demonstrated, for instance, by Shell's bitter experience in Russia. In 1994, while Boris Yeltsin was president, Shell acquired a production-sharing agreement for the Sakhalin-2 oil and natural gas field in Russia's Far East and proceeded to spend an estimated $20 billion on essential infrastructure.[25] But when Yeltsin was replaced by Vladimir Putin in 2000, Russian officials sought to bring the project under state control. Seizing Shell's facilities outright could have jeopardized Moscow's other dealings with the West, so Putin adopted a different approach: he unleashed Russia's environmental protection agency, Rosprirodnadzor, upon the enterprise. Suddenly, the normally lax Rosprirodnadzor filed a barrage of environmental complaints against the operation, halting construction work on one pretext after another. After several months of struggle, Shell finally gave up: in December 2006, the Sakhalin-2 consortium sold a majority stake to Gazprom, the state-controlled natural gas monopoly, for $7.45 billion, considerably less than the estimated market value of the oil and gas involved.[26]

As the race for what's left gains momentum, this sort of predatory behavior will become more frequent and brutal. With the number of promising projects declining and market pressures growing more intense, resource firms will see no option but to feed upon one another in the endless pursuit of valuable assets. Inevitably, many smaller and weaker companies will disappear altogether or become acquired by their more successful rivals; only the most powerful will survive.

THE WEALTH AND POWER OF NATIONS

Like the large resource companies, the world's major powers will also be forced in the coming years to compete more aggressively in the race for what's left. Because access to a wide range of natural resources is essential for continued economic vitality, every nation will have a stake in the struggle to control remaining sources of supply. Although countries, unlike corporations, are not likely to be directly attacked and absorbed by their challengers, they are destined to fight over their relative ranking in the global political and economic hierarchy—with all that this entails for the prosperity and well-being of their own citizenry. The nations that succeed in securing supplies of vital materials will gain an elevated position in the global order, while those that fail to do so will slide downward.

Of course, the desire to control natural resources has fueled international strife throughout human history. Ancient dynasties fought wars to secure more agricultural territory; European colonial empires battled one another over their resource-rich outposts overseas.[27] To a considerable extent, therefore, the race for what's left can be interpreted as just a continuation of this age-old struggle. But whereas previous centuries generally witnessed conflict between just a few dominant powers, today many more countries are industrialized or on the path to industrialization—so the number of major contenders for resources is greater than ever before. These new challengers also often harbor large and growing populations, whose desire for consumer goods of all sorts cannot be long denied. At the same time, many existing sources of supply are in decline while few new reservoirs are waiting on the horizon. With more nations in the resource race and fewer prizes to be divided among them, the competition is heating up and governments are being pressed to assume a more active role.

Even in nations like Canada and the United States, which have long relied on private companies to acquire critical materials, government agencies are now assuming greater responsibility for seeking out and securing distant resource deposits. To facilitate resource extraction in the Far North, for example, the governments of all the Arctic powers are undertaking official surveys of their maritime territories and laying claim to vast stretches of submerged continental shelf. The leaders of emerging powers such as India and China, meanwhile, now regard the task of procuring adequate supplies of raw materials—and thus sustaining their countries' economic progress—as an essential requirement for political survival.

Among the most notable manifestations of this burgeoning government involvement is the increasing use of national funds to ensure access to critical natural resources. Chinese authorities have been particularly active in this regard, offering massive loans to foreign governments and their state-owned companies as leverage for securing needed resource exports. In one such deal, concluded in February 2009, the China Development Bank (CDB) agreed to lend $25 billion to Rosneft and Transneft—Russia's state-owned oil and pipeline companies—in exchange for a Russian pledge to send China an additional 300,000 barrels of oil per day for twenty years.[28] Just a few months later, the CDB similarly awarded a $10 billion line of credit to Petrobras, which promised to supply China with up to 200,000 barrels of Brazilian oil per day.[29] The following year, yet another CDB loan—this one worth $20 billion—went to the government of Venezuela, after Hugo Chávez promised to allow the China National Petroleum Corporation (CNPC) to codevelop a major oil field in the country.[30] The Chinese mining industry, too, has benefited from the CDB's largesse: the bank has given $9 billion in loans and grants to the Democratic Republic of the Congo in exchange for valuable mineral assets, and promised $7 billion to Guinea under a similar agreement.[31]

Nor is the Chinese government alone in pursuing such agreements. When Japanese prime minister Shinzo Abe visited Abu Dhabi in April 2007, for instance, he promised the emirate a $1 billion loan from the Japan Bank for International Cooperation to finance infrastructure improvements. In return, Japanese firms were given significantly extended oil-supply agreements.[32] The government-controlled Japan Oil, Gas, and Metals National Corporation also regularly engages in such practices, providing grants to various nations that pledge to open their territory to energy and mineral extraction by Japanese companies.

In their quest for natural resources, governments eager to secure critical materials have also increasingly begun to forge strategic alliances between their own national companies and the state-owned firms of their major suppliers. Like King Abdullah's initiative to purchase farmland abroad for Saudi use, such arrangements are designed to ensure steady delivery rates and evade the vicissitudes of the global marketplace.[33] China's state-owned CNPC, for example, is now partnering with Kazakhstan's state-owned KazMunaiGaz on several major projects in that country—an arrangement worked out directly by the government officials, in what is as much a diplomatic negotiation as a commercial one.[34] The Indian government, taking inspiration from China, has also favored such partnerships, and India's state-owned Oil and Natural Gas Corporation is now allying with CNPC and Sudan's state-owned Sudapet to operate some of the major oil fields in Sudan.[35] As such state-backed deals proliferate, government policies—rather than market forces—will play an increasingly prominent role in the global distribution of vital materials.

EDGING TOWARD WAR

Financial maneuvering of the sort practiced by the China Development Bank, plus intensive diplomacy aimed at persuading resource-rich nations to increase their exports, will probably account for most of the direct government involvement in the race for what's left. As the scramble for vital resources intensifies, however, governments will also become increasingly likely to employ more forceful means. In all probability, countries with major resource deposits will receive more weapons, military training, technical assistance, and intelligence support from states that wish to curry favor or establish closer ties. At the same time, combat forces will be deployed abroad to defend friendly regimes and protect key ports, pipelines, refineries, and other critical installations. None of this will be done with the specific intent of provoking an outbreak of violent conflict; nevertheless, as more and more countries choose to rely on military tools to secure their resource needs, the risk of war is bound to increase.[36]

Indeed, we can already detect a rising curve of military involvement in key resource-supplying areas, especially Africa and Central Asia. In both of these regions, the United States and China have stepped up their deliveries of arms and military equipment, and have deployed additional military advisers, instructors, and technicians. The United States has been especially active in Nigeria, the Republic of Georgia, and the Persian Gulf kingdoms; China has been equally conspicuous in Sudan, Zimbabwe, and the Central Asian republics.[37] Even more significant, Washington and Beijing have both created new organizations to facilitate the delivery of military aid and to coordinate any future intervention by their armed forces in these areas. In 1996, China established the Shanghai Cooperation Organization (SCO), devoted to regional security in Central Asia, while in 2007 the United States inaugurated the Africa Command (AFRICOM). Although neither entity is explicitly devoted to the pursuit of energy supplies, both of them include energy security among their principal responsibilities.[38]

The Russian government, too, appears intent on employing military instruments to help secure control of critical raw materials. In doing so, it is motivated less by a need to obtain resources for the country's own domestic use—Russia is self-sufficient in oil, natural gas, and most primary metals—than by a desire to dominate the energy trade across the entire territory of the former Soviet Union, especially in Central Asia and the Caucasus. Under Soviet rule, the exploitation of natural resources in those areas had been controlled by central planners in Moscow, with any extracted materials transported to Russia for processing; after the USSR broke apart and the Central Asian republics declared their independence, the centralized system was largely disassembled. Soviet energy enterprises were then privatized, allowing Western firms such as BP, Chevron, ExxonMobil, and Shell to gain access to the region's untapped hydrocarbon reserves. Now, however, with those reserves gaining more significance as oil and gas fields decline elsewhere, Russian leaders are seeking to reassert Moscow's authority over all the regional resources.[39]

To restore their dominion, Russian leaders have employed every means at their disposal—diplomacy, cajolery, financial aid, and extensive military involvement. In Central Asia, for example, Russia has herded many of the former Soviet republics into the Collective Security Treaty Organization, a counterpart to the North Atlantic Treaty Organization (NATO) that Moscow can use to funnel weapons to local powers and deploy its armed forces throughout the region. Under CSTO auspices, Russia has integrated its air-defense network with that of Kazakhstan and has established an air base in Kyrgyzstan, near the capital Bishkek.[40] In the Caucasus, meanwhile, the Russians have fought a series of brutal wars to retain control of Chechnya, a rebellious republic within the Russian federation that sits astride several key oil and natural gas pipelines connecting the Caspian region to Russia and the Black Sea.[41]

A particularly striking demonstration of Russia's willingness to employ force in pursuit of strategic resource interests came in August 2008, when Russian forces used a skirmish over the disputed Caucasian region of South Ossetia as their pretext to invade the former Soviet republic of Georgia. The attack was meant simultaneously to punish Georgia for seeking to build closer ties with the West (rather than with Russia), and to demonstrate the vulnerability of two U.S.-backed energy projects: the Baku-Tbilisi-Ceyhan oil pipeline and the South Caucasus natural gas pipeline, both of which lay astride the main front of battle. Although Russian forces eventually withdrew from Georgia's territory, some remain deployed in South Ossetia near the Georgian border, a constant reminder of Moscow's power over any energy conduits in the region.[42]

The danger posed by Russia's belligerence has been tempered, to a certain extent, by the fact that the conflicts in the Caucasus are highly asymmetrical, pitting the heavily armed forces of a vast military apparatus against scattered guerrilla bands (Chechnya) or a minor state army (Georgia). Neither of these simmering disputes is likely to ignite a full-scale confrontation that pits leading world powers against each other. Ideally, of course, the same will remain true for all future disputes over vital resources. But as countries become more reliant on the same handful of contested supply zones, it is increasingly likely that some encounter of this sort will, in fact, trigger a clash between two major powers—especially since political leaders are very reluctant to back down in a struggle over what are seen as vital national interests.

Probably no area of the world is more likely to be the site of such a confrontation than the East and South China Seas, which are believed to sit atop significant oil and natural gas deposits. As previously mentioned, China maintains that both seas lie mostly within its territorial waters, but a large swath of the East China Sea is also claimed by Japan, while significant portions of the South China Sea are claimed by Vietnam, the Philippines, Malaysia, and Brunei. Development of the offshore oil and gas fields could provide these nations with a valuable source of energy, but it cannot go ahead without some agreement on the location of maritime boundaries, and the disputes have become deeply contentious.[43] All of the countries involved have deployed air and naval forces in the contested areas, and on occasion have engaged in provocative behavior such as seizing fishing boats or aiming guns at one another's ships and planes.[44] The United States, which maintains security ties with a number of the local powers, has also deployed military forces in the region. Should such activity continue, it is not hard to imagine how some minor incident—say, a collision between two warships, accidental or otherwise—could escalate into a major crisis.

Indeed, several recent events suggest just how easily such a scenario might unfold. On March 8, 2009, for example, a flotilla of small Chinese

SOUTH CHINA SEA

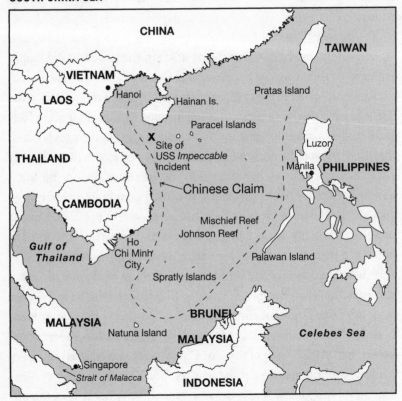

ships blocked an American naval surveillance vessel, the *Impeccable*, in the South China Sea. The *Impeccable* was towing underwater sonar cables, presumably to search for submarines; the Chinese ships attempted to sever those cables and to prevent the American vessel from leaving the area, prompting President Obama to rush a guided missile destroyer toward the site.[45] Although the *Impeccable* eventually managed to escape the Chinese dragnet on its own and no shots were fired, the incident was widely viewed as a precursor to more dangerous encounters at sea, possibly leading to armed hostilities.[46]

Just eighteen months later, such fears were renewed by another incident: the collision in the East China Sea between a Chinese fishing trawler and two Japanese coast guard vessels that eventually led China to suspend its rare earth deliveries to Japan. Although the Chinese trawler captain, Zhan Qixiong, claims that he was acting alone in resisting Japanese efforts to drive him away from the disputed Senkaku islands (claimed by both China and Japan), some analysts believe that his actions are part of a broader effort by China to assert its right to the entire region.[47] The seriousness of the affair was magnified by a treaty that obliges the United States to come to Japan's defense if it is attacked at sea; senior U.S. officials rushed to hold emergency meetings with their Japanese counterparts and suggest steps to temper the dispute.[48] As with the *Impeccable* incident, governments of all the countries involved insisted that the events were not serious enough to damage long-term relations. Many observers, though, worry about a pattern of growing Chinese aggressiveness in the area.[49]

Certainly, Chinese authorities have displayed no inclination to compromise regarding their claims to the East and South China Seas. When Secretary of State Hillary Clinton offered to facilitate talks on the subject between China and members of the Association of Southeast Asian Nations (ASEAN), she was roundly condemned by Chinese officials.[50] "China will never waive its right to protect its core interest with military means," declared the *Global Times*, an English-language newspaper published by the Communist Party.[51] To lend weight to that assertion, the Chinese navy conducted extensive military maneuvers in the South China Sea in the days immediately following Secretary Clinton's statement, deploying a fleet of missile-carrying warships and conducting live-fire exercises.[52]

China's belligerence, in turn, has led to increased hostility from other countries with vital interests in the area. The heavy-handed efforts to secure the release of Zhan Qixiong, for example, triggered unusually fervent anti-Chinese demonstrations in Tokyo and six other Japanese cities, with some protesters tossing flares or smoke bombs at local Chinese consulates.[53] The United States has also cautioned China against excessive provocation, insisting that it is fully prepared to defend its allies in the region. "We have an enduring presence here, we have an enduring responsibility," said Admiral Mike Mullen, chairman of the Joint Chiefs of Staff, during a July 2011 visit to Beijing.[54] As if in reply to Chinese demonstrations of naval force, the U.S. Navy has conducted its own set of exercises in troubled areas of the South China Sea, and in late 2011 President Obama announced the establishment of a new U.S. base at Darwin, on Australia's north coast.

There is no way to predict when, or whether, such aggressive posturing will lead to something much more serious. It is perfectly evident, however, that all key parties to the territorial disputes in the East and South China Seas are prepared to employ military means in asserting their claims to valuable offshore resource deposits, and to risk armed encounters with their rival claimants. And while it can be assumed that none of these countries specifically intends to provoke a violent clash, neither are they prepared to exercise restraint. If, in some future confrontation, commanders on the scene do not refrain from using live ammunition, and senior government officials then fail to order an immediate cease-fire, a larger outbreak of violence could conceivably follow. Many wars have erupted that way in the past, and there is no reason to assume the same cannot occur again.

As the global struggle over scarce resources intensifies, such risks will only become more common. Similar aggressive posturing by rival claimants, as we have seen, has also been occurring in the Arctic, the Falkland Islands region, and the Celebes Sea off Malaysia and Indonesia. Responding to a Russian warning of possible conflict over Arctic resources, for example, Canada's foreign minister said in 2009 that his government would "work peacefully" with other countries to resolve boundary disputes—but also added that "Canadian Forces are prepared to address future challenges and respond to any emergency" that might occur in the region.[55] Russian leaders then racheted up the tension by announcing a significant expansion of Russia's border protection forces in the Arctic region. This buildup, said Prime Minister Vladimir Putin, "will make it possible to substantially strengthen our military and border security and also increase the effectiveness of the protection of natural resources."[56] With government officials like these under increasing pressure to protect and expand their countries' resource reserves, the potential for overreaction and miscalculation—and possibly full-scale war—is bound to grow.

THE RACE TO ADAPT

On its present course, the race for what's left can end only in the eventual disappearance of many already depleted natural resources. Along the way, pristine wilderness areas will be invaded by mammoth industrial contraptions, sometimes with catastrophic results; some fraction of the major resource corporations will go bankrupt or be absorbed by their rivals, wiping out jobs and shareholders; and international armed conflict will become increasingly probable. The indigenous peoples who draw their sustenance from the remote areas now being targeted by resource firms will be the most affected, experiencing economic and cultural ruination if not actual physical harm; but in the end, all humans will suffer, as commodity prices skyrocket, certain critical materials vanish altogether, and the wheels of industry turn at an ever-diminishing pace.

There is, however, another path that humanity could take. Instead of rushing to extract whatever remains of the earth's vital resources, major political and corporate powers could engage in a *race to adapt*: a contest to become among the first to adopt new materials, methods, and devices that will free the world from its dependence on finite resource supplies. Such a race would be motivated by the realization that, sooner or later, all countries will be forced to adjust to a life of extreme resource scarcity—and that whoever can make this transition early will reap significant advantages. The race to adapt will reward the governments, companies, and communities that take the lead in developing efficient, environmentally friendly industrial processes and transportation systems, and it will punish those that persist in clinging to existing habits. Ultimately, power and wealth will come not from control over dwindling resource supplies, but from mastery of the new technologies.

It is true that eliminating our dependence on fossil fuels and other finite materials cannot be accomplished overnight—our current reliance on them is just too great. But no matter how much corporate or government officials might wish to deny it, there are not nearly enough nonrenewable resources on this planet to perpetually satisfy the growing needs of a ballooning world population; what's more, existing modes of production are causing unacceptable damage to the global environment. Eventually, continuing with current industrial practices will simply prove impossible. And precisely because implementing a whole new industrial order will be a lengthy task, any substantial delay in beginning that work will prove costly, as resources keep dwindling and their prices continue to rise.[57]

Even if the work begins now, developing all the necessary technologies will admittedly be expensive. Using well-established processes and material inputs is always cheaper in the short run than investing in experimental alternatives, and many companies and governments will balk at all the mammoth costs involved in the transition. At some stage, however, the economics of innovation will outperform the economics of procrastination—especially when the price of oil and other finite resources becomes substantially higher, as is certain to happen. When that occurs, whichever companies and governments had already embraced the new, resource-minimizing approach will start to enjoy a significant economic and political advantage over those that have not, and the race to adapt will truly gain momentum.

Replacing finite natural resources with renewables is especially critical in the energy and transportation fields, where supplies of petroleum and other fuels will fall increasingly short of demand. Over time, though, such substitution will become necessary in almost every area of human endeavor, since many other types of resources are likewise becoming increasingly depleted. New building materials, for example, will be needed to replace diminishing stocks of copper, cobalt, manganese, and other minerals widely used in the construction industry. Electrical and computer systems, too, will have to make use of innovative new materials, as all the reserves of rare earths and other specialty metals eventually become exhausted.

At the same time, the race to adapt will require a new focus on increasing efficiency, with industries of every type making an effort to extract the greatest utility from every ounce of materials that humans consume. Greater efficiency will be particularly vital in the early transition period, when many renewables are still under development and the world continues to rely to some extent on shrinking reserves of finite resources. But even after renewables become commonplace, increased efficiency will still remain prized as a way for companies, communities, and individuals to minimize waste and maximize financial return—an approach long advocated by Amory B. Lovins of the Rocky Mountain Institute.[58] Improved efficiency also provides the sole option for feeding the growing global population: only by raising crop yields while reducing inputs of water, oil, fertilizers, pesticides, and other materials can the world hope to avoid a series of devastating famines.

Besides allowing the global economy to escape from the trap of diminishing resource supplies, ultra-efficiency and the adoption of renewables would also provide political benefits. A diminished reliance on scarce materials imported from abroad, for instance, would allow many nations to free themselves from military pacts and other diplomatic arrangements currently employed to cement ties with foreign resource providers. Local initiative and innovation would instead become the key to success, as countries rush to design, test, and install advanced industrial and agricultural systems that make use of renewable domestic resources.

To succeed in these efforts, both the public and private spheres will need to make adaptation their top long-term priority. Governments will have to supply funding and research talent for projects that are not yet ready for commercial application; they will also have to establish the necessary regulatory framework, such as legislation to promote offshore wind farms and geothermal energy systems. At the same time, because governments are major consumers in their own right, they are well placed to spur commercial innovation by emphasizing renewables and efficiency in procurement contracts. Corporations, for their part, must supply the entrepreneurial vigor and technological know-how to move promising experimental systems from the laboratory to the marketplace. Universities, nonprofit organizations, and local communities will also play an important part by devising creative new solutions and supporting the introduction of new technologies.[59]

This vision may sound, to some, a bit utopian. After all, as this book has shown, it is the race for what's left—not the race to adapt—that is the dominant preoccupation among governments and businesses today. But a closer look makes it clear that the race to adapt has, in fact, already commenced. Around the world, savvy leaders of countries and corporations now frequently speak of a struggle to claim leadership in the development of "green" technology—and are taking significant steps to ensure that their country, or their firm, will be the one to prevail in this contest.[60]

China, in particular, has made no secret of its determination to become a dominant force in the green-technology field. In 2005, it instituted the Renewable Energy Law, a legislative initiative that institutes a national target for renewable energy use—with the current mandate calling for 15 percent of China's total energy consumption to come from renewable sources by 2020. This legislation has resulted in rapid expansion of wind and solar power in the country, as well as increased emphasis on the development of advanced biofuels and transportation systems.[61] The same priorities were evident in China's 2009 economic stimulus package, which devoted a significant proportion of its funds to renewable energy, high-speed rail, and an advanced electrical grid.[62]

In pursuing these initiatives, the Chinese government is aiming both to avoid problems at home and to seize an opportunity on the global market. As China's economy has expanded in recent years, so has its consumption of energy and other resources; the country has therefore become increasingly dependent on imported supplies, with all of their attendant problems and perils. What's more, China's reliance on coal and other fossil fuels to generate electricity has made it into the world's leading emitter of carbon dioxide and caused colossal environmental problems. From a domestic viewpoint, therefore, Beijing's efforts to promote energy efficiency and alternative fuels are designed to lessen the nation's reliance on imported energy and to reduce the levels of air pollution. At the same time, however, Chinese leaders have also come to view clean-energy research as a tool for stimulating economic growth and creating new jobs. Such technologies will not only satisfy a significant need at home, they believe, but also find a substantial market abroad.[63]

The importance that Chinese officials attach to green technology—for both domestic application and export abroad—is clearly evident in a recent government report on "strategic emerging industries," which designated seven such industries for intensive state support in the years ahead. Three of the seven (alternative energy, energy-efficient technology, and alternative energy vehicles) are explicitly tied to energy innovation, and the four others (advanced materials, bioengineering, next-generation information technology, and high-end equipment manufacturing) also have clear applications in the race to adapt. If all goes according to the official plan, the contribution of these seven industries to China's GDP will quintuple within a decade, rising from just 3 percent in 2010 to 15 percent by 2020.[64]

China is not alone in seeking to lead the world in clean energy technology. Germany, Italy, and Spain have all made significant contributions to the advancement of wind and solar power, while Brazil has become a major power in the production of biofuels. Many other countries, including some in the developing world, are also seeking to establish an advantage in this promising new field. "A new worldwide industry is dawning," the Pew Charitable Trusts wrote in a recent report on the "clean energy race."[65] According to the Pew study, overall investment in clean energy grew by 230 percent between 2005 and 2009, when it reached $162 billion. In a follow-up report, Pew noted that such spending then climbed another 50 percent in 2010, putting it at a whopping $243 billion.[66]

And what of the United States? America has long been a leader in the development of many key green technologies, but Pew points out that its dominance has been slipping. Whereas the United States was ranked as the world's top investor in clean energy every year through 2008, China took the lead in 2009. Even more striking, in 2010 the U.S. fell another notch in the rankings, with China again taking first place and Germany now listed in second.[67] When these figures are adjusted for GDP, the comparison is starker yet: relative to the size of its economy, the total U.S. investment in clean energy now ranks in eighth place, behind such countries as Italy, Canada, Brazil, Spain, and Australia.[68] "For a variety of reasons, the United States' competitive position appears to be eroding," the authors of the Pew report concluded, clearly troubled by their findings.[69]

Many prominent figures in the American government share this worry, including Energy Secretary Steven Chu, who has described China's green-energy advances as a modern-day "Sputnik moment" for the United States.[70] In response to such concerns, the Obama administration's 2009 stimulus package provided some $45 billion for energy conservation and renewable energy initiatives, including $14 billion for development of advanced power grid and battery technology and an equal sum for renewable energy tax incentives.[71] In 2011, President Obama also signed an executive order requiring substantial improvements in the energy efficiency of all government buildings, vehicles, and operations.[72] But many analysts believe that these and similar initiatives are not enough to make significant progress in reducing American reliance on nonrenewable energy resources. A recent report by the American Energy Innovation Council (AEIC), a group of prominent U.S. business executives, concluded that "in energy . . . America has failed the grade, and is paying a heavy price for its failure."[73]

To rectify the situation and restore America's lead in the green-technology race, the AEIC and other observers are calling on the United States government to substantially increase its investment in alternative energy systems. The AEIC's report advocates spending $16 billion per year on clean energy research, more than three times the $5 billion currently budgeted.[74] A similar proposal was advanced in November 2010 by the President's Council of Advisors on Science and

Technology, a blue-ribbon panel of scientists and corporate officials headed by presidential science adviser John P. Holdren. Like the AEIC, the Holdren panel recommended an annual budget of $16 billion for research on clean energy; it also called on the president to initiate a Quadrennial Energy Review process, akin to the Pentagon's Quadrennial Defense Review, to assess America's energy challenges and identify essential areas to focus on.[75]

It is very unlikely, however, that these measures will garner congressional support in the current political climate. Any significant increase in federal expenditures on renewable energy appears to have little chance of winning approval in the House of Representatives, where anti-spending Republicans dominate. Likewise, despite the various reports' recommendations, it seems improbable that Congress will authorize any expansion of the federal bureaucracy to oversee energy projects of this sort. No doubt some venture capitalists and private companies will put their own funds into new energy initiatives, but such investments are almost certainly not going to reach the minimum level that the President's Council of Advisors identified as necessary for continued American leadership in clean energy design. And without adequate investment, the council predicts, America is destined to become a "technology taker" rather than a technology maker, "with the implied economic and leadership consequences."[76]

The race to adapt, then, is very much upon us—though not everyone has yet come to fully appreciate its significance. While some governments and corporations have already started jockeying for dominance in the development of clean energy and renewable resources, others are still exclusively focused on winning the race for what's left. In the short term, no doubt, those who prevail in the age-old struggle for finite resource supplies will still enjoy substantial economic and political rewards, but as time goes on those rewards will prove harder and harder to come by, while the price of failure will be increasingly high. On the other hand, those who focus on the new energy and materials technologies will have to pay high start-up costs but will see greater benefits in the coming decades. The countries that pursue the path of renewables will also find themselves increasingly free from supply disruptions and from foreign military entanglements caused by excessive reliance on imported materials.

The strategic green-technology investments of the kind that the Chinese government is now undertaking—and that the AEIC and the President's Council of Advisors are recommending for the United States—will not be sufficient, by themselves, to end the global struggle for control of the world's shrinking supplies of vital materials. That task can only be accomplished through a complete transformation of industrial society, with all finite resources systematically replaced by renewable alternatives. But the AEIC report and the Chinese initiatives do demonstrate that some key leaders now see such a transformation as both necessary and desirable. Like the current scramble for the world's last remaining resources, the race to adapt will spell doom for slow-moving companies, and it will cause a grand reshuffling of the global power hierarchy. But it is not likely to end in war, widespread starvation, or a massive environmental catastrophe—the probable results of persisting with the race for what's left.

NOTES

INTRODUCTION

1. First comment is from McKenzie Funk, "Arctic Landgrab," *National Geographic*, May 2009, pp. 106–7; second is from C. J. Chivers, "Eyeing Future Wealth, Russians Plant the Flag on the Arctic Seabed, below the Polar Cap," *New York Times*, August 3, 2007. For background on the 2007 polar expedition, see Chivers, "Eyeing Future Wealth"; and David Holley, "Russians Prepare for a Deep Arctic Dive," *Los Angeles Times*, August 2, 2007.

2. From an interview with Chilingarov, *Moscow News*, July 17, 2008, retrieved at www.mnweekly.ru on September 11, 2009.

3. Ibid.

4. As quoted in Holley, "Russians Prepare for a Deep Arctic Dive."

5. As quoted in Chivers, "Eyeing Future Wealth."

6. As quoted in "General: Russia Must Guard Arctic Region," UPI.com, June 24, 2008, retrieved at www.upi.com on December 25, 2008.

7. As quoted in Chivers, "Eyeing Future Wealth."

8. As quoted in "Canadian Prime Minister Visits Arctic in an Effort to Exert Sovereignty," *International Herald Tribune*, August 8, 2007.

9. "PM Starts Fight for North," *Toronto Star*, August 10, 2007.

10. As quoted in Ian Austen, "Canada Announces Plans for 2 New Bases in Its Far North," *New York Times*, August 11, 2007.

11. As quoted in Doug Mellgren, "Denmark Joins Rush for Arctic Resources," *Seattle Times*, August 10, 2007.

12. See Guy Chazan, "Norwegian Oil Firm Goes to Energy's Last Frontier," *Wall Street Journal*, February 13, 2009.

13. As quoted in "Russia Plants Undersea Flag in Arctic," *USA Today*, August 3, 2007, retrieved at www.usatoday.com on September 17, 2011.

14. White House, Office of the Press Secretary, "National Security Presidential Directive/NSPD-66," January 12, 2009, retrieved at www.whitehouse .gov on January 15, 2009. NSPD-66 is also known as Homeland Security Presidential Directive Number 25.

15. U.S. Department of the Interior, U.S. Geological Survey (USGS), "90 Billion Barrels of Oil and 1,670 Trillion Cubic Feet of Natural Gas Assessed in the Arctic," press release, July 23, 2008, retrieved at www.usgs .gov on December 2, 2008.

16. See Guy Chazan, "Cold Comfort: Arctic Is Oil Hot Spot," *Wall Street Journal*, July 24, 2008.

17. See Brian Baskin, "Northern Exposure," *Wall Street Journal*, February 11, 2008. See also Paul Reynolds, "The Arctic's New Gold Rush," BBC News, October 25, 2005.

18. Baskin, "Northern Exposure."

19. Thomas Catan, "Remote Resource: Shell's Sakhalin Task Shows an Industry Its Daunting Future," *Financial Times*, January 9, 2006.

20. Thomas Grove and Melissa Akin, "Russian Rig Sinks, More than 50 Feared Dead," Reuters, December 18, 2011, retrieved at www.reuters.com on December 20, 2011.

21. U.S. Department of Energy, Energy Information Administration (DoE/EIA), "Brazil," Country Analysis Brief, September 2009, retrieved at www.eia.doe.gov on June 12, 2010.

22. For an optimistic perspective on the potential for unconventional oil and gas, see Daniel Yergin, *The Quest* (New York: Penguin, 2011), pp. 242–62. For a critical perspective on hydraulic fracturing, see Chris Mooney, "The Truth about Fracking," *Scientific American*, November 2011, pp. 80–85.

23. Patrick Barta, "With Easy Nickel Fading Fast, Miners Go After the Tough Stuff," *Wall Street Journal*, July 12, 2006.

24. For discussion, see Robert Guy Matthews, "Hunters Comb Globe for a Hot Metal," *Wall Street Journal*, April 4, 2008.

25. As quoted in Jeremy Page, "U.N. Clears China Sea-Floor Plan," *Wall Street Journal*, July 22, 2011. See also Page, "China Makes Milestone Dive," *Wall Street Journal*, July 27, 2011.

26. See Sohbet Karbuz, "U.S. Military Energy Consumption—Facts and Figures," Energy Bulletin, May 20, 2007, retrieved at www.energybul letin.net on February 14, 2010.

27. See Alexei Barrionuevo, "Brazil Moves for More Control of Oil Wealth beneath Its Seas," *New York Times*, August 18, 2009; Eric Watkins, "Brazil Considering Changes to Country's Oil Law," *Oil & Gas Journal*, June 22, 2009, p. 29; Watkins, "Brazil Unveils Proposed Presalt Legislation," *Oil & Gas Journal Online*, September 2, 2009, retrieved at www.ogj .com on September 9, 2009.

28. For background, see Michael T. Klare, *Rising Powers, Shrinking Planet: The New Geopolitics of Energy* (New York: Metropolitan Books, 2008), pp. 73–77, 132–37, 164–71, 194–201.

29. See A. J. Graham, *Colony and Mother City in Ancient Greece* (New York: Barnes and Noble, 1964), pp. 1–9.

30. See Peter Garnsey, *Famine and Food Supply in the Graeco-Roman World* (Cambridge: Cambridge University Press, 1988), pp. 182–243.

CHAPTER 1: DRIVEN BY DEPLETION

1. For background on Cantarell, see "Cantarell Oil Field, Gulf of Mexico, Mexico," Offshore-Technology.com, retrieved at www.offshore -technology.com on March 8, 2011; David Luhnow, "Mexico Tries to Save a Big, Fading Oil Field," *Wall Street Journal*, April 5, 2007; and Tom Standing, "Mexico Cantarell Field: How Long Will It Last?" Energy Bulletin, retrieved at www.energybulletin.net on March 8, 2011.

2. See DoE/EIA, "Mexico," Country Analysis Brief, July 2011, retrieved at www.eia.doe.gov on August 15, 2011, and earlier editions of this document.

3. See Alan R. Hildebrand et al., "Chicxulub Crater: A Possible Cretaceous/Tertiary Boundary Impact Crater on the Yucatán Peninsula, Mexico," *Geology*, vol. 19, no. 1 (September 1991), pp. 867–71.

4. See Manik Talwani, *Oil and Gas in Mexico: Geology, Production Rates, and Reserves* (Houston: Rice University, James A. Baker III Institute for Public Policy, 2011), pp. 21–22.

5. See DoE/EIA, "Mexico," July 2011. See also Carola Hoyos, "Mexico's Pemex Struggles with Oil Decline," *Financial Times*, March 30, 2010; and "Mexico's Pemex Top Crude-Oil Fields to Remain Stable—CEO," Dow Jones Newswire, June 9, 2011, retrieved at online.wsj.com on June 13, 2011.

6. BP, *Statistical Review of World Energy June 2010* (London: BP, 2010), p. 8. Data for 2010 from DoE/EIA, "International Energy Statistics: Production: Petroleum," retrieved at www.eia.doe.gov on June 12, 2011. For discussion, see David Luhnow, "Mexico's Fading Oil Output Squeezes Exports and Spending," *Wall Street Journal*, September 9, 2009.

7. DoE/EIA, *International Energy Outlook 2010* (Washington, D.C.: DoE/EIA, 2010), Tables A5 and G1, pp. 136, 235.

8. As quoted in Luhnow, "Mexico's Fading Oil Output."

9. Luhnow, "Mexico Tries to Save a Big, Fading Oil Field."

10. See discussion in International Energy Agency (IEA), *World Energy Outlook 2008* (Paris: IEA, 2008), pp. 221–48.

11. Angus Maddison, *The World Economy: Historical Statistics* (Paris: Organization for Economic Cooperation and Development, 2003), Table 8b, p. 259.

12. USGS, *Minerals Yearbook 2000*, vol. 1, various entries; and U.S. Department of the Interior, Bureau of Mines (BoM), *Minerals Yearbook 1952*, vols. 1 and 2, various entries. (The *Minerals Yearbook* is published annually by the U.S. Government Printing Office, usually a year or two after the year given in the title; more recent editions are available online at www.usgs.gov.)

13. For background, see Daniel Yergin, *The Prize* (New York: Touchstone, 1993), pp. 395–96, 429.

14. For background on Aramco and the U.S. concession in Saudi Arabia, see ibid., pp. 280–92, 298–302, 391–99, 410–19.

15. IEA, *World Energy Outlook 2008*, Table 10.1, p. 225.

16. See Yergin, *The Prize*, pp. 409, 437–43, 515, 666.

17. Ibid., pp. 525–30.

18. Ibid., pp. 429, 669.

19. Ibid., p. 669.

20. For background, see ibid., pp. 569–74, 665–66.

21. BoM, *Minerals Yearbook 1957*, vol. 2, p. 322. (Production data covers the years 1952–56.)

22. Ibid.

23. BoM, *Minerals Yearbook 1976*, vol. 1, p. 887; BP Amoco, *Statistical Review of World Energy 2000* (London: BP Amoco, 2000), p. 23.

24. Ibid.

25. BoM, *Minerals Yearbook 1969*, vol. 1, p. 458.

26. BoM, *Minerals Yearbook 1960*, pp. 1129–35.

27. BoM, *Minerals Yearbook 1952*, p. 329.

28. A 1965 entry in the *Minerals Yearbook* noted, "The use of tantalum, primarily in capacitors and other electronic applications, increased significantly in response to the military needs developed by the Viet-Nam conflict." BoM, *Minerals Yearbook 1965*, vol. 1, p. 337.

29. Ibid., pp. 347–49.

30. David S. Painter, "Oil, Resources, and the Cold War, 1945–1962," in Melvyn P. Leffler and Odd Arne Westad, *The Cambridge History of the Cold War*, vol. 1 (Cambridge: Cambridge University Press, 2010), pp. 487–88.

31. DoE/EIA, "Crude Oil Production and Crude Oil Well Productivity, Selected Years, 1954–2008," retrieved at www.eia.doe.gov on October 31, 2009.

32. DoE/EIA, *Annual Energy Outlook 2011* (Washington, D.C.: DoE/EIA, 2011), Table A11, p. 137.

33. BP, *Statistical Review of World Energy 2010*, p. 8.

34. Production data from ibid. For background, see DoE/EIA, "Russia," Country Analysis Brief, May 2008, retrieved at www.eia.doe.gov on November 21, 2009.

35. BP, *Statistical Review of World Energy 2010*, p. 8.

36. DoE/EIA, *International Energy Outlook 2010*, Table G2, p. 236.

37. IEA, *World Energy Outlook 2008*, pp. 221–48.

38. Ibid., pp. 242–46.

39. Ibid., pp. 244–45.

40. Ibid., pp. 245–47.

41. Ibid., pp. 225–27.

42. IEA, *World Energy Outlook 2010* (Paris: IEA, 2010), p. 119.

43. See IEA, *World Energy Outlook* 2008, pp. 293–94. For projections to 2035, see DoE/EIA, *International Energy Outlook 2009*, Table 5, p. 39.

44. DoE/EIA, "Russia," May 2008. See also Christian Wüst, "How Long Will Siberia's Gas Last?" *Spiegel Online*, December 18, 2007, retrieved at www .spiegel.de on December 13, 2009.

45. USGS, "Copper," *Minerals Yearbook 2007*, chap. 20, p. 22. (Data for 1990 from 1986 edition.)

46. USGS, "Copper," *Minerals Yearbook 2007*, chap. 20, pp. 21–22.

47. Comisión Chilena del Cobre, "Desafíos Estratégicos de la Política Minera," August 18, 2008, retrieved at www.cochilco.cl on December 17, 2009.

48. Commodity Research Bureau (CRB), *CRB Commodity Yearbook 2009* (Hoboken, N.J.: Wiley, 2009), p. 50. See also USGS, "Copper," *Minerals Yearbook 2007*, chap. 20, p. 6.

49. CRB, *CRB Commodity Yearbook 2009*, p. 50.

50. Ibid., pp. 36, 179.

51. USGS, "Cobalt," *Minerals Yearbook 2007*, chap. 19, pp. 1–7 and Table 8; USGS, "Nickel," ibid., chap. 51, pp. 1–8 and Table 13.

52. USGS, "Titanium," *Minerals Yearbook 2007*, chap. 78, pp. 1–5.

53. USGS, "Lithium," *Minerals Yearbook 2007*, chap. 44, pp. 1–4; USGS, "Niobium (Columbium) and Tantalum," ibid., chap. 52, pp. 1–4; and USGS, "Platinum-Group Metals," ibid., chap. 57, pp. 1–7.

54. See USGS, "Rare Earths," *Minerals Yearbook 2008*, chap. 60, pp. 1–6.

55. Michel Rademaker and Jaakko Kooroshy, "The Global Challenge of Mineral Scarcity," Report for the Conference "Enriching the Planet, Empowering Europe," The Hague, April 26–27, 2010.

56. DoE/EIA, *International Energy Outlook 2011*, Table A3, p. 160. Represents GDP as measured in purchasing power parity.

57. Ibid., Tables A5 and A6, pp. 162–63.

58. Ibid.

59. For background on the role of China's state-owned firms in the pursuit of overseas resources, see Klare, *Rising Powers, Shrinking Planet*, pp. 75–76, 132–37, 164–71, 194–201.

60. CRB, *CRB Commodity Yearbook 2009*, pp. 1–4, 50–55, 151–55.

61. The global market for lithium batteries, for example, has been grow-

ing by more than 20 percent per year. USGS, "Lithium," *Minerals Yearbook 2007,* chap. 44, p. 4.

62. David Menzie, Pui-Kwan Tse, Mike Fenton, John Jorgenson, and Hendrik van Oss, *China's Growing Appetite for Minerals,* USGS Open-File Report 2004–1374, retrieved at pubs.usgs.gov on December 19, 2009. See also USGS, "China," *Minerals Yearbook 2008,* vol. 3, chap. 9, pp. 1–5.

63. For discussion, see USGS, "China," *Minerals Yearbook 2008,* chap. 9, pp. 1–14.

64. See official Web site of Japan Oil, Gas, and Metals National Corporation, www.jogmec.go.jp.

65. UN Population Division, "World Population Prospects: The 2008 Revision," retrieved at esa.un.org/UNPP on January 25, 2011.

66. For background on this phenomenon, see Klaus Deininger and Derek Byerlee, *Rising Global Interest in Farmland* (Washington, D.C.: World Bank, 2011).

CHAPTER 2: DEEP-OFFSHORE OIL AND GAS

1. Lord John Browne, "Sustainability: A Practical Agenda," speech at the University of Michigan, Ann Arbor, November 14, 2006, retrieved at www.bp.com on March 21, 2010.

2. Ed Crooks, "Back to Petroleum," *Financial Times,* July 8, 2009. On the transition from Browne to Hayward, see Heather Timmons, "BP Names Its Next Chief; Succession Pace Stepped Up," *New York Times,* January 13, 2007.

3. Tony Hayward, "The Challenge of Energy Security," speech at London Business School, February 4, 2010, retrieved at www.bp.com on March 16, 2010.

4. Andy Inglis, "IOC's: A Strategy for Growth," speech at Howard Weil Conference, New Orleans, March 22, 2010, retrieved at www.bp.com on March 23, 2010.

5. BP, *Annual Review 2009* (London: BP), p. 13.

6. For background, see National Commission on the BP *Deepwater Horizon* Oil Spill and Offshore Drilling (National Commission), *Deep Water* (Washington, D.C.: National Commission, January 2011), pp. 45–51.

7. Clifford Krauss, "BP Finds Giant Oil Field Deep in Gulf of Mexico," *New York Times*, September 3, 2009.

8. For background on these events, see National Commission, *Deep Water*.

9. See excerpts from the congressional testimony of other senior oil company executives in John M. Broder, "Oil Executives Break Ranks in Testimony," *New York Times*, June 16, 2010.

10. National Commission, *Deep Water*, p. 40.

11. Datamonitor, "Global Offshore Drilling Fully Recovered by 2011," press release, March 1, 2010, retrieved at about.datamonitor.com on June 7, 2010.

12. John Westwood, "Global Offshore Prospects," PowerPoint presentation to British Chamber of Commerce, Singapore, March 22, 2010, retrieved at www.dw-1.com on June 5, 2010.

13. See Russell Gold, "In Gulf of Mexico, Industry Closes In on New Oil Source," *Wall Street Journal*, September 5, 2006; and Steven Mufson, "U.S. Oil Reserves Get a Big Boost," *Washington Post*, September 6, 2006.

14. As quoted in Mufson, "U.S. Oil Reserves Get a Big Boost."

15. See Jad Mouawad, "Going Deep: The Gulf of Mexico Holds a Lot of Oil, but Recovering It Isn't Easy," *New York Times*, November 8, 2006.

16. Chevron Corp., "Tahiti," from 2008 *Annual Report*, retrieved at www.chevron.com on June 9, 2010.

17. See Mouawad, "Going Deep."

18. National Commission, *Deep Water*, pp. 49–50.

19. Ibid., p. 50.

20. Chevron Corp., "Chevron Announces Discovery in the Deepest Well Drilled," press release, December 20, 2005, retrieved at www.chevron.com on March 20, 2006.

21. Chevron Corp., "Chevron Announces Record Setting Well Test at Jack," press release, September 5, 2006, retrieved at www.chevron.com on June 6, 2010.

22. Royal Dutch Shell, "Shell Starts Production at Perdido—World's Deepest Offshore Drilling and Production Facility," press release, March 31, 2010, retrieved at www.shell.com on April 17, 2010.

23. See Peter Elkind and David Whitford, "'An Accident Waiting to Happen,'" *Fortune*, February 7, 2011, pp. 107–32. See also Ben Casselman

and Russell Gold, "Unusual Decisions Set Stage for BP Disaster," *Wall Street Journal*, May 27, 2010; and Ian Urbina, "BP Chose Riskier of Two Options for Well Casing," *New York Times*, May 27, 2010.

24. For an assessment of what caused the April 20 blowout, see National Commission, *Deep Water*, pp. 89–127. See also John M. Broder, "Report Links Gulf Oil Spill to Shortcuts," *New York Times*, September 15, 2011. This article refers to a new report on the causes of the disaster produced by a joint task force of the Bureau of Ocean Energy Management, Regulation, and Enforcement and the Coast Guard.

25. See Ben Casselman, "Rig Owner Had Rising Tally of Accidents," *Wall Street Journal*, May 10, 2010; Casselman and Guy Chazan, "Disaster Plans Lacking at Deep Rigs," *Wall Street Journal*, May 18, 2010; Russell Gold and Casselman, "Far Offshore, a Rash of Close Calls," *Wall Street Journal*, December 9, 2010; and Clifford Krauss, "Accidents Don't Slow Gulf of Mexico Drilling," *New York Times*, April 22, 2010.

26. National Commission, *Deep Water*, p. ix.

27. DoE/EIA, "Outer Continental Shelf Deep Water Royalty Relief Act of 1995," retrieved at www.eia.doe.gov on June 7, 2010.

28. See Russell Gold and Stephen Power, "Regulator Ceded Oversight of Rig Safety to Oil Drillers," *Wall Street Journal*, May 7, 2010; and Ian Urbina, "U.S. Said to Allow Drilling Without Needed Permits," *New York Times*, May 14, 2010.

29. National Commission, *Deep Water*, p. 126.

30. White House, Office of the Press Secretary, "Remarks by the President on Energy Security at Andrews Air Force Base," March 31, 2010, retrieved at www.whitehouse.gov on June 6, 2010.

31. As quoted in "Obama Unchanged on Offshore Drilling Despite Spill," Reuters, April 23, 2010, retrieved at www.nytimes.com on April 25, 2010.

32. National Commission, *Deep Water*, p. vii.

33. For background, see Ben Casselman and Daniel Gilbert, "Drilling Is Stalled Even after Ban Lifted," January 3, 2011. See also Ed Crooks and Sheila McNulty, "Exxon Urges U.S. to Allow Deep-Sea Drilling," *Financial Times*, February 28, 2011; and Tennille Tracy and Ryan Tracy, "Pressures Mount to Resume Drilling," *Wall Street Journal*, February 25, 2011.

34. John M. Broder and Clifford Krauss, "Judge Tells Government to Resume Permits for Drilling," *New York Times*, February 18, 2011.

35. John M. Broder and Clifford Krauss, "Oil Drilling to Resume in the Gulf's Deep Waters," *New York Times*, March 1, 2011. See also Nick Snow, "BHP Billiton Latest to Get Drilling Permit from BOEMRE," *Oil & Gas Journal Online*, March 14, 2010, retrieved at www.ogj.com on March 22, 2011.

36. As quoted in Guy Chazan, "BP Plans to Return to Gulf This Year," *Wall Street Journal*, April 28, 2011.

37. As quoted in Curtis Williams, "Macondo Will Someday Be Produced, BP Executive Says," *Oil & Gas Journal Online*, April 27, 2011, retrieved at ogj.com on May 3, 2011.

38. U.S. Department of the Interior, Minerals Management Service (MMS), "Lease Sale 220," retrieved at www.mms.gov on June 10, 2010. See also Cynthia Dizikes, "First Step toward New Oil Drilling," *Los Angeles Times*, November 13, 2008.

39. See Nick Snow, "U.S. House Passes Bill Requiring DOI to Hold Cancelled OCS Lease Sales," *Oil & Gas Journal Online*, May 5, 2011, retrieved at www.ogj.com on May 9, 2011; and John M. Broder, "In a Shift, Obama Moves to Speed Drilling for Oil and Gas on Public Lands," *New York Times*, May 15, 2011.

40. DoE/EIA, "Canada," Country Analysis Brief, July 2009, retrieved at www.eia.doe.gov on June 10, 2010.

41. See Clyde H. Farnsworth, "Canada's High-Risk Oil Venture," *New York Times*, April 26, 1994.

42. Douglas Martin, "Oil Drillers off Canada Battle Nature and Politics," *New York Times*, March 15, 1981.

43. "84 Feared Dead as Oil-Drilling Rig Reportedly Sinks in North Atlantic," Associated Press, *New York Times*, February 16, 1982; Dudley Clendinen, "Inquiry Is Started on Rig That Sank," *New York Times*, April 21, 1982.

44. See "Hibernia, Jeanne d'Arc Basin," Offshore-technology.com, retrieved at www.offshore-technology.com on September 17, 2011.

45. "ExxonMobil to Develop Hebron Oil Field off Canada," *Oil & Gas Journal Online*, May 3, 2011, retrieved at www.ogj.com on May 4, 2011.

46. DoE/EIA, "Canada," July 2009. See also Nina M. Rach, "New Projects Develop in Canadian Maritimes," *Oil & Gas Journal*, November 20, 2006, pp. 47–52.

47. "Deep Drilling Starts off Newfoundland," CBC News, May 10, 2010, retrieved at www.cbc.ca January 29, 2011.

48. "Halt Deep-Water Drilling Project: N.L. Opposition," CBC News, May 11, 2010, retrieved at www.cbc.ca on January 29, 2011.

49. Matt Muffett and Bernd Radowitz, "Brazil Discovers Large Oil Reserve in Deep Waters of Atlantic," *Wall Street Journal*, November 9, 2007.

50. As quoted in Carlos Caminada and Jeb Blount, "Petrobras' Tupi Oil Field May Hold 8 Billion Barrels," *Bloomberg News*, November 8, 2007, retrieved at www.bloomberg.com on September 14, 2011.

51. Eric Watkins, "Petrobras Approves 5-year, $225 Billion Investment Plan," *Oil & Gas Journal Online*, July 28, 2011, retrieved at ww.ogi.com on August 23, 2011. For discussion, see Alexei Barrionuevo, "Brazil Discovers an Oil Field Can Be a Political Tool," *New York Times*, November 19, 2007; Barrionuevo, "Brazil Moves for More Control"; and Matt Moffett, "How a Sleeping Oil Giant Became a World Player," *Wall Street Journal*, August 30, 2007.

52. As quoted in Eric Watkins, "Brazil Sets Sights on Increasing Oil Production," *Oil & Gas Journal Online*, June 29, 2008, retrieved at www.ogj .com on July 2, 2008.

53. See Watkins, "Brazil Unveils Proposed Offshore Presalt Legislation"; and Watkins, "Brazil Approves Oil Laws, Opens Presalt Region to Development," *Oil & Gas Journal*, December 13, 2010, pp. 26–27.

54. As quoted in Watkins, "Brazil Approves Oil Laws," p. 27.

55. DoE/EIA, "Brazil," September 2009. See also Jonathan Wheatley, "Critics Warn Plan Will Deter Investors," *Financial Times*, September 8, 2009.

56. See "Preparing to Spend a 'Millionaire Ticket' from Offshore," *Economist*, September 5, 2009, pp. 42–43; and Alexei Barrionuevo, "Rio de Janeiro Is at Center of Fight over Shares of Brazil's Oil Riches," *New York Times*, March 18, 2010.

57. As quoted in Wheatley, "Critics Warn Plan Will Deter Investors."

58. Dilma Rousseff, "Brazil Aims to Avoid Long-Term Oil 'Curse,'" *Oil & Gas Journal*, November 9, 2009, pp. 18–19.

59. White House, Office of the Press Secretary, "Remarks of the President at U.S.-Brazil Business Summit," Brasília, Brazil, March 19, 2011, retrieved at projects.washingtonpost.com on April 23, 2011.

60. As quoted in Jeff Grocott, "Liberian Leader Vows Responsible Oil Plan," *Wall Street Journal*, September 22, 2010.

61. "Ghana's Latest Discovery Hints at Growing Potential," *Oil & Gas Journal*, December 8, 2008, pp. 40–41.

62. For background, see Rudolf ten Hoedt, "Ghana: A Race against the Oil Curse," *European Energy Review*, April 16, 2010, retrieved at www.euro peanenergyreview.eu on May 11, 2010.

63. "Tullow Oil: Ghana Jubilee Field 1st Oil 4Q 2010," Dow Jones Newswire, April 13, 2010, retrieved at online.wsj.com on April 14, 2010.

64. "Ghana's Latest Discovery"; Eric Watkins, "Ghana Ports Authority Prepares for Oil Production," *Oil & Gas Journal Online*, August 11, 2009, retrieved at www.ogj.com on August 18, 2009.

65. See "Ghana's Latest Discovery"; "Tullow Oil: Ghana Jubilee Field"; and Uchenna Izundu, "Ghana Approves First Jubilee Development Phase," *Oil & Gas Journal*, July 27, 2009, p. 35.

66. Will Connors, Simon Hall, and David Winning, "Exxon Ends Ghana Plan," *Wall Street Journal*, August 19, 2010.

67. Rakesh Sharma and Isabel Ordóñez, "Bid for Ghana Oil Field Rebuffed," *Wall Street Journal*, November 2, 2010.

68. See, for example, William Wallis, "Ghana Seeks Way out of Oilfields Dispute," *Financial Times*, July 19, 2010.

69. As quoted in ten Hoedt, "Ghana: A Race against the Oil Curse."

70. As quoted in ibid.

71. Alan Petzet, "Discovery off Sierra Leone May Set Up 700-Mile Play," *Oil & Gas Journal*, September 28, 2009, pp. 36–37.

72. For discussion, see "Is Offshore West Africa the World's Next Frontier for Oil?" in DoE/EIA, *International Energy Outlook 2010*, pp. 28–29.

73. See Adrian Croft, "UK Files Claim to Seabed Around the Falklands," *Washington Post*, May 11, 2009; and "Sea Lion Hailed as Giant Falklands Oil Find," *Oil & Gas Journal Online*, June 7, 2010, retrieved at www .ogj.com on June 10, 2010.

74. "South Falklands Prospects High-Graded," *Oil & Gas Journal*, March 2, 2009, pp. 36–37.

75. See "Sea Lion Hailed as Giant Falklands Oil Find"; and "Falklands Find Appraised as Commercial Oil Field," *Oil & Gas Journal Online*, August 2011, retrieved at www.ogj.com on August 12, 2011.

76. See Eric Watkins, "BHP Exits Falklands," *Oil & Gas Journal*, November 1, 2010, pp. 60–61.

77. David Blair, "Britain and Argentina Lodge Rival Claims to Seabed around Falklands," *Telegraph*, May 12, 2009.

78. Ian Drury, "Flashpoint the Falklands," *Mail Online*, February 20, 2010, retrieved at www.dailymail.co.uk on June 14, 2010.

79. Eric Watkins, "Argentina Closes Ports to Ships Visiting Falklands," *Oil & Gas Journal*, February 22, 2010, p. 28.

80. Ginger Thompson, "Clinton Urges Talks on the Falkland Islands," *New York Times*, March 1, 2010.

81. DoE/EIA, *International Energy Outlook 2011*, Table A1, p. 157.

82. As quoted in Bambang Dwi Djanuarto, "Indonesia to Fight Malaysia's Ambalat Oil Claims," *Jakarta Globe*, October 22, 2009, retrieved at www.thejakartaglobe.com on June 21, 2010.

83. Ibid. See also Eric Watkins, "Malaysia Downplays Territorial Dispute with Indonesia," *Oil & Gas Journal*, November 3, 2008, p. 32.

84. See DoE/EIA, "East China Sea," Country Analysis Brief, March 2008, retrieved at www.eia.doe.gov on June 21, 2010; and "South China Sea," Country Analysis Brief, March 2008, retrieved at www.eia.doe.gov on June 21, 2010.

85. For background, see James Manicom, "China's Claims to an Extended Continental Shelf in the East China Sea: Meaning and Implications," *China Brief*, Jamestown Foundation, July 9, 2009, pp. 9–11; and Mark J. Valencia, *Foreign Military Activities in Asian EEZs: Conflict Ahead?* NBR Special Report No. 27 (Seattle: National Bureau of Asian Research, May 2011).

86. For background, see Klare, *Rising Powers, Shrinking Planet*, pp. 221–24. See also James Brooke, "Drawing the Line on Energy," *New York Times*, March 29, 2005; and Brooke, "For Japan and China, Strains from a Line in the Sea," *New York Times*, April 14, 2005.

87. On incidents at sea, see "Oil and Gas in Troubled Waters," *Economist*, October 2005, pp. 52–53. See also Mure Dickie and Kathrin Hille, "Japan Urges China Warships Probe," *Financial Times*, April 14, 2010. This article refers to an incident in the East China Sea in which a Chinese ship-based helicopter came within 300 feet of a Japanese destroyer.

88. Martin Fackler, "China and Japan Agree to End Offshore Gas Dispute," *New York Times*, June 18, 2008.

89. See "Oil and Gas in Troubled Waters"; and Dickie and Hille, "Japan Urges China Warships Probe."

90. For background, see DoE/EIA, "South China Sea," March 2008. See also Michael T. Klare, *Resource Wars: The New Landscape of Global Conflict* (New York: Metropolitan Books, 2001), pp. 109–37.

91. As quoted in Paula Dittrick, "OTC: BP Calls Deepwater Drilling 'Indispensable,'" *Oil & Gas Journal*, May 9, 2011, p. 19.

CHAPTER 3: INVADING THE ARCTIC

1. "Largest Drillship Visits Medserv Malta," *Times of Malta*, October 23, 2009, retrieved at www.timesofmalta.com on July 22, 2010.

2. "Oil, Gas Shows off Greenland Encourage Cairn," *Oil & Gas Journal*, November 1, 2010, p. 10. See also Uchenna Izundu, "Gambling on Greenland," *European Energy Review*, January 10, 2011, retrieved at www.europeanenergyreview.eu on January 12, 2011.

3. James Herron, "Cairn to Spend $600 Million on Greenland Oil Drilling," *Wall Street Journal*, May 24, 2011.

4. "Greenland Awards Seven Licenses in Baffin Bay," *Oil & Gas Journal*, January 3, 2011, p. 71.

5. Marianne Stigset, "Greenland Oil Rush Looms as Exxon Eyes Cairn," *Bloomberg Businessweek*, May 5, 2010, retrieved at www.businessweek.com on July 21, 2010. See also Izundu, "Gambling on Greenland."

6. Economist Intelligence Unit, "World Oil: Into Greenland's Waters," January 7, 2010, retrieved at viewswire.eiu.com on July 21, 2010.

7. "Greenland: BMP to License Area off Northeast," *Oil & Gas Journal Online*, April 12, 2011, retrieved at www.ogj.com on April 18, 2011.

8. See Andrew Ward and Sylvia Pfeifer, "Greenland Sees Oil as Key to Independence," *Financial Times*, August 27, 2010.

9. Spencer Swartz, "Oil-Exploration Prospects Divide Greenland," *Wall Street Journal*, April 26, 2010.

10. As quoted in Krista Mahr, "Will the Arctic Oil Rush Be Spoiled by a Spill?" *Time*, July 10, 2010, retrieved at www.time.com on July 21, 2010.

11. Ibid.

12. See Izundu, "Gambling on Greenland."

13. "Greenpeace Cairn Rig Activists Arrested off Greenland," BBC News, September 2, 2010, retrieved at www.bbc.co.uk on April 23, 2011.

14. "Greenpeace Abandons Cairn Energy Rig off Istanbul," Associated Press, April 22, 2011, retrieved at fuelfix.com on April 23, 2011.

15. As quoted in Patrick White, "Politicians, Activists Raise Alarm over Greenland's Ambitious Drilling Program," *Globe and Mail*, May 19, 2010.

16. Alexandra Stephenson, "Arctic Survey Data Trigger Worldwide Warning," *Financial Times*, October 15, 2009. For further background on the impact of warming on drilling prospects in the Arctic, see Ronald O'Rourke, *Changes in the Arctic: Background and Issues for Congress*, Congressional Research Service (CRS) Report for Congress (Washington, D.C.: CRS, July 7, 2011).

17. USGS, "Circum-Arctic Resource Appraisal: Estimates of Undiscovered Oil and Gas North of the Arctic Circle," USGS Fact Sheet 2008–3049 (Washington, D.C.: USGS, 2008), p. 1.

18. Ibid.

19. As quoted in Jad Mouawad, "Oil Survey Says Arctic Has Riches," *New York Times*, July 24, 2008.

20. DoE/EIA, *Annual Energy Review 2008* (Washington, D.C.: DoE/EIA, 2009), Table 5.2, p. 131.

21. USGS, "Arctic National Wildlife Refuge, 1002 Area: Petroleum Assessment, 1998, Including Economic Analysis," USGS Fact Sheet FS-028–01, April 2001 (Washington, D.C.: USGS, 2001), p. 4.

22. As cited in "Presidential Candidates' Views on ANWR—The Democrats," ANWR.org, retrieved at www.anwr.org on July 29, 2010.

23. Peter Canby, "The Specter Haunting Alaska," *New York Review of Books*, November 17, 2005, retrieved at www.nybooks.com on June 23, 2011.

24. Broder, "In a Shift, Obama Moves to Speed Drilling for Oil and Gas."

25. MMS, *Report to Congress: Comprehensive Inventory of U.S. OCS Oil and Natural Gas Resources* (Washington, D.C.: MMS, February 2006), p. vii.

26. MMS, "Sale Day Statistics," Chukchi Sea Sale Number 193, February 7, 2008, retrieved at alaska.boemre.gov on July 29, 2010.

27. BP, *BP in Alaska* (Anchorage, Alaska: BP), p. 34.

28. See Kristen Nelson, "BP Spending Three-Quarters of a Million Dollars a Day at Northstar," *Petroleum News*, March 28, 2000, retrieved at www.petroleumnews.com on July 30, 2010.

29. See Kristen Nelson, "Northstar-Bound Barge Heads for Island—Again," *Petroleum News*, August 28, 2000, retrieved at www.petroleumnews.com on July 30, 2010. See also Andrew Mullins, "Greenpeace Hijacks Barge in Protest at Arctic Oil Drilling," *Independent*, August 8, 2000.

30. Jim Burke, "Inspectors Say BP's Alaska Pipeline Needs Attention," *Alaska Dispatch*, May 19, 2010, retrieved at alaskadispatch.com on July 30, 2010.

31. See BP Exploration (Alaska), Inc., *Reaching Out to Liberty* (Anchorage, Alaska: BP, n.d.). See also Rhonda McBride, "BP's Massive New Drill Rig Arrives at Beaufort Sea," KTUU.com, August 6, 2009, retrieved at www.ktuu.com on July 30, 2010; and Ian Urbina, "BP Is Pursuing Alaska Drilling Some Call Risky," *New York Times*, June 23, 2010.

32. Reliance on u-ERD "eliminates the offshore impacts of island and pipeline construction," the company noted in a 2007 development plan submitted to the MMS. See BP Exploration (Alaska) Inc., *Liberty Development Project—Development and Production Plan* (Anchorage, Alaska: BP, April 2007), pp. 1–2.

33. Urbina, "BP Is Pursuing Alaska Drilling."

34. See Tim Dickinson, "BP's Next Disaster," *Rolling Stone*, July 8–22, 2010, pp. 61–64. On the problem of addressing an oil spill in the Arctic, see O'Rourke, *Changes in the Arctic*, pp. 22–25.

35. Patti Epler, "BP Slows Down Plans for Liberty Oil Field," *Alaska Dispatch*, July 6, 2010, retrieved at alaskadispatch.com on July 30, 2010. See also Rhonda McBride, "BP's Liberty Project Delayed Again," KTUU.com, February 1, 2011, retrieved at www.ktuu.com on April 23, 2011.

36. "The Liberty project is really untested cutting-edge technology," said Rebecca Noblin, the Alaska director for the Center for Biological Diversity, an environmental watchdog. "This is at the frontiers of their technology and we think we really need to take a closer look to make sure all the environmental reviews are done." As quoted in Epler, "BP Slows Down Plans for Liberty Oil Field."

37. Nick Snow, "U.S. Court Rejects Bid to Halt Shell's Alaskan Offshore Program," *Oil & Gas Journal Online*, May 17, 2010, retrieved at www.ogj.com on May 17, 2010.

38. Clifford Krauss, "Royal Dutch Shell Abandons Plans to Drill in Arctic Waters," *New York Times*, February 4, 2011.

39. As quoted in Clifford Krauss, "Shell Prepares for Drilling in Arctic," *New York Times*, November 6, 2010.

40. John M. Broder and Clifford Krauss, "U.S. Taking Steps to Open Drilling in Arctic Ocean," *New York Times*, August 5, 2011.

41. As quoted in "Alaska Politicians Praise Drilling Decision," *Alaska Dispatch*, June 22, 2010, retrieved at alaskadispatch.com on July 31, 2010.

42. As quoted in Yereth Rosen, "Court Order Halts Chukchi Oil and Gas Activity," Reuters, July 22, 2010, retrieved at af.reuters.com on July 31, 2010.

43. BP, *Statistical Review of World Energy June 2011* (London: BP, 2011), pp. 6, 8, 22.

44. For background, see DoE/EIA, "Norway," Country Analysis Brief, August 2011, retrieved at www.eia.doe.gov on August 31, 2011. See also earlier editions of Norway country brief.

45. "Snøhvit Gas Field, Barents Sea, Norway," Offshore-Technology.com, retrieved at www.offshore-technology.com on July 14, 2011.

46. See Guy Chazan, "Norwegian Oil Firm Goes to Energy's Last Frontier," *Wall Street Journal*, February 13, 2009; Jay Mouawad, "A Quest for Energy in the Globe's Remote Places," *New York Times*, October 9, 2007; and "StatoilHydro Shutting Down Hammerfest LNG for 3 Months," *Oil & Gas Journal*, September 7, 2009, p. 33.

47. "Snøhvit—Unlocking Resources in the Frozen North," November 23, 2009, retrieved at www.statoil.com on February 17, 2010.

48. Statoil, "Snøhvit Made the Impossible Possible," press release, June 4, 2010, retrieved at www.statoil.com on August 1, 2010.

49. "Statoil Getting Ready for More Drilling in Barents Sea," *Barents Observer*, July 27, 2010, retrieved at www.barentsobserver.com on July 31, 2010.

50. DoE/EIA, "Norway," August 2011.

51. WWF, *The Barents Sea—An Sea of Opportunities . . . and Threats: A WWF-Norway Report*, Executive Summary, April 4, 2003, retrieved at www.panda.org on August 1, 2010.

52. Erik Watkins, "Norway Launches New Licensing Round," *Oil & Gas Journal*, March 8, 2010, pp. 30–31.

53. Norwegian Ministry of Petroleum and Energy, "Announcement—21st Licensing Round," press release, June 23, 2010, retrieved at www.regjeringen.no on July 31, 2010.

54. For background, see DoE/EIA, "Russia," May 2008.

55. USGS, "Circum-Arctic Resource Appraisal," USGS Fact Sheet 2008–3049, p. 4.

56. From a transcription of a *Science* magazine podcast, May 29, 2009, retrieved at podcasts.aaas.org on August 1, 2010.

57. "Arctic Resources Central to Russia's Energy Security—Medvedev," *RIA Novosti*, September 17, 2008, retrieved at en.rian.ru on December 27, 2008.

58. Roger McDermott, "Russia Planning Arctic Military Grouping," *Eurasia Daily Monitor*, Jamestown Foundation, April 15, 2009, retrieved at www.jamestown.org on April 24, 2009. See also "Russia Outlines Arctic Force Plan," BBC News, March 27, 2009, retrieved at newsvote.bbc.co.uk on December 22, 2010.

59. For background and discussion, see Philip Budzik, "Arctic Oil and Natural Gas Potential," DoE/EIA, October 2009, retrieved at www.eia.doe.gov on July 31, 2010.

60. See "Prirazlomnoye Oilfield—Barents Sea, Russia," Offshore-Technology.com, retrieved at www.offshore-technology.com on August 3, 2010.

61. See Budzik, "Arctic Oil and Natural Gas Potential," p. 11.

62. "Gazprom Board of Directors Approves Adjusted Investment Program," *Russia-Media*, Murmansk & Shtokman News, October 3, 2011, retrieved at russia-media.ru on October 28, 2011.

63. "'Iceberg Threat' Looms over Shtokman," Upstreamonline.com, April 27, 2007, retrieved at www.upstreamonline.com on August 3, 2010.

64. "Floating Removable Platforms for Shtokman Field," *Barents Observer*, January 31, 2008, retrieved at www.barentsobserver.com on August 3, 2010.

65. Uchenna Izundu, "Shtokman Phase 1 Development Contracts Awarded," *Oil & Gas Journal Online*, March 27, 2008, retrieved at www.ogj.com on March 31, 2008.

66. "Shtokman Partners Delay Production Start," *Oil & Gas Journal*, February 8, 2010, retrieved at www.ogj.com on August 3, 2010.

67. Alan Petzet, "Explorers Directing Efforts at Frontier, Underexplored, Nonproducing Basins," *Oil & Gas Journal*, April 4, 2011, pp. 49–50.

68. BP, "Major Arctic Projects and Share Swap," press announcement, January 14, 2011, retrieved at www.bp.com on January 29, 2011.

69. See Andrew E. Kramer and Clifford Krauss, "Court Blocks BP-

Rosneft Arctic Deal," *New York Times*, March 25, 2011; and Catherine Belton and Sylvia Pfeifer, "BP Frozen Out as the Landscape Shifts," *Financial Times*, May 18, 2011.

70. Andrew E. Kramer, "Exxon Reaches Oil Deal with Russians," *New York Times*, August 31, 2011.

71. For background on these developments, see O'Rourke, *Changes in the Arctic*; and Reginald R. Smith, "The Arctic: A New Partnership Paradigm of the Next 'Cold War'?" *Joint Forces Quarterly*, no. 62 (3rd quarter 2011), pp. 111–24.

72. As quoted in Chivers, "Eyeing Future Wealth."

73. For background on these developments, see O'Rourke, *Changes in the Arctic*, pp. 40–55.

74. See Chip Cummins, "Canada Presses Claims Over a Chunk of Arctic," *Wall Street Journal*, September 28, 2011; and Jacob W. Kipp, "Russian Strategic Interests Expand in the Arctic," *Eurasia Daily Monitor*, September 21, 2011, retrieved at www.jamestown.org on September 21, 2011.

75. See O'Rourke, *Changes in the Arctic*, pp. 34–40. See also Steven Lee Myers, "Cooperation Is Pledged by Nations of the Arctic," *New York Times*, May 13, 2011.

76. For background, see Kaj Hober, "Territorial Disputes and Natural Resources: The Melting of the Ice and Arctic Disputes," *Oil & Gas Journal*, February 7, 2011, pp. 54–60; and O'Rourke, *Changes in the Arctic*, pp. 11–13.

77. See Paul Reynolds, "The Arctic's New Gold Rush," BBC World News, October 25, 2005, retrieved at newsvote.bbc.co.uk on December 25, 2008.

78. "We will assert our right to enforce Canadian law in our territory," Prime Minister Stephen Harper said of the Beaufort Sea wedge prior to a September 2009 official visit to Washington. As quoted in Randy Boswell, "NDP Press Harper to Raise U.S.-Canada Boundary Dispute with Obama," Canwest News Service, September 15, 2009, retrieved at www.canada.com on August 7, 2010.

79. See Reynolds, "The Arctic's New Gold Rush."

80. For background, see Hober, "Territorial Disputes and Natural Resources."

81. See Jessa Gamble, "Drawing Lines in the Sea: Nations Stake Claims on Arctic Ocean Riches," *Scientific American*, November 10, 2008, retrieved at www.scientificamerican.com on June 28, 2009.

82. As quoted in Eric Watkins, "Arctic Conferences Point to 'Cold War' over Oil," *Oil & Gas Journal*, December 6, 2010, p. 81.

CHAPTER 4: TAR SANDS, SHALE GAS, AND OTHER UNCONVENTIONAL HYDROCARBONS

1. DoE/EIA, "Canada," Country Analysis Brief, April 2011, retrieved at www.eia.doe.gov on April 25, 2011.

2. For background, see Marc Humphries, *North American Oil Sands: History of Development, Prospects for the Future*, CRS Report for Congress (Washington, D.C.: CRS, January 17, 2008); Robert Kunzig, "The Canadian Oil Boom: Scraping Bottom," *National Geographic*, March 2009, pp. 37–59; and Abraham Lustgarten, "The Dark Magic of Oil Sands," *Fortune*, October 3, 2005, pp. 136–48.

3. Kunzig, "The Canadian Oil Boom," p. 44.

4. See Humphries, *North American Oil Sands*, pp. 10–11; and Lustgarten, "The Dark Magic of Oil Sands."

5. See Clifford Krauss, "In Canada's Wilderness, Measuring the Cost of Oil Profits," *New York Times*, October 9, 2005; and Kunzig, "The Canadian Oil Boom."

6. Ian Austen, "An Oil Sandstorm," *New York Times*, January 7, 2009.

7. Ibid. See also Kunzig, "The Canadian Oil Boom"; and Tim Reiterman, "Canada's Black Gold Glimmers but Tarnishes," *Los Angeles Times*, July 8, 2007.

8. See DoE/EIA, "Canada," April 2011; and Humphries, *North American Oil Sands*, pp. 12–13.

9. As quoted in Krauss, "In Canada's Wilderness."

10. See Humphries, *North American Oil Sands*, pp. 21–22.

11. As quoted in Krauss, "In Canada's Wilderness."

12. Ana Campoy, "Oil-Sands Obstacle: Emissions," *Wall Street Journal*, April 25, 2007.

13. See Humphries, *North American Oil Sands*, p. 21. See also Ian Austen, "Canada Announces Exit from Kyoto Climate Treaty," *New York Times*, December 13, 2011.

14. "Suncor Plans $20.6 Billion Oil Sands Expansion," *Oil & Gas Journal Online*, February 1, 2008, retrieved at www.ogj.com on February 5, 2008.

15. Sheila McNulty, "Sinopec Buys Conoco's 9% Stake in Syncrude," *Financial Times*, April 13, 2010.

16. For background, see Paul W. Parfomak, Neelesh Nerurkar, Linda Luther, and Vanessa K. Burrows, *Keystone XL Pipeline Project: Key Issues* (Washington, D.C.: CRS, March 4, 2011).

17. See Kunzig, "The Canadian Oil Boom," p. 43; and Guntis Moritis, "Alberta Bitumen Development Continues Its Rapid Expansion," *Oil & Gas Journal*, July 9, 2007, p. 43.

18. As quoted in Clifford Krauss and Elisabeth Rosenthal, "Mired in Canada's Oil Sands," *New York Times*, May 19, 2010.

19. As quoted in Russell Gold, "As Prices Surge, Oil Giants Turn Sludge into Gold," *Wall Street Journal*, March 27, 2006.

20. "The Next Trillion Barrels," *Next*, no. 2 (2007), p. 21. For discussion, see Yergin, *The Quest*, pp. 242–62, 325–32; and Clifford Krauss, "The Energy Picture, Redrawn," *New York Times*, October 26, 2011.

21. IEA, *World Energy Outlook 2010*, Table 3.3, p. 119.

22. DoE/EIA, *Annual Energy Outlook 2011* (Washington, D.C.: DoE/EIA, 2011), Table A14. On international shale gas options, see Krauss, "The Energy Picture, Redrawn."

23. Steve Gelsi, "Exxon Mobil to Buy XTO Energy in $41 Billion Deal," *MarketWatch*, December 14, 2009, retrieved at www.marketwatch.com on August 12, 2010; and Russell Gold, "Exxon Bets Big on Gas with Deal for XTO," *Wall Street Journal*, December 15, 2009.

24. See Nick Snow, "Forum: Alberta Oil Sands 'Source of Strategic Value,'" *Oil & Gas Journal*, May 24, 2010, pp. 30–31. For discussion of the potential national security advantages of increased U.S. reliance on Canadian tar sands, see Michael A. Levi, *The Canadian Oil Sands: Energy Security vs. Climate Change* (New York: Council on Foreign Relations, 2009).

25. As quoted in Krauss and Rosenthal, "Mired in Canada's Oil Sands."

26. See Geoff Dyer and Carola Hoyos, "Sinopec and BP Explore China Gas Venture," *Financial Times*, January 19, 2010.

27. "It's not true to say . . . that we are running out of hydrocarbons," said Tony Hayward, then BP's chief executive officer, in February 2009. In addition to all the oil and gas deposits still waiting to be discovered, "there are vast quantities of unconventional hydrocarbons, including oil sands, heavy oil, and unconventional gas." Opening speech to the Cambridge

Energy Research Association, Houston, Tex., February 10, 2009, retrieved at www.bp.com on March 16, 2010.

28. USGS, "An Estimate of Recoverable Heavy Oil Resources of the Orinoco Oil Belt, Venezuela," USGS Fact Sheet 2009–3028, October 2009, retrieved at www.usgs.gov on August 13, 2010.

29. BP, *Statistical Review of World Energy June 2011*, p. 6.

30. Brian Clark et al., "Heavy Oil," Topic Paper no. 22, Working Document of the National Petroleum Council Global Oil and Gas Study, July 18, 2007, retrieved at www.npc.org on August 13, 2010.

31. Richard F. Meyer and Emil D. Attanasi, "Heavy Oil and Natural Bitumen—Strategic Petroleum Resources," USGS Factsheet 70–03, August 2003, retrieved at www.usgs.gov on August 13, 2010.

32. USGS, "An Estimate of Recoverable Heavy Oil Resources of the Orinoco Oil Belt."

33. See Simon Romero, "Chávez Reopens Oil Bids to West as Prices Plunge," *New York Times*, January 15, 2009.

34. As quoted in Eric Watkins, "Two Consortia Awarded Orinoco Carabobo Blocks," *Oil & Gas Journal*, February 22, 2010, p. 34.

35. Chevron Corp., "Venezuela Fact Sheet," March 2010, retrieved at www.chevron.com on August 13, 2010. See also Michael Lynch, "Chevron Expanding Operations in Risky Venezuela," Gerson Lehrman Group, February 11, 2010, retrieved at www.glgroup.com on August 13, 2010.

36. Watkins, "Two Consortia Awarded Orinoco Carabobo Blocks," p. 34.

37. Ibid.

38. As quoted in Simon Romero, "Chávez Says China to Lend Venezuela $20 Billion," *New York Times*, April 18, 2010.

39. DoE/EIA, "Venezuela," Country Analysis Brief, February 2010, retrieved at www.eia.doe.gov on August 13, 2010.

40. USGS, "Technical Assessment: U.S. Oil Shale Assessments Updated," press release, April 2, 2009, retrieved at www.usgs.gov on August 15, 2010.

41. USGS, "In-Place Oil Shale Resources Underlying Federal Lands in the Piceance Basin, Western Colorado," USGS Fact Sheet 2010–041, June 2010; and USGS, "Assessment of In-Place Oil Shale Resources of the Green River Formation, Uinta Basin, Utah and Colorado," USGS Fact Sheet 010–3010, May 2010.

42. Khosrow Biglarbigi, Hitesh Mohan, and James Killen, "Oil Shale:

U.S., World Possess Rich Resource Base," *Oil & Gas Journal*, January 19, 2009, p. 57.

43. Ibid., pp. 56–57.

44. For a survey of the environmental risks involved in oil shale extraction and possible methods for mitigating these risks, see Emily Knaus and James Killen, "Technology May Control Adverse Environmental Effects," *Oil & Gas Journal*, February 9, 2009, pp. 42–45. See also Julie Cart, "Water, Oil Don't Mix in Rockies," *Los Angeles Times*, December 28, 2008.

45. Guntis Moritis, "Western U.S. Commercial Oil Shale Leasing Still Years Away," *Oil & Gas Journal Online*, retrieved at www.ogj.com on October 16, 2008.

46. Stephen Power, "Interior Secretary Scraps Oil-Shale Leasing," *Wall Street Journal*, February 25, 2009.

47. Nick Snow, "Salazar Announces Oil Shale Lease Round, Addenda Inquiry," *Oil & Gas Journal*, October 26, 2009, pp. 20–21.

48. Peter Crawford et al., "Oil Shale: New Approaches Overcome Past Technical Issues," *Oil & Gas Journal*, January 26, 2009, pp. 45–46. See also Jon Birger, "Oil from a Stone," *Fortune*, November 12, 2007, pp. 105–16.

49. Crawford et al., "New Approaches Overcome Past Technical Issues," p. 46.

50. Ibid., pp. 46–47. See also Telis Demos, "The World of Oil Shale," *Fortune*, November 12, 2007, p. 114.

51. Amy Myers Jaffe, "How Shale Gas Is Going to Rock the World," *Wall Street Journal*, May 10, 2010.

52. DoE/EIA, *International Energy Outlook 2010*, pp. 41–42. See also Krauss, "The Energy Picture, Redrawn."

53. For background on the hydrofracking technique, see Mooney, "The Truth about Fracking." See also Ben Casselman and Russell Gold, "Drilling Technique Unleashes a Trove of Natural Gas—And a Backlash," *Washington Post*, January 21, 2010.

54. For background on the development of shale gas, see Daniel Yergin, "Stepping on the Gas," *Wall Street Journal*, April 2–3, 2011.

55. Scott Stevens and Vello Kuuskraa, "Seven Plays Dominate North America Activity," *Oil & Gas Journal*, September 28, 2009, pp. 39–55.

56. "Shale Plays Push Up U.S. Gas Resource Estimate," *Oil & Gas Journal Online*, June 18, 2009, retrieved at www.ogj.com on August 16, 2010.

57. Stevens and Kuuskraa, "Seven Plays Dominate North American Activity," pp. 45–46.

58. "An Unconventional Glut," *Economist*, March 13, 2010, pp. 72–74. See also Thomas Kaplan, "Chevron to Buy Atlas in a Competition for Natural Gas," *New York Times*, November 10, 2010.

59. See Gelsi, "Exxon Mobil to Buy XTO Energy"; and Gold, "Exxon Bets Big on Gas with Deal for XTO."

60. As quoted in Jad Mouawad and Clifford Krauss, "Tapping the New Gusher," *New York Times*, December 15, 2009.

61. "WoodMac: Majors Buying into Shale Gas Plays," *Oil & Gas Journal*, October 11, 2010, pp. 18–20.

62. For discussion, see Carola Hoyos, "Europe the New Frontier in Shale Gas Rush," *Financial Times*, March 8, 2010.

63. See "ConocoPhillips, Lane to Explore Polish Shale Gas," *Oil & Gas Journal*, September 21, 2009, p. 52; and Doris Leblond, "European Shale Gas Prospects Heat Up," *Oil & Gas Journal Online*, May 29, 2009, retrieved at www.ogj.com on June 2, 2009.

64. For background and discussion, see Mark Fischetti, "The Drillers Are Coming," *Scientific American*, July 2010, pp. 82–85; Paul Hagemeier and Jason Hutt, "Hydraulic Fracturing, Water Use Issues Under Congressional, Public Scrutiny," *Oil & Gas Journal*, July 6, 2009, pp. 18–25; Mooney, "The Truth about Fracking"; and Mark Zoback, Saya Kitasei, and Brad Copithorne, *Addressing the Environmental Risks from Shale Gas Development* (Washington, D.C.: Worldwatch Institute, July 2010).

65. See Zoback, Kitasei, and Copithorne, *Addressing the Environmental Risks from Shale Gas Development*, pp. 7–11. See also Jay Mouawad and Clifford Krauss, "Dark Side of a Natural Gas Boom," *New York Times*, December 8, 2009; Steven Mufson, "Drilling Right into a Heated Environmental Debate," *Washington Post*, December 3, 2009; and Ian Urbina, "Regulation Lax as Gas Wells' Tainted Water Hits Rivers," *New York Times*, February 26, 2011.

66. As quoted in Mouawad and Krauss, "Dark Side of a Natural Gas Boom."

67. As quoted in Casselman and Gold, "Drilling Tactic Unleashes a Trove of Natural Gas."

68. See Mouawad and Krauss, "Dark Side of a Natural Gas Boom"; and Mufson, "Drilling Right into a Heated Environmental Debate." See also

Nick Snow, "Cabot, Pennsylvania DEP Reach New Accord for 19 Dimock Households," *Oil & Gas Journal Online*, December 21, 2010, retrieved at www.ogj.com on January 3, 2011.

69. Joel Kirkland, "Concerns Spread over Environmental Costs of Producing Shale Gas," ClimateWire, July 9, 2010, retrieved at www.nytimes.com on August 17, 2010.

70. "Gas Well Spews Polluted Water," Associated Press, *New York Times*, April 20, 2011.

71. Urbina, "Regulation Lax as Gas Wells' Tainted Water Hits Rivers."

72. As quoted in ibid.

73. Ibid.

74. Statement of Benjamin L. Cardin before the hearing on "Natural Gas Drilling: Public Health and Environmental Impacts," Subcommittee on Water and Wildlife, Senate Environment and Public Works Committee, Washington, D.C., April 12, 2011, retrieved at epw.senate.gov on May 8, 2011.

75. White House, *Blueprint for a Secure Energy Future* (Washington, D.C.: White House, March 30, 2011), p. 9.

76. John M. Broder, "Energy Dept. Panel to Revise Standards for Gas Extraction," *New York Times*, May 6, 2011.

77. For background, see Ian Urbina, "Insiders Sound an Alarm Amid a Natural Gas Rush," *New York Times*, June 25, 2011.

78. As quoted in ibid.

79. On the Bakken formation, see USGS, "Assessment of Undiscovered Oil Resources in the Devonian-Mississippian Bakken Formation, Williston Basin Province, Montana and North Dakota, 2008," USGS Fact Sheet 2008–3021, April 2008. On Eagle Ford, see Paula Dittrick, "Industry Expects Rapid Gains in Eagle Ford Shale Output," *Oil & Gas Journal*, July 4, 2011, pp. 40–42.

80. See "New Drilling Method Opens Vast U.S. Oil Fields," Associated Press, February 10, 2011, retrieved at www.foxnews.com on May 25, 2011.

81. See USGS, "Coal-Bed Methane: Potential and Concerns," USGS Fact Sheet 123–00, October 2000, retrieved at www.usgs.gov on August 18, 2010.

82. Ibid.

83. Ibid.

84. DoE/EIA, *Annual Energy Outlook 2011*, Table A14, p. 143.

85. "WSJ: Exxon Lured by Gas Potential," Dow Jones, November 11, 2009, retrieved at www.energytribune.com on August 18, 2010. See also Jack Williams, "Shale Gas: The Keys to Unlocking Its Full Potential," speech delivered at SPE Unconventional Gas Conference, Houston, Tex., June 14, 2011, retrieved at www.exxonmobil.com on July 20, 2011.

86. ConocoPhillips, "Australia and Timor-Leste," retrieved at www .conocophillips.com on August 18, 2010.

87. See "China Wants to Hasten Coalbed Methane Development," *Oil & Gas Journal*, September 6, 2010, pp. 84–87.

88. "The Next Trillion Barrels," p. 23.

89. See DoE, "Methane Hydrate—The Gas Resources of the Future," retrieved at www.fossil.energy.gov on August 18, 2010.

90. As noted by a special task force of the National Research Council, "Complex scientific challenges, which may require the development of new technologies, remain before methane from methane hydrate can be realized as an energy resource." See Committee on Earth Sciences, National Research Council (NRC), *Realizing the Potential of Methane Hydrate for the United States* (Washington, D.C.: National Academies Press, 2010), p. 1.

91. Ibid., p. 161.

92. DoE, "Methane Hydrate—The Gas Resources of the Future."

93. Japan Oil, Gas, and Metals National Corporation (JOGMEC), "Promoting the Development of Methane Hydrates," retrieved at www.jogmec .go.jp on May 8, 2011.

94. Michael Fitzpatrick, "Japan to Drill for Controversial 'Fire Ice,'" *Guardian*, September 27, 2010.

95. As quoted in "The Next Trillion Barrels," p. 25.

CHAPTER 5: MINING'S NEW FRONTIERS

1. For background, see Lydia Polgreen, "Pristine African Park Faces Development," *New York Times*, February 22, 2009.

2. USGS, "Gabon," *Minerals Yearbook 2008*, vol. 3, chap. 17, pp. 1–2.

3. See David Lewis, "Special Report: In Africa, Can Brazil Be the Anti-China?" Reuters, February 23, 2011, retrieved at www.reuters.com on May 14, 2011.

4. Antoine Lawson, "Gabonese Hope for Windfall as Chinese Develop Iron Ore Deposit," *New York Times*, February 26, 2007.

5. As quoted in ibid.

6. As quoted in Lewis, "Special Report."

7. Polgreen, "Pristine African Park Faces Development."

8. Ibid. See also "Gabon: Ivindo National Park," retrieved at www.tripadviser.com on September 9, 2010.

9. As quoted in Polgreen, "Pristine African Park Faces Development."

10. "Gabon to Review China's Belinga Deal, Vale Hovers," Reuters, April 13, 2010, retrieved at www.miningweekly.com on August 31, 2010.

11. Ibid.

12. For discussion, see "Belinga Iron Ore Project," BankTrack.org, retrieved at www.banktrack.org on August 31, 2010.

13. See USGS, "Iron" and "Copper," from *Minerals Yearbook 2008*.

14. Lorraine Turner, "Rio Tinto Gets 3-Month Extension to Mine Rights at Simandou," Reuters, February 24, 2011, retrieved at www.mineweb.com on September 17, 2011.

15. See David Gauthier-Villars, "Mining Fight Shows Pressure on Multinationals," *Wall Street Journal*, January 27, 2011.

16. Ibid. See also Turner, "Rio Tinto Gets 3-Month Extension to Mine Rights at Simandou."

17. Jessica Brice, "Vale Buys Rio's Seized Guinea Assets for $2.5 Billion," *Bloomberg Businessweek*, April 30, 2010, retrieved at www.businessweek.com on August 31, 2010.

18. Bate Felix, "Rio Does $700 Million Simandou Iron Ore Deal with Guinea," Reuters, April 22, 2011, retrieved at www.mineweb.com on April 26, 2011. See also Bettina Wassener, "Rio Tinto and Chinalco in Deal for Iron Project," *New York Times*, March 20, 2010.

19. See Shai Oster, "China Fund's $7 Billion Deal with Guinea Draws Scrutiny," *Wall Street Journal*, November 2, 2009.

20. Saliou Samb, "Key Political Risks to Watch in Guinea—Factbox," Reuters, July 7, 2011, retrieved at www.forexyard.com on July 23, 2011.

21. Institute for Security Studies (Tshwane/Pretoria), "Guinea: Presidential Guards Thwart Attack on Conde," AllAfrica.com, July 20, 2011, retrieved at allafrica.com on July 23, 2011.

22. For background, see Lydia Polgreen, "Battle Unfolds in a Poor Land for the Riches beneath the Soil," *New York Times*, December 15, 2008.

23. Andrew McGregor, "Niger's Uranium Industry Threatened by Rebels," *Terrorism Focus*, Jamestown Foundation, July 31, 2007, retrieved at www.jamestown.org on October 7, 2007.

24. International Energy Agency, "Key World Energy Statistics 2010," retrieved at www.iea.org on July 30, 2011.

25. For background, see "Uranium in Niger," World Nuclear Association, December 2009, retrieved at www.world-nuclear.org on February 8, 2010.

26. Ibid. See also "Niger's President Opens Work on New Uranium Plant," Agence France-Presse, May 4, 2009, retrieved at www.google.com on August 5, 2011; and "Work Begins on Niger Uranium Mine," BBC News, May 4, 2009, retrieved at newsvote.bbc.co.uk on February 8, 2010.

27. See McGregor, "Niger's Uranium Industry Threatened by Rebels." For background on the Tuaregs and their dispute with Areva, see Peter Gwin, "Lost Lords of the Sahara," *National Geographic*, September 2011, pp. 137–52.

28. As quoted in Polgreen, "Battle Unfolds in a Poor Land."

29. McGregor, "Niger's Uranium Industry Threatened by Rebels."

30. "French Uranium Employees Kidnapped in Niger," *World Nuclear News*, June 23, 2008, retrieved at www.world-nuclear-news.org on May 16, 2011.

31. See "Niger's President Opens Work on New Uranium Plant."

32. "France Confirms al-Qaeda Kidnap at Niger Uranium Mine," BBC News, September 22, 2010, retrieved at www.bbc.co.uk on May 16, 2011.

33. "Al-Qaeda Parade French Hostages Seized in Niger," BBC News, April 27, 2011, retrieved at www.bbc.co.uk on May 16, 2011.

34. DoE/EIA, "China," Country Analysis Brief, November 2010, retrieved at www.eia.doe.gov on May 17, 2011.

35. "First Uranium from Niger Mine," *World Nuclear News*, January 4, 2011, retrieved at www.world-nuclear-news.org on May 16, 2011.

36. See Andrew McGregor, "Mining for Energy: China's Relations with Niger," *China Brief*, Jamestown Foundation, October 3, 2007, retrieved at www.jamestown.org on September 17, 2011.

37. See James Risen, "World's Mining Companies Covet Afghan Riches," *New York Times*, June 18, 2010; and Sarah Simpson, "Afghanistan's Buried Riches," *Scientific American*, October 2011, pp. 58–64.

38. James Risen, "U.S. Discovers Mineral Riches in Afghanistan," *New York Times*, June 14, 2010.

39. USGS, "Preliminary Assessment of Non-Fuel Mineral Resources of Afghanistan," USGS Fact Sheet 2007–3063, October 2007, retrieved at www .usgs.gov on September 22, 2010. See also USGS, "Afghanistan," *Mineral Yearbook 2008*, vol. 3, chap. 2.

40. Risen, "U.S. Discovers Mineral Riches in Afghanistan."

41. As quoted in Alissa J. Rubin, "Afghan Officials Elated by Minerals Report," *New York Times*, June 15, 2010.

42. As quoted in Risen, "U.S. Discovers Mineral Riches in Afghanistan."

43. As quoted in Donald G. McNeil Jr., "Next for Afghanistan, the Curse of Plenty?" *New York Times*, June 19, 2010.

44. See "China Wins Right to Explore Afghan Copper Mine," Agence France-Presse, November 21, 2007, retrieved at www.sinodaily.com on September 27, 2011; and Ron Synovitz, "Afghanistan: China's Winning Bid for Copper Rights Includes Power Plant, Railroad," Radio Free Europe/Radio Liberty, November 24, 2007, retrieved at www.rferl.org on September 17, 2011.

45. See Joshua Partlow, "Afghan Minister Accused of Taking Bribe," *Washington Post*, November 18, 2009; and Michael Wines, "China Is Willing to Spend Big in Afghanistan, on Commerce," *New York Times*, December 30, 2009.

46. See Adrienne Mong, "Resource-Hungry China Heads to Afghanistan," *World Blog*, MSNBC, October 14, 2009, retrieved at worldblog.msnbc .com on November 19, 2009.

47. Ibid.

48. See Eltaj Najazfizada, "Afghanistan Seeks New Hajigak Iron Bids, Other Mine Investment," *Bloomberg Businessweek*, June 17, 2010, retrieved at www.businessweek.com on July 20, 2010.

49. As quoted in Wines, "China Is Willing to Spend Big in Afghanistan."

50. Emma Graham-Harrison, "Afghanistan Opens Giant Iron Ore Deposit to Tender," Reuters AlertNet, April 4, 2009, retrieved at www.alertnet .org on September 23, 2010.

51. See Dorothy Kosich, "Mongolian Trilateral Agreement Aimed at Easing Mining-Stakeholder Conflicts," Mineweb.com, January 4, 2011, retrieved at www.mineweb.com on January 24, 2011. See also Mark Storry and Alexandra Ashikhimina, "Mongolia: Open for Business," *Engineering*

and Mining Journal, August 11, 2010, retrieved at www.e-mj.com on August 30, 2010.

52. For background and discussion, see "Mongolia's Mining Boom: Nomads No More," *Economist*, October 23, 2010, p. 52; and James T. Areddy, "Mining Fuels Mongol Hoard," *Wall Street Journal*, June 2, 2011.

53. USGS, "Mongolia," *Minerals Yearbook 2007*, chap. 18, p. 2.

54. Chris Morrissey, "Digging Up the Elephant," *Rio Tinto Review*, September 2010, pp. 14–18. See also USGS, "Mongolia," *Minerals Yearbook 2008*, chap. 18, pp. 2–3.

55. Storry and Ashikhimina, "Mongolia: Open for Business."

56. Ivanhoe Mines, "Oyu Tolgoi Investment Agreement Takes Full Legal Effect Following Completion of Conditions Precedent," press release, March 31, 2010, retrieved at www.ivanhoemines.com on September 24, 2010.

57. Storry and Ashikhimina, "Mongolia: Open for Business."

58. See Patrick Barta and Jason Leow, "Political Unrest in Mongolia May Hinder Mining Investment," *Wall Street Journal*, July 5–6, 2008; Edward Wong, "In Election Dispute, a Challenge for Mongolia's Democracy," *New York Times*, July 8, 2008; and Jim Yardley, "Mongolia Enforces Martial Law in Capital Amid Political Unrest," *New York Times*, July 3, 2008.

59. Ivanhoe Mines, "Ivanhoe Mines Reports Construction of Oyu Tolgoi Copper-Gold Complex on Schedule for Initial Test Production in 2012," press release, September 7, 2010, retrieved at finance.yahoo.com on September 17, 2011.

60. See "Mongolian Coal," *New York Times*, February 23, 2011.

61. Ibid. See also Yuko Inoue, "Mitsui, Shenhua to Join Together on Coal, May Bid for Tavan Tolgoi," Reuters, September 14, 2010, retrieved at www.mineweb.com on September 19, 2010; and David Stanway, "Mongolian PM Confirms Tavan Tolgoi Decision," Reuters, February 8, 2010, retrieved at www.mineweb.com on September 24, 2010.

62. Leslie Cook, "Shenhua Wins Race for Coking Venture," *Financial Times*, July 6, 2011. See also "Japan Files Complaint with Mongolia over Tavan Tolgoi Bidding Process," Reuters, July 22, 2011, retrieved at www.mineweb.com on July 30, 2011.

63. Khan Resources, "Dornod Uranium Project," retrieved at www.khanresources.com on September 26, 2010.

64. See "Khan Resources Gets Mongolia Agency Breather, Shares Up,"

Reuters, September 21, 2010, retrieved at www.reuters.com on September 26, 2010. See also Melissa Pistilli, "Khan Resources: Center of Russian-Chinese Resource War in Mongolia," Uranium Investing News, May 3, 2010, retrieved at uraniuminvestingnews.com on September 26, 2010.

65. USGS, "Alaska," *Minerals Yearbook 2007*, vol. 2, chap. 4, p. 1.

66. See Dorothy Kosich, "Alaska's Pebble Copper-Gold Project of Global Importance," Mineweb.com, February 24, 2011, retrieved at www.mineweb.com on February 25, 2011.

67. "Pebble Project," Alaska Department of Natural Resources, retrieved at dnr.alaska.gov on May 18, 2011.

68. Ibid.

69. Kosich, "Alaska's Pebble Copper-Gold Project."

70. See Lisa W. Drew, "Prospect of a Mine Near Salmon Fishery Stirs Worry in Alaska," *New York Times*, April 26, 2005; and Kenneth Miller, "The Midas Touch," *Mother Jones*, May/June 2006, retrieved at motherjones.com on May 18, 2011.

71. For background on Pebble, see Edwin Dobb, "Alaska's Choice: Salmon or Gold," *National Geographic*, December 2010, retrieved at ngm.nationalgeographic.com on May 18, 2011; Drew, "Prospect of a Mine"; and Miller, "The Midas Touch."

72. Miller, "The Midas Touch." See also William Yardley, "Vote in Alaska Puts Question: Gold or Fish?" *New York Times*, August 23, 2008.

73. Dobb, "Alaska's Choice."

74. As quoted in Yardley, "Vote in Alaska Puts Question."

75. See Michael Powell and Jo Becker, "Palin's Hand Seen in Battle over Mine in Alaska," *New York Times*, October 22, 2008.

76. As quoted in Miller, "The Midas Touch."

77. See Yardley, "Vote in Alaska Puts Question."

78. As quoted in Manuel Quinones, "Battle over Alaska Mining Project Heads to Washington," *New York Times*, March 18, 2001.

79. As quoted in Drew, "Prospect of a Mine."

80. Vale Inc., "Voisey's Bay Development," retrieved at www.vbnc.com on September 28, 2010.

81. Kosich, "Vale, Unions Finally Settle on Voisey's Bay Contract," Mineweb.com, February 1, 2011, retrieved at www.mineweb.com on September 17, 2011.

82. See Louise Egan, "Interest Grows in Baffinland Iron Ore Project: CEO," Reuters, February 5, 2010, retrieved at www.reuters.com on September 28, 2010. See also Baffinland Iron Mines Corp., "The Mary River Project," retrieved at www.baffinland.com on September 28, 2010.

83. See "Baffin Island Residents Resist Proposed Iron Mine Plans," CBC News, April 7, 2008, retrieved at www.cbc.ca on September 28, 2010.

84. "LKAB Expands Iron Mining in Northern Sweden," Barents Observer, May 11, 2010, retrieved at www.barentsobserver.com on September 29, 2010.

85. "Large Mineral Deposits in Finnmark," Barents Observer, August 20, 2010, retrieved at www.barentsobserver.com on September 29, 2010.

86. USGS, "Russia," Minerals Yearbook 2008, vol. 3, chap. 35.

87. "Sami Parliament Fights Norwegian Government over Mining Rights," Barents Observer, June 12, 2009, retrieved at www.barentsobserver .com on September 29, 2010. For background on the Sami people and their relationship to reindeer, see Jessica Benko, "Sami: The People Who Walk with Reindeer," National Geographic, November 2011, pp. 62–81.

88. Quadra FNX Mining, "About Quadra FNX," retrieved at www .quadrafnx.com on September 29, 2010.

89. Proactive Investors, "Greenland Eases Uranium-Mining Ban, Greenland Minerals & Energy to Benefit," One News Page, September 10, 2010, retrieved at www.onenewspage.com on September 29, 2010.

90. See Stephen Pax Leonard, "Greenland's Race for Minerals Threatens Culture on the Edge of Existence," Guardian, February 6, 2011.

CHAPTER 6: RARE EARTHS AND OTHER CRITICAL MINERALS

1. Keith Bradsher, "Amid Tension, China Blocks Vital Exports to Japan," New York Times, September 22, 2010.

2. As quoted in Martin Fackler and Ian Johnson, "Arrest in Disputed Seas Riles China and Japan," New York Times, September 20, 2010.

3. Martin Fackler and Ian Johnson, "Japan Retreats with Release of Chinese Boat Captain," New York Times, September 24, 2010.

4. Yuka Hayashi and James T. Areddy, "Japan Scrambles for Rare Earth," Wall Street Journal, October 16–17, 2010.

5. As quoted in ibid.

6. Ibid. See also "Mongolia Could Help Break China's Grip on Key Materials," *Asahi Shimbun,* October 4, 2010, retrieved at www.ashahi.com/english on October 4, 2010; "Japan and Vietnam Agree on Mining of Rare Earths," Associated Press, *New York Times,* October 31, 2010; and Cindy Hurst, "Japan's Approach to China's Control of Rare Earth Elements," *China Brief,* Jamestown Foundation April 22, 2011, retrieved at www.james town.org on April 22, 2011.

7. See "Nations Wary of Dependence on China's Rare Earths," Associated Press, October 4, 2010, retrieved at www.cbsnews.com on October 6, 2010; Tom Doggett, "U.S. Aims to End China's Rare Earths Metals Monopoly," Reuters, September 30, 2010, retrieved at www.reuters.com on October 4, 2010; and Nathan Hodge and James T. Areddy, "China Hold on Metals Worries Washington," *Wall Street Journal,* September 24, 2010.

8. The Rare Earths and Critical Materials Revitalization Act of 2010.

9. Statement of David Sandalow before the Subcommittee on Energy, Senate Committee on Energy and Natural Resources, Washington, D.C., September 30, 2010, retrieved at energy.senate.gov on October 4, 2010.

10. See Keith Bradsher, "China Is Said to Resume Shipping Rare Earth Minerals," *New York Times,* October 28, 2010.

11. See Keith Bradsher, "China Restarts Rare Earth Shipments to Japan," *New York Times,* November 20, 2010; and Bradsher, "China to Cut Rare Earth Trade in 2011," *New York Times,* December 29, 2010.

12. For background, see USGS, "Rare Earths," *Minerals Yearbook 2008,* vol. 1, chap. 60; and USGS, "Rare Earth Elements—Critical Resources for High Technology," USGS Fact Sheet 087–02, 2002, retrieved at pubs.usgs .gov on October 4, 2010.

13. USGS, "Rare Earth Elements—Critical Resources for High Technology."

14. DoE, *Critical Materials Strategy* (Washington, D.C.: DoE, December 2010), p. 6.

15. USGS, "Rare Earth Elements—Critical Resources for High Technology." See also DoE, *Critical Materials Strategy,* pp. 14–26.

16. Steve Gorman, "As Hybrid Cars Gobble Rare Metals, Shortage Looms," Reuters, August 31, 2009, retrieved at www.reuters.com on October 7, 2010.

17. U.S. Government Accountability Office (GAO), "Rare Earth Mate-

rials in the Defense Supply Chain," Briefing for Congressional Committees, April 1, 2010, GAO-10–617R, retrieved at www.gao.gov on October 4, 2010.

18. Hodge and Areddy, "China Hold on Metals Worries Washington."

19. Sandalow statement before the Subcommittee on Energy, Senate Committee on Energy and Natural Resources, September 30, 2010. See also Hodge and Areddy, "China Hold on Metals Worries Washington."

20. GAO, "Rare Earth Materials in the Defense Supply Chain."

21. On the environmental hazards associated with rare earths processing, see Keith Bradsher, "Earth-Friendly Elements, Mined Destructively," *New York Times*, December 26, 2009; and Bradsher, "After Rare Earth Embargo, a New Calculus," *New York Times*, October 30, 2010.

22. Pui-Kwan Tse, *China's Rare-Earth Industry*, USGS Open-File Report 2011–1042, 2011, retrieved at www.usgs.gov on May 21, 2011.

23. Tse, *China's Rare-Earth Industry*, pp. 6–7. See also Keith Bradsher, "China Tightens Grip on Rare Minerals," *New York Times*, September 1, 2009; Bradsher, "Backpedaling, China Eases Proposal to Ban Exports of Some Vital Minerals," *New York Times*, September 4, 2009; and Chuin-Wei Yap, "Will China Tighten 'Rare Earth' Grip?" *Wall Street Journal*, September 3, 2009.

24. See James T. Areddy, "China Cites Pollution in Tightening Rare-Earth Exports," *Wall Street Journal*, November 15, 2010; Bradsher, "China to Cut Rare Earths Trade in 2011"; and Keith Bradsher, "China Acts to Tighten Grasp on Rare Earth Production," *New York Times*, February 17, 2011. See also Tom Miles, "Dramatic Fall in China Rare Earth Exports," Reuters, May 23, 2011, retrieved at www.mineweb.com on May 26, 2011.

25. See Yap, "Will China Tighten 'Rare Earth' Grip?" See also Keith Bradsher, "China Seizes Rare Earth Mine Areas," *New York Times*, January 21, 2011; and Bradsher, "Chasing Rare Earths," *New York Times*, August 25, 2011.

26. Office of Rep. Mike Coffman, "Coffman Introduces RESTART Act to Develop Rare Earths Supply Chain," press release, March 17, 2010, retrieved at coffman.house.gov on October 4, 2010.

27. Office of Rep. Mike Coffman, "Coffman RESTART Act Creates Rare Earths Supply Chain," press release, April 6, 2011, retrieved at coffman.house.gov on July 24, 2011.

28. For background and commentary, see David Gauvey Herbert, "Wither Heat-Seeking Missiles," *Burn After Reading*, blog entry, May 12, 2010, retrieved at burnafterreading.nationaljournal.com on October 4, 2010.

29. Tim Folger, "The Secret Ingredients of Everything," *National Geographic*, June 2011, p. 144.

30. See Hiroko Tabquchi, "The Hunt for Rare Earths," *New York Times*, November 25, 2011; and Shirley Won, "Investors Taking a Shine to Rare Earth Metals," *Globe and Mail*, September 28, 2010.

31. For background, see Keith Bradsher, "A Mine Owner's Risky Bet on Rare Minerals," *New York Times*, April 22, 2010.

32. See James T. Areddy, "Rare-Earth Miner in U.S. Tackles China, Its Own Past," *Wall Street Journal*, December 20, 2010; Dorothy Kosich, "Molycorp Approves Mountain Pass Expansion, Combined Stock Offering," Mineweb.com, January 25, 2011, retrieved at www.mineweb.com on January 25, 2011; and Kosich, "Molycorp Reports Soaring Rare Earth Oxide Sales and Demand," Mineweb.com, March 10, 2011, retrieved at www.mineweb.com on March 14, 2011.

33. Arafura Resources, "Nolans Project," Fact Sheet 02, retrieved at www.arafuraresources.com.au on May 22, 2011.

34. Yuko Inoue, "Japanese Trading House Forges Rare Earth Procurement Deal with Lynas," Reuters, November 24, 2010, retrieved at www.mineweb.com on November 29, 2010.

35. See Bradsher, "China Tightens Grip on Rare Minerals"; and Yap, "Will China Tighten 'Rare Earth' Grip?" See also Rob Taylor, "China Drops Lynas Bid, Further Strains Australia-China Relations," Reuters, September 24, 2009, retrieved at www.mineweb.com on October 10, 2010.

36. See Keith Bradsher, "The Fear of a Toxic Rerun," *New York Times*, June 29, 2011; and Bradsher, "Rare Earth Refinery Meets Standards, Atomic Agency Says," *New York Times*, July 1, 2011.

37. As quoted in "Nations Wary of Dependence on China's Rare Earths."

38. As quoted in Yoshio Takahashi, "Japan, Mongolia to Cooperate on Rare Earth," *Wall Street Journal*, October 3, 2010.

39. "Mongolia Could Help Break China's Grip on Key Materials."

40. "Japan and Vietnam Agree on Mining of Rare Earths."

41. Hurst, "Japan's Approach to China's Control of Rare Earth Elements."

42. "Toshiba and Kazatomprom Sign JV to Develop Rare Earth Metals," Domain-b.com, June 5, 2010, retrieved at www.domain-b.com on October 11, 2010.

43. "Malawi: A Fresh Source of Rare Earths," *Africa Mining Intelligence*, April 13, 2011, retrieved at www.africaintelligence.com on May 22, 2011.

44. See Simpson, "Afghanistan's Buried Riches"; and Proactive Investors, "Greenland Eases Uranium-Mining Ban, Greenland Minerals & Energy to Benefit."

45. William J. Broad, "Mining the Seafloor for Rare-Earth Minerals," *New York Times*, November 9, 2010.

46. For background, see NRC, Committee on Critical Mineral Impacts on the U.S. Economy, *Minerals, Critical Minerals, and the U.S. Economy* (Washington, D.C.: National Academies Press, 2008). See also DoE, *Critical Materials Strategy*, pp. 14–26.

47. Statement of Roderick G. Eggert before the Senate Committee on Energy and Natural Resources, Subcommittee on Energy, September 30, 2010, retrieved at energy.senate.gov on October 4, 2010.

48. NRC, *Minerals, Critical Minerals, and the U.S. Economy*. See also Roderick G. Eggert, "Critical Minerals and Emerging Technologies," *Issues in Science and Technology*, Summer 2010, retrieved at www.issues.org on October 11, 2010.

49. NRC, *Minerals, Critical Minerals, and the U.S. Economy*.

50. Liam Pleven, "Pentagon in Race for Raw Materials," *Wall Street Journal*, May 3, 2010.

51. European Commission, *Critical Raw Materials for the EU*, Report of the Ad-hoc Working Group on Defining Critical Raw Materials (Brussels: EC, June 2010).

52. JOGMEC, "JOGMEC's Activities," retrieved at www.jogmec.go.jp/english on October 15, 2010.

53. JOGMEC, "JFE Steel, Nippon Steel, Sojitz, JOGMEC, POSCO and NPS Form Japan-Korea Partnership Group to Invest in Brazilian Producer of Niobium," press release, March 4, 2011, retrieved at www.jogmec.go.ja on July 29, 2011.

54. USGS, "Japan," *Minerals Yearbook 2008*, vol. 3, chap. 3, p. 1.

55. DoE, *Critical Materials Strategy*, p. 17; USGS, "Lithium," *Minerals Yearbook 2008*, vol. 1, chap. 44, pp. 1–2.

56. "Building a Better Car Battery," *Fortune*, March 1, 2010, p. 94.

57. USGS, "Lithium," *Minerals Yearbook 2008*, vol. 1, chap. 44, p. 5.

58. Marc Gunther, "Warren Buffett Takes Charge," *Fortune*, April 13, 2009, retrieved at money.cnn.com on October 15, 2010.

59. Ibid.

60. See David Barboza, "China to Invest Billions in Electric and Hybrid Cars," *New York Times*, August 19, 2010.

61. USGS, "Lithium," *Minerals Yearbook 2008*, vol. 1, chap. 44, p. 5.

62. White House, Office of the Press Secretary, "Remarks by the President in Phone Call to Recovery Act Advanced Battery Grant Recipient, A123 Systems in Livonia, MI," September 13, 2010, retrieved at www.whitehouse.gov on October 15, 2010.

63. For discussion, see Clifford Krauss, "The Lithium Chase," *New York Times*, March 10, 2010.

64. Rory Carroll, "Multinationals Eye Up Lithium Reserves beneath Bolivia's Salt Flats," *Guardian*, June 17, 2009.

65. Ibid. See also Simon Romero, "In Bolivia, Untapped Bounty Meets Nationalism," *New York Times*, February 3, 2009; and Lawrence Wright, "Lithium Dreams," *New Yorker*, March 22, 2010, pp. 48–59.

66. For background, see USGS, "Bolivia," *Minerals Yearbook 2008*, vol. 3, chap. 3. See also Romero, "In Bolivia, Untapped Bounty Meets Nationalism"; and Wright, "Lithium Dreams."

67. As quoted in Carroll, "Multinationals Eye Up Lithium Reserves."

68. As quoted in Wright, "Lithium Dreams," p. 52.

69. As quoted in Carroll, "Multinationals Eye Up Lithium Reserves."

70. USGS, "Lithium," *Minerals Yearbook 2008*, vol. 1, chap. 44, p. 3.

71. Dorothy Kosich, "Toyota Tsusho/Orocobre Argentine Lithium Deal Critical to Hybrid Auto Development," Mineweb.com, January 21, 2010, retrieved at www.mineweb.com on October 11, 2010.

72. Risen, "U.S. Discovers Mineral Riches in Afghanistan."

73. International Platinum Group Metals Association, "Platinum Group Metals—The Power to Improve Lives," retrieved at www.ipa-news.com on October 27, 2010.

74. USGS, "Platinum-Group Minerals, *Minerals Yearbook 2008*, vol. 1, p. 1.

75. NRC, *Minerals, Critical Minerals, and the U.S. Economy*, pp. 137–39.

76. USGS, "Platinum-Group Metals," *Mineral Commodities Summaries*, January 2011 (Washington, D.C.: USGS, 2011), p. 120.

77. USGS, "Platinum-Group Minerals, *Minerals Yearbook 2008*, vol. 1, Table 5, p. 3; USGS, "Platinum-Group Metals," *Mineral Commodities Summaries*, January 2011, p. 120.

78. USGS, "Platinum-Group Metals," *Mineral Commodities Summaries*, January 2011, p. 120.

79. See "Toxic Truth of Secretive Siberian City," BBC News, April 5, 2007, retrieved at news.bbc.co.uk on October 30, 2010.

80. Blacksmith Institute, "The World's Worst Polluted Places," September 2007, retrieved at www.blacksmithinstitute.org on October 30, 2010. See also Andrew Kramer, "For One Business, Polluted Clouds Have Silvery Linings," *New York Times*, July 12, 2007.

81. USGS, "Platinum-Group Minerals," *Minerals Yearbook 2008*, vol. 1, p. 5.

82. "Strike Hits SA Platinum Producer," BBC News, September 30, 2004, retrieved at news.bbc.co.uk on October 30, 2010.

83. See Angus Stickler, "Who Pays the Price of Platinum?" BBC News, March 25, 2008, retrieved at news.bbc.co.uk on September 17, 2011.

84. Tawanda Karombo, "Anglo Platinum Forges Ahead with New Zimbabwe Platinum Mine," Mineweb.com, April 28, 2008, retrieved at www.mineweb.net on October 30, 2010; "Impala Vague on U.S. $500 Million Expansion," AllAfrica.com, August 27, 2010, retrieved at allafrica.com on October 30, 2010.

85. See Agnieszka Flak and Ed Stoddard, "Impala Platinum Cuts Output Targets, Zim Worries Weigh," Reuters, May 18, 2011, retrieved at www.mineweb.com on May 26, 2011; and Jason Moyo, "Zimbabwe's Political Elite Eyes Mines," *Mail & Guardian Online*, May 13, 2011, retrieved at mg.co.za on May 25, 2011.

86. NRC, *Minerals, Critical Minerals, and the U.S. Economy*, pp. 156–59.

87. USGS, "Niobium (Columbium) and Tantalum," *Minerals Yearbook 2008*, vol. 1, chap. 52.

88. Ibid., p. 1.

89. Ibid.

90. Ibid., Table 6, p. 12. See also USGS, "Tantalum," *Mineral Commodities Summaries, January 2011*, pp. 111, 163.

91. For background on this ongoing conflict, see Gérard Prunier, *Africa's World War* (Oxford: Oxford University Press, 2009); and Jason Stearns, *Dancing in the Glory of Monsters: The Collapse of the Congo and the Great War of Africa* (New York: PublicAffairs, 2011).

92. GAO, *The Democratic Republic of the Congo: U.S. Agencies Should Take Further Actions to Contribute to the Effective Regulation and Control of the Minerals Trade in the Eastern Democratic Republic of the Congo*, Report to Congress, GAO-10-1030 (Washington, D.C.: GAO, September 2010), pp. 6–10.

93. Lydia Polgreen, "Congo's Riches, Looted by Renegade Troops," *New York Times*, November 16, 2008.

94. See Jeffrey Gettleman, "Congo Army Helps Rebels Get Arms, U.N. Finds," *New York Times*, November 25, 2009. (The UN study was not made public, but reporters from the *New York Times* were shown a copy.) See also UN Department of Public Information, "Press Conference on Democratic Republic of Congo Expert Group Report," December 12, 2008, retrieved at www.un.org on January 19, 2009.

95. As quoted in Jeffrey Gettleman, "Clinton Presses Congo on Illicit Minerals," *New York Times*, August 11, 2009.

96. Section 1502 of the Wall Street Reform and Consumer Protection Act of 2010 (the Dodd-Frank Act).

97. As noted in a September 2010 GAO assessment, "The minerals trade cannot be effectively monitored, regulated, or controlled as long as armed groups and some units of the Congolese national military continue to commit human rights violations and exploit the local population at will." GAO, *The Democratic Republic of the Congo*, p. 32.

98. NRC, *Minerals, Critical Minerals, and the U.S. Economy*, pp. 148–52 and 160–63.

99. Ibid., pp. 1–2.

100. Indeed, China has already begun reducing its export quotas of indium. See USGS, "Indium," *Minerals Yearbook 2008*, vol. 1, chap. 35, p. 4.

CHAPTER 7: GLOBAL "LAND GRABS" AND THE STRUGGLE FOR FOOD

1. "Two falcons gifted to King Abdullah," *Dawn*, February 3, 2006, retrieved at dawn.com on August 4, 2011; Elisabeth Rosenthal, "Pope Meets

King of Saudi Arabia," *New York Times*, November 6, 2007, retrieved at www.nytimes.com on August 4, 2011.

2. Saudi Ministry of Foreign Affairs, "Custodian of the Two Holy Mosques Receives Minister of Commerce and Industry," press release, January 26, 2009, retrieved at farmlandgrab.org on July 30, 2011.

3. For background, see Thomas W. Lippman, "Saudi Arabia's Quest for 'Food Security,'" *Middle East Policy*, vol. 17, no. 1, pp. 90–92.

4. For background on Al Amoudi, see Andrew Rice, "Is There Such a Thing as Agro-Imperialism?" *New York Times,* November 22, 2009, retrieved at www.nytimes.com on December 17, 2010.

5. Saudi Ministry of Foreign Affairs, "Custodian of the Two Holy Mosques."

6. See Wudineh Zenebe, "Al-Amoudi Solicits Additional Arable Land," *Addis Fortune*, December 7, 2009, retrieved at farmlandgrab.org on December 17, 2009; and William Davison, "Saudi Billionaire's Company Will Invest $2.5 Billion in Ethiopia Rice Farm," *Bloomberg News*, March 23, 2011, retrieved at farmlandgrab.org on May 26, 2011.

7. See Syed Rashid Husain, "Saudi Arabia Looks to Foreign Farmlands to Feed Itself," *Dawn*, April 26, 2009, retrieved at farmlandgrab.org on May 30, 2011; and "Saudi Hail Starts Farm Investment Abroad in Sudan," Reuters, February 16, 2009, retrieved at af.reuters.com on December 1, 2010.

8. See Maram Mazen, "Sudan Looks to Attract Middle Eastern Investment in Farmland," *Bloomberg News*, December 17, 2009, retrieved at farmlandgrab.org on January 5, 2010.

9. Nancy Macdonald, "What's the New Global Source for Fresh, Shiny Produce? Famine-Ridden Ethiopia," *Maclean's*, August 19, 2010, retrieved at farmlandgrab.org on August 30, 2010.

10. For background, see Shepard Daniel and Anuradha Mittal, *The Great Land Grab* (Oakland: Oakland Institute, 2009); Deutsche Gesellschaft für Technische Zusammenarbeit (GTZ), *Foreign Direct Investment (FDI) in Land in Developing Countries* (Eschborn, Germany: GTZ, December 2009); Michael Kugelman and Susan L. Levenstein, eds., *Land Grab? The Race for the World's Farmland* (Washington, D.C.: Woodrow Wilson International Center for Scholars, 2009); and Deininger and Byerlee, *Rising Global Interest in Farmland*. See also Naveen Thukral, "Farm Private Invest-

ment Seen Doubling in Two Years," *Reuters*, April 26, 2011, retrieved at farmlandgrab.org on May 26, 2011.

11. For background on the issue, see "The 9 Billion-People Question," *Economist*, February 26, 2011, pp. 3–16. See also Joel K. Bourne Jr., "The End of Plenty," *National Geographic*, June 2009, pp. 26–59.

12. For such an assessment, see World Bank, *Global Economic Prospects 2009: Commodities at the Crossroads* (Washington, D.C.: World Bank, 2009), pp. 79–85.

13. Lester R. Brown, "Could Food Shortages Bring Down Civilization?" *Scientific American*, May 2009, pp. 50–57.

14. See, for example, SilverStreet Capital, "The Case for Agricultural Investments," retrieved at silver.uk.endis.com on November 28, 2010.

15. Helen Avery, "Agriculture: Farmland Is the New Gold," *Euromoney*, December 1, 2008, retrieved at euromoney.com on August 6, 2011.

16. UN Department of Economic and Social Affairs, "World Population Prospects: The 2010 Revision," retrieved at esa.un.org on July 31, 2011.

17. As quoted in "Al-Amoudi's Efforts to Initiate Saudi Agro Investments," *Addis Fortune*, November 24, 2009, retrieved at farmlandgrab.org on July 30, 2011.

18. See, for example, Ed Butler, "Land Grab Fears for Ethiopian Rural Communities," BBC News, December 15, 2010, retrieved at farmlandgrab .org on July 30, 2011.

19. As quoted in Davison, "Saudi Billionaire's Company Will Invest $2.5 Billion in Ethiopia Rice Farm."

20. "Saudis to Invest $500 Million in Brazil Agriculture," Qatar News Agency, October 5, 2010, retrieved at farmlandgrab.org on November 18, 2010.

21. For background and discussion, see "Arabs Mull $65bn Food Security Plan," *Emirates 24/7*, July 28, 2010, retrieved at farmlandgrab.org on August 30, 2010; and Aya Lowe, "Investing Abroad to Secure Food at Home," *Gulf News*, March 9, 2011, retrieved at farmlandgrab.org on September 17, 2011.

22. David Lepeska, "In Bid for Security, Qatar Sows Seeds Globally," *The National*, September 2, 2010, retrieved at farmlandgrab.org on September 9, 2010. See also "Qatar in Talks to Buy Argentina, Ukraine Farmland," *Reuters*, October 13, 2010, retrieved at farmlandgrab.org on November 18, 2010.

23. "UAE Has over 2,800 sq km in Sudan Farms," *Emirates 24/7*, retrieved at farmlandgrab.org on November 18, 2010.

24. Lowe, "Investing Abroad to Secure Food at Home." See also "Jenaan to Focus on Developing Farmland," Reuters, November 25, 2010, retrieved at farmlandgrab.org on June 3, 2011.

25. "UAE's MEC in Talks to Lease Indonesian Farmland," Reuters, February 14, 2010, retrieved at farmlandgrab.org on February 15, 2010.

26. For discussion and background, see Alexandra Spieldoch and Sophia Murphy, "Agricultural Land Acquisitions: Implications for Food Security and Poverty Alleviation," in Kugelman and Levenstein, *Land Grab?* pp. 40–43.

27. Dave Durbach, "Korea's Overseas Development Backfires," *Korea Times*, December 4, 2009, retrieved at farmlandgrab.org on December 17, 2010.

28. As cited in Sungwoo Park, "S. Korea to Increase Overseas Farming on Record Food Costs," *Bloomberg News*, March 10, 2011, retrieved at farmlandgrab.org on May 26, 2011.

29. Ibid. See also "S. Korea to Secure More Overseas Farmland," Yonhap, March 10, 2011, retrieved at farmlandgrab.org on May 26, 2011.

30. See "Outsourcing's Third Wave," *Economist*, May 23, 2009, pp. 61–63.

31. Daniel and Mittal, *The Great Land Grab*, p. 4.

32. Ed Cropley, "Daewoo Finds Africa Land Is a Risky Business," Reuters, March 20, 2009, retrieved at www.reuters.com on November 25, 2010.

33. As quoted in ibid.

34. Kim Se-jeong, "Korea Will Grow Wheat in Sudan," *Korea Times*, June 15, 2008, retrieved at www.koreatimes.co.kr on November 25, 2010.

35. "Hyundai Heavy Reaps Corn, Soybeans at Its Russian Farmland," Yonhap, April 15, 2010, retrieved at farmlandgrab.org on November 25, 2010.

36. Matheus Magenta, "Hyundai Wants to Buy Land in Brazil," *Folha de S. Paulo*, September 5, 2010, retrieved at farmlandgrab.org on November 25, 2010.

37. See Sungwoo Park, "South Korea to Expand Overseas Farming on Rising Food Costs," *Bloomberg News*, July 10, 2011, retrieved at farmland grab.com on July 30, 2011.

38. Rana Kapoor, "Food Security Needs Beckon Investment in Transnational Farming," *Hindu Business Line*, October 18, 2010, retrieved at farmlandgrab.org on November 18, 2010.

39. As quoted in Utpal Bhaskar, "Indian Firms Find Africa Fertile Ground for Contract Farming," Livemint.com, October 19, 2010, retrieved at farmlandgrab.org on November 27, 2010.

40. William Davison, "Karuturi Global Eyes East African Markets for Crops Grown on Ethiopia Land," *Bloomberg News*, November 12, 2010, retrieved at farmlandgrab.org on November 18, 2010.

41. For background on China's agricultural dilemma, see Elizabeth C. Economy, *The River Runs Black: The Environmental Challenge to China's Future* (Ithaca, N.Y.: Cornell University Press, 2010). On China's pursuit of foreign cropland, see "China Farms the World to Feed a Ravenous Economy," Associated Press, May 4, 2008, retrieved at farmlandgrab.org on May 30, 2011.

42. As quoted in Chuin-Wei Yap, "China Beidahuang Planning Large Farmland Buys Overseas," Dow Jones, March 11, 2011, retrieved at farmlandgrab.org on May 26, 2011.

43. Li Xin, "Chongqing Grain Seeks State Firms to Back $2.47 bln Brazil Soybean Facility," China Business Newswire, March 1, 2011, retrieved at farmlandgrab.org on May 26, 2011.

44. Alexei Barrionuevo, "China's Farming Pursuits Make Brazil Uneasy," *New York Times*, May 27, 2011.

45. See GRAIN, "Mauritius Leads Land Grabs for Rice in Mozambique," September 1, 2009, retrieved at farmlandgrab.org on December 19, 2010.

46. "China Farms the World to Feed a Ravenous Economy."

47. See Joachim Von Braun and Ruth Meinzen-Dick, "'Land-Grabbing' by Foreign Investors in Developing Countries: Risks and Opportunities," IFPRI Policy Brief 13, International Food Policy Research Institute, Washington, D.C., April 2009, pp. 5–8.

48. Yap, "China Beidahuang Planning Large Farmland Buys Overseas."

49. As quoted in "Chinese Agricultural Group to Acquire 200K Hectares of Land Globally," Freshfruitportal.com, March 15, 2011, retrieved at farmlandgrab.org on May 26, 2011.

50. See Von Braun and Meinzen-Dick, "'Land-Grabbing' by Foreign Investors in Developing Countries," pp. 5–8.

51. Soyatech, "Global AgInvesting 2011, May 2–4, 2011," retrieved at events.soyatech.com on May 30, 2011.

52. Soyatech, "Global AgInvesting 2011: Companies Attending," retrieved at events.soyatech.com on May 30, 2011.

53. Marcia Zarley Taylor, "Land Investors Crowd the Waiting Room," *DTN/The Progressive Farmer*, May 11, 2011, retrieved at farmlandgrab.org on May 26, 2011.

54. Soyatech, "3rd Annual Global AgInvesting Opens to a Sold Out Audience in New York," press release, May 3, 2011, retrieved at www.press releasepoint.com on May 29, 2011.

55. Africa Investor, "Cultivating Investment in Africa," Agribusiness Investment Summit and Awards 2010, Conference Programme, retrieved at www.africa-investor.com on December 17, 2010.

56. Laura MacInnis, "Bankers, Funds Try to Cope with Demand for Farms," Reuters, November 9, 2010, retrieved at farmlandgrab.org on November 18, 2010.

57. Paul Kanitra, "Visionary Alternatives to Boost Food Security," *The National*, February 8, 2011, retrieved at farmlandgrab.org on February 16, 2011.

58. As quoted in "Land May Become Top Asset Class—Beating Shares," *Agrimoney*, May 28, 2010, retrieved at farmlandgrab.org on November 29, 2010.

59. Laura MacInnis, "South America Tops Farmland Investor's Wish-List," Reuters, November 10, 2010, retrieved at farmlandgrab.org on November 18, 2010.

60. Diana B. Henriques, "Food Is Gold, So Billions Invested in Farming," *New York Times*, June 5, 2008.

61. See Andrew Rice, "Is There Such a Thing as Agro-Imperialism?" *New York Times Magazine*, November 22, 2009, p. 51.

62. Deininger and Byerlee, *Rising Global Interest in Farmland*, p. xiv.

63. Ibid., p. 35.

64. For discussion, see Caroline Henshaw, "Private Sector Interest Grows in African Farming," *Wall Street Journal*, October 29, 2010. See also

Drew Hinshaw, "The Great African Land Rush," *Atlantic*, April 14, 2011, retrieved at www.theatlantic.com on September 17, 2011.

65. For discussion, see Chido Makunike, "Large-Scale Agricultural Investment in Africa: Points to Ponder," in Kugelman and Levenstein, *Land Grab?* pp. 85–94.

66. As quoted in Rice, "Is There Such a Thing as Agro-Imperialism?"

67. As quoted in Henriques, "Food Is Gold."

68. As cited in Henshaw, "Private Sector Interest Grows in African Farming."

69. As quoted in Rice, "Is There Such a Thing as Agro-Imperialism?"

70. For discussion, see Butler, "Land Grab Fears for Ethiopian Rural Communities."

71. Horand Knaup and Juliane von Mittelstaedt, "The New Colonialism: Foreign Investors Snap Up African Farmland," *Der Spiegel*, July 30, 2010, retrieved at farmlandgrab.org on November 30, 2010.

72. Katie Hunt, "Africa Investment Sparks Land Grab Fear," BBC News, August 5, 2009, retrieved at newsvote.bbc.co.uk on November 21, 2010.

73. Quoted in ibid.

74. See Macdonald, "What's the New Global Source for Fresh, Shiny Produce?"

75. See "China Farms the World to Feed a Ravenous Economy"; and "DRC: Oil Palm Invasion Era," *Africa Bulletin*, January 6, 2011, retrieved at farmlandgrab.org on May 26, 2011.

76. Arsène Séverin, "South African Farmers Set Up in Congo," Inter-Press Service, March 26, 2011, retrieved at farmlandgrab.org on May 26, 2011.

77. Tracy McVeigh, "Biofuels Land Grab in Kenya's Tana Delta Fuels Talk of War," *Guardian*, July 2, 2011, retrieved at farmlandgrab.org on July 30, 2011.

78. Xan Rice, "Qatar Looks to Grow Food in Kenya," *Guardian*, December 2, 2008, retrieved at www.guardian.co.uk on November 29, 2010.

79. As quoted in McVeigh, "Biofuels Land Grab in Kenya's Tana Delta."

80. Alphonso Toweh, "Sime Darby to Invest $3.1 bln in Liberia Project," Reuters, May 19, 2011, retrieved at farmlandgrab.org on May 26, 2011.

81. As cited in "Halt Sime Darby Plantation Expansion," *Analyst*, July 14, 2011, retrieved at farmlandgrab.org on July 30, 2011.

82. See Fred Pearce, "Africa's Flourishing Niger Delta Threatened by Libya Water Plan," *Environment 360*, February 3, 2011, retrieved at farm landgrab.org on February 16, 2011.

83. See Neil MacFarquhar, "African Farmers Displaced as Investors Move In," *New York Times*, December 22, 2010.

84. As quoted in ibid.

85. Amena Bakr, "Senegal in Talks to Lease Farmland to Saudi," Reuters, December 6, 2010, retrieved at farmlandgrab.org on December 9, 2010.

86. Ibid. See also "Saudi Investors Posed to Take Control of Rice Production in Senegal and Mali?" GRAIN, November 29, 2010, retrieved at farmlandgrab.org on December 2, 2010.

87. As quoted in Hinshaw, "The Great African Land Rush."

88. For an inventory of such acquisitions, see Von Braun and Meinzen-Dick, "'Land-Grabbing' by Foreign Investors in Developing Countries," pp. 5–8.

89. Slindile Khanyile, "African Farms Lure Overseas Investment," *Business Report* (South Africa), September 1, 2010, retrieved at farmland grab.org on November 30, 2010.

90. "Qatar in Talks to Buy Argentina, Ukraine Farmland."

91. Deininger and Byerlee, *Rising Global Interest in Farmland*, p. 35.

92. See Carl Atkin, "Investment in Farmland and Farming in Central and Eastern Europe and the Former Soviet Union—Current Trends and Issues," in Kugelman and Levenstein, *Land Grab?* pp. 109–19. See also Andrew E. Kramer, "Russia's Collective Farms: Hot Capitalist Property," *New York Times*, August 31, 2008, retrieved at farmlandgrab.org on August 10, 2011.

93. See Eleonore Dermy, "Black Earth Stirs Investors in Russia," Agence France-Presse, October 12, 2009, retrieved at farmlandgrab.org on December 18, 2010.

94. Ibid.

95. As quoted in Kramer, "Russia's Collective Farms."

96. Ibid.

97. BEF, "BEF History," retrieved at blackearthfarming.com on December 19, 2010.

98. See Von Braun and Meinzen-Dick, "'Land-Grabbing' by Foreign Investors in Developing Countries," pp. 5–8.

99. Jenia Ustinova, "Time Is Ripe to Develop Agribusiness," *Moscow Times*, September 13, 2010.

100. Ibid.

101. Laetitia Van Eeckhout, "Ukraine: Forgotten Granary of Europe," *Guardian Weekly*, July 20, 2010, retrieved at farmlandgrab.org on December 18, 2010.

102. Santosh Menon, "Enter the New Farmers," Reuters, June 25, 2008, retrieved at farmlandgrab.org on December 20, 2010.

103. See Nicoleta Banila and Michael Bird, "Foreign Farmland Ownership Rises over Ten Percent," *The Diplomat*, March 2011, retrieved at farmlandgrab.org on May 26, 2011.

104. Ibid.

105. "UAE to Look at Farmland Deals in Ukraine," Maktoob, November 17, 2009, retrieved at farmlandgrab.org on November 28, 2010.

106. "Qatar in Talks to Buy Argentina, Ukraine Farmland."

107. See "UAE Company to Invest in Bulgarian Agriculture," *Standart News*, July 23, 2010, retrieved at farmlandgrab.org on August 30, 2010; and Pratap John, "Qatar Eyes Farm, Energy Investment in Moldova," *Gulf Times*, May 31, 2010, retrieved at farmlandgrab.org on November 28, 2010.

108. See Anna Minaeva, "Acquisition of Land for Agricultural Purposes—Legal Aspects," *Moscow Times*, November 23, 2010, retrieved at farmland grab.org on August 1, 2011; and Kateryna Choursina, "Ukraine Should Not Sell Farmland to Foreigners, Minister Says," *Bloomberg News*, June 16, 2011, retrieved at farmlandgrab.org on August 1, 2011.

109. "After Land Reform, Land Ownership Will Remain Ukrainian," press release, Ukrainian Ministry of Agrarian Policy, June 15, 2011, retrieved at www.minagro.kiev.ua on August 9, 2011.

110. As quoted in Duan Yan and Bao Chang, "Agricultural Group Seeks More Overseas Expansion," *China Daily*, March 14, 2011, retrieved at www.chinadaily.com.cn on August 1, 2011.

111. Anwar Elshamy, "Ghana Presents $700mn Investment Proposals to Qatar Food Firm," *Gulf Times*, May 3, 2010, retrieved at farmlandgrab .org on May 11, 2010.

112. As quoted in Hunt, "Africa Investment Sparks Land Grab Fear."

113. As quoted in Henshaw, "Private Sector Interest Grows in African Farming."

114. Deininger and Byerlee, *Rising Global Interest in Farmland*, p. 46.

115. Ibid.

116. As quoted in William Davison, "Ethiopia Plans to Rent Out Belgium-Sized Land Area to Produce Cash Crops," *Bloomberg News*, October 26, 2010, retrieved at farmlandgrab.org on November 16, 2010.

117. As quoted in Butler, "Land Grab Fears for Ethiopian Rural Communities."

118. As quoted in ibid.

119. As quoted in McVeigh, "Biofuels Land Grab in Kenya's Tana Delta."

120. See the postings at farmlandgrab.org.

CHAPTER 8: SHAPING THE COURSE OF HISTORY

1. David J. O'Reilly, "U.S. Energy Policy: A Declaration of Interdependence," Keynote Address, CERA Week, Houston, Tex., February 15, 2005, retrieved at www.chevron.com on June 5, 2011.

2. Ben Casselman, "Facing Up to the End of 'Easy Oil,'" *Wall Street Journal*, May 24, 2011.

3. Ibid.

4. Daniel Gross, "Going to Extremes," *Newsweek*, June 14, 2010, p. 29.

5. As quoted in Kirk Johnson, "Facing the Multiple Risks of Newer, Deeper Mines," *New York Times*, August 16, 2007.

6. As quoted in ibid.

7. Barta, "With Easy Nickel Fading Fast."

8. Ibid.

9. See Lawrence Williams, "New Caledonia's Huge Goro Nickel Project Under Siege Again," Mineweb.com, February 18, 2008, retrieved at www.mineweb.com on June 6, 2011; "Acid Spill at Vale Inco's Giant $3.2 bn Goro Nickel Project," Reuters, April 8, 2009, retrieved at www.mineweb.com on June 6, 2011; and "Acid Spill Halts Commissioning Work on Vale's Goro Nickel Operation," Reuters, April 27, 2010, retrieved at www.mineweb.com on June 6, 2011.

10. See "The 9 Billion-People Question"; Bourne, "The End of Plenty";

and Justin Gillis, "A Warming Planet Struggles to Feed Itself," *New York Times*, June 5, 2011.

11. World Bank, *Global Economic Prospects 2009*, p. 61.

12. As quoted in "Algeria: Youths Clash with Police during Protests over Food Prices and Chronic Unemployment," Reuters, January 6, 2011, retrieved at www.itnsource.com on March 5, 2011.

13. "Global 500: Our Annual Ranking of the World's Largest Corporations," *Fortune*, July 20, 2009, retrieved at money.cnn.com on January 6, 2011.

14. See John Schwartz, "Weighing the Possibility of Bankruptcy for BP," *New York Times*, July 10, 2010.

15. Ibid. See also Terry Macalister, "Vultures Circle BP over Fears Its Days Are Numbered in US," *Guardian*, June 30, 2010, retrieved at www .guardian.co.uk on January 6, 2011.

16. See Michael Peel, "Eagles and Vultures," *Financial Times*, July 2, 2010; John Schwartz, "Costs to BP Would Soar Under Criminal Charges," *New York Times*, June 17, 2010; and Schwartz, "Liability Issues Loom for BP et al.," *New York Times*, June 25, 2010.

17. As quoted in Broder, "Oil Executives Break Ranks in Testimony."

18. Alex Brummer, "Royal Dutch Shell Eyed a Move for BP After Oil Spill," *Daily Mail*, January 3, 2011, retrieved at www.dailymail.co.uk on January 6, 2011; Danny Fortson and Dominic O'Connell, "Exxon Weighs £100bn Bid for BP," *Times*, July 11, 2010, retrieved at www.thetimes.co.uk on January 6, 2011.

19. See "ExxonMobil Purchase of BP Is Unlikely, Barclay Says," *Bloomberg News*, July 14, 2010, retrieved at www.businessweek.com on January 6, 2011.

20. See "BP Fast Becoming a Takeover Target," *New York Times*, April 11, 2011.

21. See Macalister, "Vultures Circle BP."

22. Guy Chazan and Gina Chon, "BP Sells $7 Billion of Assets to Help Fund Cleanup," *Wall Street Journal*, July 21, 2010; Brian Swint and Heather Walsh, "BP Agrees on $1.9 Billion Colombia Sale to Ecopetrol, Talisman," *Bloomberg News*, August 3, 2010, retrieved at www.bloomberg.com on January 6, 2011; Michael J. de la Merced, "BP to Sell Big Stake in Oil Asset," *New York Times*, November 29, 2010.

23. See William MacNamara and Christopher Thompson, "Congo Seizes First Quantum Mineral's Assets," *Financial Times*, August 31, 2010.

24. Alex MacDonald, "First Quantum Sues ENRC over Disputed Kolwezi Project in Congo," Dow Jones Newswires, December 6, 2010, retrieved at www.tradingmarkets.com on January 8, 2011. See also Andrea Hotter, "First Quantum Sues ENRC over Congo Mines," *Wall Street Journal*, September 15, 2010.

25. For background on these events, see Klare, *Rising Powers, Shrinking Planet*, pp. 98–100.

26. See Andrew E. Kramer, "Russians Buy Control of an Oil Field," *New York Times*, December 22, 2006.

27. This history is related with particularly great insight and gusto by Paul Kennedy in his landmark study *The Rise and Fall of the Great Powers* (New York: Random House, 1987).

28. David Winning, Shai Oster, and Alex Wilson, "China, Russia Strike $25 Billion Oil Pact," *Wall Street Journal*, February 18, 2009.

29. "Brazil, China Agree on $10 Billion Loan Package," *Oil & Gas Journal*, May 25, 2009, p. 35.

30. Simon Romero, "China's Offer of $20 Billion in Loans to Venezuela Extends Needed Cash to Chávez," *New York Times*, April 19, 2010.

31. See Tim Whewell, "China to Seal $9bn DR Congo Deal," BBC News, April 14, 2008, retrieved at newsvote.bbc.co.uk on September 18, 2010; and Oster, "China Fund's $7 Billion Deal with Guinea Draws Scrutiny."

32. David Pilling, "Japan to Give $1bn in Loans for Gulf Oil Supply," *Financial Times*, April 30, 2007.

33. For background on such arrangements, see James A. Baker III Institute for Public Policy (Baker Institute), "The Changing Role of National Oil Companies in International Energy Markets," *Baker Institute Policy Report*, Rice University, March 2007; and Robert Pirog, *The Role of National Oil Companies in the International Oil Market*, CRS Report for Congress (Washington, D.C.: CRS, August 21, 2007).

34. DoE/EIA, "Venezuela," February 2010; DoE/EIA, "Kazakhstan," Country Analysis Brief, November 2010, retrieved at www.eia.doe.gov on August 14, 2011.

35. DoE/EIA, "India," Country Analysis Brief, August 2010, retrieved at www.eia.doe.gov on August 14, 2011.

36. For discussion, see Klare, *Rising Powers, Shrinking Planet*, pp. 210–37.

37. Ibid., pp. 211–19.

38. Ibid., pp. 173–7, 215–16, 230–31. For background on AFRICOM, see Lauren Ploch, *Africa Command: U.S. Strategic Interests and the Role of the U.S. Military in Africa*, CRS Report for Congress (Washington, D.C.: CRS, March 11, 2011). For background on the SCO, see Jim Nichol, *Central Asia's Security: Issues and Implications for U.S. Interests*, CRS Report for Congress (Washington, D.C.: CRS, March 11, 2010), pp. 18–20.

39. For discussion, see Klare, *Rising Powers, Shrinking* Planet, pp. 128–32. See also Nichol, *Central Asia's Security*, pp. 21–26.

40. For background, see Klare, *Rising Powers, Shrinking* Planet, pp. 215–17. On CSTO, see Nichol, *Central Asia's Security*, pp. 17–18. On the Russian base at Kant, see Steven Lee Myers, "Russia to Deploy Air Squadron in Kyrgyzstan, Where U.S. Has Base," *New York Times*, December 4, 2002.

41. For discussion, see Klare, *Blood and Oil*, p. 130. See also Robert D. Kaplan, "Why Russia Risks All in Dagestan," *New York Times*, August 17, 1999.

42. For background, see Jim Nichol, *Armenia, Azerbaijan, and Georgia: Political Developments and Implications for U.S. Interests*, CRS Report for Congress (Washington, D.C.: CRS, April 15, 2011), pp. 11–14.

43. For background, see Klare, *Rising Powers, Shrinking Planet*, pp. 221–25; and Valencia, *Foreign Military Activities in Asian EEZs*. On the East China Sea, see "Oil and Gas in Troubled Waters," *Economist*, October 2005, pp. 52–53; Brooke, "Drawing the Line on Energy"; Brooke, "For Japan and China, Strains from a Line in the Sea"; and Manicom, "China's Claims to an Extended Continental Shelf." On the South China Sea, see DoE/EIA, "South China Sea," March 2008.

44. On clashes in the East China Sea, see "Oil and Gas in Troubled Waters." For a chronology of clashes in the South China Sea, see "Major Clashes in the South China Sea Since 1970," in DoE/EIA, "South China Sea."

45. Thom Shanker and Mark Mazzetti, "China and U.S. Clash on Naval Fracas," *New York Times*, March 11, 2009. See also Ann Scott Tyson, "Destroyer to Protect Ship Near China," *Washington Post*, March 13, 2009.

46. See Ian Storey, "Impeccable Affair and Renewed Rivalry in the South China Sea," *China Brief*, Jamestown Foundation, April 30, 2009,

retrieved at www.jamestown.org on June 8, 2011; and Valencia, *Foreign Military Activities in Asian EEZs*, p. 10.

47. See Edward Wong, "Chinese Civilian Boats Roil Disputed Waters," *New York Times*, October 5, 2010. See also Manicom, "China's Claims to an Extended Continental Shelf."

48. See Fackler, "China and Japan Agree to End Offshore Dispute"; and Mark Landler, "U.S. Works to Ease China-Japan Conflict," *New York Times*, October 30, 2010.

49. See, for example, Valencia, *Foreign Military Activities in Asian EEZs*, pp. 7–8.

50. See Mark Landler, "Offering to Aid Talks, U.S. Challenges China on Disputed Islands," *New York Times*, July 24, 2010; and Andrew Jacobs, "Stay Out of Island Dispute, Chinese Warn the U.S.," *New York Times*, July 27, 2010.

51. As cited in Jacobs, "Stay Out of Island Dispute."

52. See Russell Hsiao, "PLA Posturing for Conflict in the South China Sea?" *China Brief*, August 5, 2010, retrieved at www.jamestown.org on August 6, 2010. A photograph of a Chinese missile firing from this exercise appeared in the *Wall Street Journal* for September 23, 2010.

53. Yoree Koh, "Tokyo Protests Blast China's Response to Collision," *Wall Street Journal*, October 3, 2011.

54. As quoted in Jeremy Page, "U.S. Presses China on Regional Maritime Disputes," *Wall Street Journal*, July 11, 2011.

55. "Canada Gives Tough Message to Russians over Arctic Sovereignty," Canwest News Service, May 15, 2009, retrieved at www.canada .com on May 18, 2009.

56. As quoted in Kipp, "Russian Strategic Interests Expand in Arctic."

57. For a comprehensive overview of the challenges ahead and options for overcoming them, see United Nations, Department of Economic and Social Affairs (DESA), *World Economic and Social Survey 2011: The Great Green Technological Revolution* (New York: United Nations, 2011).

58. See Amory B. Lovins, *Reinventing Fire: Bold Business Solutions for the New Energy Era* (White River Junction, Vt.: Chelsea Green, 2011).

59. For discussion of the respective roles that could be played by governments and the private sector in such efforts, see American Energy Innovation

Council (AEIC), *A Business Plan for America's Energy Future* (Washington, D.C.: AEIC, 2010).

60. For an inventory of such endeavors in the energy field, see Pew Charitable Trusts (Pew), *Who's Winning the Clean Energy Race? 2010 Edition* (Washington, D.C.: Pew, 2011). See also Michael Levi, Elizabeth C. Economy, Shannon O'Neil, and Adam Segal, "Globalizing the Energy Revolution," *Foreign Affairs*, vol. 86, no. 6 (November/December 2010), pp. 111–21.

61. Richard J. Campbell, *China and the United States—A Comparison of Green Energy Programs and Policies*, CRS, Report for Congress (Washington, D.C.: CRS, June 14, 2010), pp. 1–2, 5–6. See also Evan Osnos, "Green Giant: Beijing's Crash Program for Clean Energy," *New Yorker*, December 21, 2009, retrieved at www.newyorker.com on June 8, 2011.

62. Campbell, *China and the United States—A Comparison of Green Energy Programs and Policies*, pp. 7–10, 18. See also Bradsher, "China Leading the Race to Make Clean Energy," *New York Times*, January 31, 2010; and Lisa Mastny, *Renewable Energy and Energy Efficiency in China: Current Status and Prospects for 2020*, Worldwatch Report 182 (Washington, D.C.: Worldwatch Institute, 2010).

63. "China recognizes that given the growing demand for energy at home, developing its domestic renewable energy industry and building manufacturing capacity can lead to advantages in future export markets." Campbell, *China and the United States—A Comparison of Green Energy Programs and Policies*, pp. 17–18. See also Jiahua Pan, Haibing Ma, and Ying Zhang, *Green Economy and Green Jobs in China*, Worldwatch Report 185 (Washington, D.C.: Worldwatch Institute, 2011).

64. See "Strategic Emerging Industries Likely to Contribute 8% of China's GDP by 2015," *People's Daily Online*, October 9, 2010, retrieved at english.peopledaily.com.cn on November 1, 2010.

65. Pew, *Who's Winning the Clean Energy Race? Growth, Competition and Opportunity in the World's Largest Economies* (Philadelphia and Washington, D.C.: Pew, March 25, 2010), p. 6. For additional background on the green energy initiatives of various states, see DESA, *World Economic and Social Survey 2011*, pp. 41–47.

66. Pew, *Who's Winning the Clean Energy Race? 2010 Edition*, p. 2.

67. Ibid., p. 11.

68. Ibid., p. 12.

69. Ibid., p. 14.

70. As cited in U.S. Department of Energy, "Secretary Chu: China's Clean Energy Success Represent a New 'Sputnik Moment' for America," press release, November 29, 2010, retrieved at www.energy.gov on December 9, 2010.

71. Campbell, *China and the United States—A Comparison of Green Energy Programs and Policies*, p. 14.

72. White House, Council on Environmental Quality, "Federal Leadership in Environment, Energy and Economic Performance—Executive Order 13514," retrieved at www.whitehouse.gov on January 22, 2011.

73. AEIC, *A Business Plan for America's Energy Future*, p. 5.

74. Ibid., pp. 16–31.

75. Executive Office of the President (EOP), President's Council of Advisors on Science and Technology, *Report to the President on Accelerating the Pace of Change in Energy Technologies Through an Integrated Federal Energy Policy* (Washington, D.C.: EOP, November 2010).

76. Ibid., p. 2.

ACKNOWLEDGMENTS

Writing the acknowledgments to this volume is a special pleasure. Up until now, this book has focused on what I see as potent and deadly threats to human well-being, but here, at long last, I can rest for a moment and speak of more pleasant things: the gratitude I feel for all those who helped me in one way or another to make this book possible. I may not do an adequate job of communicating my appreciation, but the feeling is strong nonetheless.

As always, my greatest debt is owed to my partner, Andrea Ayvazian, and to my son, Sasha Klare-Ayvazian. Without their constant love and support, I would not possess the stamina and peace of mind to undertake and complete a project of this magnitude. I'm sure they sometimes wondered at my determination to pursue such a demanding project, but I know that they consistently supported my endeavors—and I am very grateful for their understanding and perseverance.

Next, I wish to highlight the crucial roles performed by my publisher, Sara Bershtel of Metropolitan Books, and my editor, Grigory Tovbis. Sara was instrumental from the start, encouraging me to pursue this project and helping to devise the book's overall design. I am especially grateful for the clarity she brought to our discussions over the shape and structure of the book—a contribution that was absolutely essential.

Grigory's contribution was no less significant. Not only did he work closely with Sara Bershtel in suggesting improvements to the overall shape and structure of the book, but he did an extraordinary job in editing the manuscript—line by line, word by word. As we began to work together, I came to trust his guidance in constructing language to express my core arguments, and this book reflects both his artistry and superb judgment. I am extremely grateful for his assistance in bringing this project to fruition, and I am sure that my readers will be the beneficiaries of his outstanding work.

I also wish to recognize several other individuals who helped me in my research and thinking on this project. My friend Daniel Volman provided information on the scramble for resources in Africa and helped me enhance my analysis of the overall situation. Another friend, Edward Connelly, supplied a constant stream of news reports on all things resource-related. The editor of my periodic online essays, Tom Engelhardt of TomDispatch .com, encouraged me to pursue these themes and provided excellent advice on how best to shape my arguments. These are precious gifts, and I am very grateful to each of them for their invaluable assistance. Equally valuable and appreciated is the financial assistance I received from the Samuel Rubin Foundation, for support of my research endeavors.

Finally, I wish to acknowledge the continuing support of my students and colleagues at Hampshire College and the other members of the Five College consortium—Amherst, Mount Holyoke, and Smith Colleges and the University of Massachusetts at Amherst. I have benefited from dialogue with many students and faculty at these institutions, but I particularly wish to acknowledge the many rewarding conversations I've had with Professors Peter Haas and Laura Reed of the University of Massachusetts, Professor Betsy Hartmann of Hampshire College, and Zilong Wang, my teaching assistant at Hampshire. Not only have I received unwavering endorsement for my research and teaching in this field but also an extraordinary degree of personal warmth and encouragement. These, too, are precious gifts, and I feel very, very blessed to receive them.

INDEX

Page numbers in *italics* refer to maps and tables.